XIT

∾

XIT
A Story of Land, Cattle, and Capital in Texas and Montana

MICHAEL M. MILLER

UNIVERSITY OF OKLAHOMA PRESS : NORMAN

This book is published with the generous assistance of the McCasland Foundation, Duncan, Oklahoma.

Portions of this book, particularly chapter 6, appeared in an earlier form in Michael M. Miller, "Cowboys and Capitalists: The XIT Ranch in Texas and Montana, 1885–1912," *Montana: The Magazine of Western History* 65 (Winter 2015): 3–28.

LIBRARY OF CONGRESS CATALOGING-IN-PUBLICATION DATA

Names: Miller, Michael Mark, 1956– author.
Title: XIT : a story of land, cattle, and capital in Texas and Montana / Michael M. Miller.
Description: Norman : University of Oklahoma Press, [2020] | Includes bibliographical references and index. | Summary: "The history of the XIT Ranch connecting Texas politics and the American beef business with global Gilded Age economics"—Provided by publisher.
Identifiers: LCCN 2020017093 | ISBN 978-0-8061-6716-9 (hardcover)
Subjects: LCSH: Capitol Freehold Land and Investment Company—History. | Cattle trade—West (U.S.)—History—19th century. | Land tenure—Texas—History. | Capitalists and financiers—United States—History—19th century. | XIT Ranch (Tex.)—History.
Classification: LCC F392.X2 M55 2020 | DDC 338.1/7620978—dc23
LC record available at https://lccn.loc.gov/2020017093

The paper in this book meets the guidelines for permanence and durability of the Committee on Production Guidelines for Book Longevity of the Council on Library Resources, Inc. ∞

1 2 3 4 5 6 7 8 9 10

To the memory of my dad,
Lynn H. Miller
He loved this sort of thing.

Contents

Illustrations

Maps

Charts

Tables

Acknowledgments

I started this project about ten or so years ago with the vague idea of writing something about homesteading in eastern Montana. Born there, I spent twelve years in Wolf Point and often visited the countryside stretching between the Missouri and Yellowstone rivers. I spent several summers on my uncle's ranch on the northern edge of the "Big Open." I worked for a custom harvest crew traveling from Oklahoma to Montana following in the path of the northbound cattle trails of the nineteenth century along the western edge of the Great Plains. In conversations, older friends and relatives sometimes talked about the early days there and the big ranches in the country. I could only remember a couple of them—the Circle, CK, and N-N. I decided maybe I might need to start with the cattle business to really explain the homesteading boom there. It is an incredibly fascinating and complex story. The problem was that I was in Texas. I remembered hearing about an "IT" ranch or something like that. Then I came across J. Evetts Haley's *XIT Ranch of Texas.* I thought it a pretty good place to start. I had found a story that brings together Texas and Montana into a story about the American West. The homesteaders' story in Montana will have to wait. The XIT story takes many trails. I have not followed them all. I tried here to tell an important story about the XIT, but it isn't the only story.

I happily acknowledge the contributions the following people and organizations have made toward this book. Michael Wise became a forceful guide and mentor in my attempts to understand what I was trying to say. F. Todd Smith taught me not to get shook up about things. Neilesh Bose and Glen Sample Ely provided detailed critical reviews during this manuscript's evolution. Leland Turner and William Green gave the green light on this project and offered valued commentary. James E. Sherow and Joshua Specht read and offered their advice on the next-to-last draft. Warm appreciation goes out to them. Much thanks, too, for my sister, Bonnie Miller, niece, Becky Taylor, and, son, Blair Miller for reading and commenting on this in its manuscript form. I am grateful, too, for the assistance of my youngest son, Caleb, who traveled with me in the earliest days of this project. His hen-scratch notes from our research proved invaluable. I owe much to my mentor and friend Dr. Rick McCaslin. This project could not have been completed without his interest and attention. His stunning knowledge of the breadth of Texas history continually amazes me. His editing skills can be seen in all the best parts of this story.

My deep thanks to Byron Price and Kent Calder at the University of Oklahoma Press. Byron was one of my earliest supporters of this effort. Kent championed the project and patiently guided me through it with his calming influence. His encouragement and advice made this a lot easier job than what it seemed to be during the panic attacks all this sometimes brought me. Thanks to the managing editor turning this into a final product, Steven Baker; to my copyeditor, John Thomas, whose humor, patience, and genius are immeasurable; and to all the folks at OU Press who helped so much on making this real. Much gratitude to Carol Zuber-Mallison, who listened to me ramble and studied some lousy photos I showed her, then created some fabulous maps depicting exactly what I imagined.

Much of my gratitude regarding this effort is reserved for the people throughout the country working to preserve remnants of our history. Often faceless, librarians, archivists, and assistants in Chicago, Minneapolis, Washington, Laramie, Austin, Lubbock, Midland, and Denton have contributed their lives making it easier for me to find things I did not know existed. I owe particular gratitude to Warren Stricker and his staff at the research center at the Panhandle-Plains Historical Museum in Canyon, Texas, and to Molly Kruckenberg, Brian Shovers, and their staff at the Montana Historical Society research center in Helena, Montana. Much gratitude is owed Cathy Smith at the Nita Stewart Haley Library in Midland. She opened the collection to me and has probably spent hours chasing memories and bad notes I asked about over the phone and via email. Many thanks to the people I met along the "Montana Trail" at the XIT Museum in Dalhart, Texas, at the Sand Creek Massacre site, and in Brush, Colorado; Moorcroft, Wyoming; Fallon, Montana; and sometimes just along a road somewhere where I found someone who had something to say about the XIT. Thanks to Glen Heitz and the other volunteers at the Prairie County Museum in Terry, Montana, and many thanks to Bunny and Gary Miller at Range Riders Museum in Miles City, Montana. I also want to acknowledge the assistance of staff at the offices of treasurer and clerk and recorder, Dawson and Prairie County, Montana.

Much thanks to committee members of the Bradley Fellowship at the Montana Historical Society. The benefits of receiving the Bradley award to my work are immeasurable. Not only did it give me the opportunity to undertake critical research and to meet some fascinating people, it also led to publication of an article in a prestigious journal and an award from a respected organization. Thanks to then-editor Molly Holz and her staff at *Montana: The Magazine of Western History* and to the board and staff of Western Writers of America. Thanks to the University of North Texas history department, Toulouse Graduate School, College of Arts and Science, and all the donors contributing to scholarship for the generous support I received during my studies there.

Thanks to all my friends and family who have supported me for many years, even those who questioned, if not my sanity, my judgment. To my wife, Maureen, and my sons, Keegan, Blair, and Caleb, thanks for the support, tolerance, and love over the many years none of us probably thought would go the way they did. Forgive me for leaving out anyone. Thanks to the people reading this, too!

ﻋﻨﻮ

Cowboys and Capitalists

Arguably, modern America is a result of the actions and events of the Gilded Age. Although American industrialism is most associated with the teeming metropolises of the Northeast and Midwest, belching smoke from their coal-powered forges and factories, Americans often forget that feeding the industrial might emerging from those forges and factories were the minerals, forests, and pasturelands of the relatively recently settled American West. A hallmark of the story of the American West are the cattle trails that wound north out of Texas in the wake of the Civil War. What is less known is how the largest ranch in the Lone Star State, the almost mythical XIT, also, for a time, dominated the landscape of the Rocky Mountain Front Range. Operating much like the more familiar factories and financial organizations of the Gilded Age, the XIT Ranch for a brief time became one of the most productive cattle operations in the West. It thus established a legend that further obscures the true story of how the backup plan for a group of Chicago land developers, with the support of an international cartel of investors, grew into a cattle ranch that sprawled from Texas to Montana.

From 1885 to 1912, the three-million-acre XIT Ranch of Texas reigned as "truly a nation in itself, an empire." At its height, the XIT controlled as many as 140,000 cattle in at least five states. The ranch sold hundreds of thousands of cattle for millions of dollars in revenue. Its network of ownership relied on $10 million in British investment and the managerial skills of a small syndicate of Illinois capitalists. Their ambassadors—legislators, congressmen, senators, members of Parliament, and other officials—in Washington, London, and Austin looked out for the group's interests in those places. An office building in downtown Chicago represented the empire's capitol. To the men there, the cattle business was a scheme to keep their finances moving forward until they could collect on the true goal of their investment—land sales. As Karl Marx pointed out, "The original meaning of the word capital is cattle." Cattle represented money, on the hoof, and the men in charge of the project's success aimed to keep their investment growing.[1] Words like "pecuniary" and "peculiar" originated from similar old English words that meant both finance and cattle. The history of the ranch certainly lends many opportunities to apply both of those terms. Its operation highlights the "growing appetite of American capitalism," as H. W. Brands has written. The cattle business on the American Plains, he wrote, "was a business . . . driven by the same imperatives that governed the oil business and the steel business."[2]

A network of finance and politics created a virtual empire of meat across the country during the 1880s and 1890s. An oligarchy of the largest livestock growers created the foundation for a beef trust whose operations affected Americans, arguably, more intimately and broadly than any other notable industrial activity of the late nineteenth century. The meat on the table, the oleo spread on one's bread, the lard in the pantry, and the shoes on American feet all demonstrated the pervasiveness of the livestock industry in everyday life. In the "Golden West," those people who sought a garden spot of their own on the prairies stretching to the Rocky Mountain foothills found the reality of their dream stifled, not simply by an unforgiving climate but by powerful financial and government organizations that preceded them.[3]

The XIT Ranch in Texas fenced in the Capitol Reservation, the huge Panhandle land grant set aside by the Texas constitution and legislature to pay for a new statehouse in Austin. The state certainly received one of the finest capitol buildings in the United States. From the outset of the project in 1882, however, for the Capitol Syndicate ("the Syndicate," as the ownership group came to be called) controversy followed controversy. Contractual disputes permeated the building's construction timeline. The nature of and source for materials for the capitol and the title status of the three million acres in the reservation dominated those conflicts. Political winds in Texas buffeted the Syndicate continuously. It was often a populist wind that brought storms of questions, criticism, and resentment of an outsider's ownership of so much land. Internally, ownership of the huge tract twisted and evolved, burdened by corporate entanglement and lawsuit upon lawsuit. Completed in 1888 by Abner Taylor, Syndicate member and the designated contractor, the capitol continues to stand as both a monument to Texas and a symbol for many of the small-government, limited-regulation ideals sweeping the statehouses of the United States.[4]

Construction costs for the capitol swelled to about $3,250,000, more than doubling the original estimates. The State of Texas provided an extra half million, to put the building's final construction cost at around $3,750,000. At the same time, the Syndicate quickly discovered that three million acres of land in the Texas Panhandle may not have been the bargain for which they hoped.

Originally imagining their reserve to become covered by small farms and towns of industrious settlers, the Syndicate soon found prospects for that limited. Although small tracts for town lots and railroad use sold sporadically over the next decade, the first large land sales did not come until the early years of the twentieth century. As costs on the capitol project ran over budget and land sales prospects began to look distant, "pending the arrival of the farming settler," a cattle-ranching scheme seemed the best solution to address the cash flow problems of the group. With American investors leery of western opportunities, the Syndicate sought them out in Great Britain. The British investment boom of the early 1880s had subsided, but many there continued to be enamored of a mythological West based on travelogues, popular literature, and over-the-top prospectuses from eager, if not always honest, fiscal suitors. Established in London in June 1885, Capitol Freehold Land and Investment Company, Limited, drew immediate funds to the operation through its new stakeholders. By the end of that summer, thousands of mongrel cattle brought in bunches from other parts of Texas or from Indian Territory stocked what a few in its early days called the Capitol Ranch.[5]

In 1901 the first substantial land sales brought the operation $2.40–$2.50 per acre—what the Syndicate imagined they might receive in 1883. But during the last decade of the nineteenth century ranching operations in the reservation returned nearly $5 million to British investors and paid over $20,000 per year in property taxes. The Syndicate's climb to profitability, as well as the state's recovery of its costs on the capitol, was long and slow, and it started with the sale of cattle, not real estate.[6]

The market for cattle, particularly Texas cattle, collapsed at the beginning of 1885. The trail industry—as a distinct business made obsolete by railroads, livestock quarantines, and settlement—fell into the hands of larger ranches, generally financed by nonlocal entities. A few of the once independent drovers who took millions of cattle to Kansas railheads became the owners or, more likely, ranch managers for absentee owners and hundreds of thousands of cattle by then ranging throughout the West. These factors shaped early decisions by the Syndicate members concerning their millions of acres in the Panhandle.[7]

The West many people think they know continues to be somewhat a "fictional world . . . set in a mythical distant past before corporations took over the people and the land."[8] Despite popular memories of the period, the cattle trail era depicted in old movies featuring bar fights and gunplay wound down quickly after the displacement of Indians and bison from the country's vast grassland. Clinging to a rural sense of their own history,[9] Americans stylized the Old West to include a quaint image of a rustic cabin on a luscious plain alongside a bright, gurgling stream and beneath the shade of a mighty tree. Shadowed from rainfall by the Rocky Mountains, the Great Plains, until cattle displaced bison, was a place perhaps high on the travelogue list of European elites, but not somewhere most people hoped would afford them an affluent future.[10]

As Richard White has written, the wild days of rounding up a bunch of maverick longhorns and driving them to railheads in dusty Kansas cow towns passed quickly. By 1880, "large-scale and sometimes corporate organizations, absentee owners, professional management, mechanization, and specialized production" dominated the western cattle industry. Legendary cattlemen like Charles Goodnight and Granville Stuart project the romance and legend of the period, but they were part of its reality, too. These pioneers of the western cattle business became middlemen for larger interests. Texas's Goodnight and Montana's Stuart realized that the only way to really make money in the range cattle business at the time was to control a lot of land and own a lot of cattle. The XIT Ranch and similar ranches were often simply arms of those interests. Capitalist actors in the East or in Europe invested in a resource promising spectacular rewards at little cost. The reality was much different. This story is about the "business" of cattle ranching.[11]

Goodnight and Stuart understood that, in the interim between the federal government nominally acquiring the vastness of the interior West and the government actually controlling the land, they could fill those public lands with cattle while also limiting competitors who did not get there fast enough. It took money, however, to make money—even when the land was "free." The owners of the land that became the XIT Ranch—the Syndicate—found themselves legally in control of a vast amount of land which, at the time, seemed most useful for raising cattle. But even three million acres could not sustain the thousands of cattle they hoped would bring great wealth.[12]

Often remembered as the last gasp of the open range, the winter of 1886–87, known commonly as the "Big Die-Up," affected livestock growers throughout the Great Plains. Hundreds of thousands of animals died. It struck particularly hard in Montana, the Dakotas, and Wyoming. The Big Die-Up ruined large and small stock growers alike. Challenging winters, though, did not surprise those experienced in the vagaries of Great Plains weather. Summers there do not always bring much relief, either. The winter of 1886–87 was not the first and would not be the last killing snowstorm. The western range cattle business developed where it did precisely because of the Great Plains' limitations and hazards. The men who drove cattle herds into places like the Texas Panhandle and the eastern sections of Montana and Wyoming on the heels of the U.S. Army hoped that the wildness and obstacles of those territories would reduce their competition—at least for the time being.[13] The infamous winter meant change and an end to the cattle business for some. It meant opportunity for others. The cattle business worked that way. Just the year before, winter storms had brought similar devastation across the South Plains, including to the XIT. The ranch saw its best years after the Big Die-Up, or perhaps because of it. Another terrible winter twenty years later, in 1906–7, ushered in the ranch's closing act.[14]

The Oregon country, Territory of Utah, and northern territories of Montana, Wyoming, and the Dakotas challenged Texas's claim as the country's prime cattle production region. Quarantines, farmers, railroads, better breeding, and more competition after 1885 limited demand for Texas cattle on northern ranches and at midwestern slaughterhouses. Government action to bar leasing of Indian lands to grazing greatly affected Texas livestock owners. The successive extreme winters and dry summers throughout the Great Plains added high cattle losses to the already huge market losses caused by the collapse in beef prices. By then, too, livestock associations enforced selective access and use in western cattle regions. Many operations embraced barbed wire, hay cultivation, and winter feeding. In the Texas Panhandle, beyond the area restricted by northern quarantines, owners with the deepest pockets consolidated their operations, and as an added hedge against a market preference for northern beef nearly every major southwestern ranch sought stock range in Wyoming, the Dakotas, Montana, and even in

Canada. Vast tracts of government and railroad land remained available for sale or leasing there. Most who came, with cattle, sheep, or a plow, however, at first paid little or nothing for where they located. Very little of eastern Montana had yet been surveyed; it would be the next century before that task was completed. Legitimate land authorities were slow to take control and other interests filled the need.[15] The XIT, among many southwestern ranches, trailed thousands of cattle from Texas to Montana from 1889 to 1897, years beyond common beliefs about the close of the cattle trails. The "northern range," as livestock operators knew the region, was not so much free as it was available to those with the strongest connections to deep pockets and political wherewithal.[16]

The gilded finish of the "beef bonanza" had worn quite thin by the time the XIT Ranch sold its first cattle. Production shifted to match market demands, and the maintenance of large herds of open range cattle was found to be financially and environmentally unsustainable. Both the marketplace and government policy now discouraged the large-scale ranching predominant in the waning days of the nineteenth-century American West. Rapid settlement encouraged by government and the railroads wrested back control of the great swaths of the northern range, thus limiting the largest ranches' use.[17]

Entering the twentieth century, the cattle industry was dependent on a triad of railroads, stockyards, and packers. A small number of gigantic corporations dominated the national economy's major sectors of banking, manufacturing, meat packing, oil refining, railroads, and steel. The XIT Ranch, however, like a few other great ranches, managed to, if not flourish, project a powerful image of success in the 1890s and into the 1900s that continues to mark American imaginations. But the men responsible for the XIT Ranch were not, for the most part, rugged, adventurous individualists; they were shrewd capitalists and astute businessmen not so much interested in what they were doing for the nation as what they were doing for their own fortune and legacy.[18]

Today, people are surprised to learn that the "fabulous" XIT Ranch operated for less than thirty years. The descendants of the original Syndicate men had no interest in the cattle business. They were happy to sell the iconic outfit's last cattle in 1912, happy to reap the income of the sales from their still substantial Texas land holdings. The XIT Ranch certainly left its mark in the places where it operated. The great operation continues to stir the imaginations of people from Texas to Montana and most of the places in between. There are celebrations, museums, roads, and businesses named for the XIT. The ranch brought towns and people to the Texas Panhandle and helped establish a culture in eastern Montana that continues in many ways to uphold some of the same principles held when Texas longhorns covered its hills and prairies.[19]

None of the principals of the XIT thought of themselves as great "cattle barons," although few of those among the latter could boast of a larger commitment to the beef industry. The men of the Syndicate simply were capitalists who sought money and influence. Each, throughout their careers, had been flexible in their lines of interests and business. For the time being, they found ranching to be just another way of making money—or at least keeping money on the move. Undoubtedly, there was some further reward for owners, perhaps the cachet claimed from owning a Texas cattle ranch.[20] But that was not their goal. Throughout much of its operation, the XIT Ranch bore the antipathy and antagonism of neighbors, competitors, Texas politicians, and even its partners and stockholders. Yet today the XIT Ranch, for those even slightly aware of its one-time existence, is viewed with near reverence.[21]

The XIT emerged after a West remembered most for a cattle business built on local, individual enterprise had transformed into a "corporate enterprise capitalized from alien sources."[22] No cattle bore the famous XIT brand before 1885. Many of the cattle initially purchased by the ranch were lost in the first two years when drought, fire, fences, and fierce winter storms created a fatal combination for the outfit's unprepared cattle. The XIT was just getting its start when the Old West revered by people today was ending.[23]

The rise of the XIT occurred within the context of the settling of the last frontiers in the contiguous United States. The American West's range cattle era straddles the transformation of the great American "Zahara" into the "Great American Breadbasket." The Great Plains were the last obstacle in the way of expanding America's population into every portion of the country. The great ranches that reached from Texas to Montana exemplify what Elliott West called "the recent and the older folded neatly into the new."[24] Cattle ranching on the Great Plains created an economic relationship along a north-south axis that guided the influx of settlers to the last great tracts of public lands left for them. In eastern Montana, most of the triangle of ground lying between the confluences of the Missouri and Yellowstone rivers, Texans' northern range, was either federal, state, or railroad land. Land ownership and management there were complicated as the federal territories were adopted as states. Most official surveys were completed by 1910 and thousands of acres were open for homesteading under several federal acts. The federal government did not withdraw from the land sale business, however, and the states and railroads were eager to sell their land as well. In Texas, where there was no federal land, where people could own as much as three million acres, and where railroad companies also controlled great amounts of land, landowners and the railroads worked closely to bring settlers to the Panhandle. Texline, Dalhart, Channing, Friona, Hereford, and Farwell are among the several towns obliged to count the XIT as a prime contributor to their existence.[25]

The beef bonanza expanded the market economy in the American West. Yet it carried with it capitalism's propensity to destroy as it creates. Writing nearly fifty years ago, Alfred Crosby, in his seminal *Columbian Exchange,* contemplated the arrival of Europeans in the New World in the late fifteenth century. Lacking much optimism, Crosby wrote, "We, all the life of this planet, are the less for Columbus." Crosby concluded that the introduction of horses, cattle, and pigs to the Americas brought "wild oscillation of the balance of nature." Far from a benevolent gift to aboriginal people, Crosby saw cattle as the champion of conquest. "The frontier of European civilization," he wrote, "advancing in the interior of the Americas has been that of the cattle industry," and this resulted in "the squandering of riches" from erosion, overgrazing, and predator management. Crosby's outlook seems not to deter modern Americans, however; recent news reports suggest that overall meat consumption in the United States is rising to unprecedented levels.[26]

The American West plays a prominent role in the origin story of the United States as many, both Americans and others around the world, envision it. Stories like this can have villains as well as heroes. This one is intended to make a point, but it purposely leaves room for interpretation and judgment. Over the years, reading the letters and records left behind by people featured in this story, one gets to know something about them, to begin to understand what kind of people they were, to perhaps even care for them. For the most part, the men featured here approached life no differently than anyone else might have during the late nineteenth century.[27]

Although the capitol continues to serve Texas, the ranch that developed on the land that the state gave to pay for it is long gone. The cattle business was challenging, and the fast money the Syndicate initially envisioned coming from land sales proved unrealistic until much later. According to one observer of the XIT, the principal ranch owners later offered that, if they had it to do again, they would have passed on the deal. Charles Farwell, another Syndicate member, a one-time U.S congressman and senator, at one point offered to sell the whole thing back to Texas. An Austin newspaper set an early tone for the long-running debate over whether Texas or the capitol's builders got the best of the bargain:

> We Texans are proud of our state house and think we have good value for the $3,000,000 it cost us—at least that we believe was the value of the land we gave in exchange for it. It will come as a surprise to some that our capitol building cost us $20,000,000. Such is at least the statement of one of the contractors, ex-Senator Farwell of Chicago, who is booming his property. . . . It would be interesting to know on [what] valuation Farwell & Co. pay taxes. This is a matter that Panhandle assessors should look into.[28]

~~

Crooked Lines

Texas legislators in 1879 set aside the three-million-acre Capitol Reservation in the northwest Texas Panhandle as the funding source for the largest state capitol building in the country. The huge tract, which became better known as the XIT Ranch, traced its origins to the 1876 Texas constitution. Almost as an afterthought, the delegates at the constitutional convention had inserted a section in the document allowing for the exchange of a portion of the state's dwindling unappropriated public lands "for the purpose of erecting a new State Capitol and other necessary public building at the seat of government." Unlike most of the states accepted as one of the United States of America after implementation of the U.S. Constitution, Texas, by virtue of the Compromise of 1850, had retained control of its vast unclaimed regions. Despite state leaders' intentions to preserve its public lands for the benefit of its residents and actual settlers, substantial portions of that land wound up under the control of a variety of syndicates, combines, and corporations often controlled from beyond the state's boundaries. This included the syndicate that developed the XIT Ranch.[1]

Texas officials, through grants and very low prices, distributed some 150 million acres of public land from 1850 to 1890. Legislation enacted liberal state land policies in the late 1870s and the early 1880s. Although many of the writers of the 1876 constitution intended their actions regarding land policy to benefit small farmers and encourage settlement, many of the men left with the task of implementing the constitution held different ideas on how best to encourage that settlement. Railroad land grants, a topic dominating debate during the convention, continued generously at a ratio of sixteen sections of Texas real estate for every mile built of track. The federal government, with the Pacific Railway Act of 1862, initially allocated five alternate sections per mile of track laid on each side of the road's right-of-way. The new Texas constitution reaffirmed an 1873 law requiring that half of all remaining public lands proceeds go to public education. It allocated two million acres to support a Texas university. They set aside the Capitol lands in optimistic hope that it would attract settlement. Few of those gathered in Austin in late 1875 expected those lands to so soon pass into the hands of other than actual settlers. Eastern and foreign ownership in Texas seemed anathema to them. The same attitudes seemed to prevail after about 1883, but for a short period Texas offered a free-for-all to land speculators and deep-pocketed syndicates lured to Texas by a somewhat mythical "beef bonanza."[2]

Over thirty-two million acres of land grants went to railroad companies that came and went, seldom achieving their promises but nevertheless earning the coveted land allotments granted on track mileage. The Texas constitution limited to twelve years the amount of time that railroads maintained their land rights, at which point the certificate reverted to the state. Yet few of these grants ever returned to state control. Most were purchased from the grantee for pennies on the acre by speculators and cattle operators. Besides railroad grants and the Capitol Reservation, Texas allocated about five million acres for internal developments, primarily for waterway improvements, the promotion of industry, a central road, and even shipbuilding projects. The failure of many of these projects often presented a financial burden to Texas. Later legislatures attempted to apply time restrictions upon foreign or out-of-state corporate ownership to stem domination of Texas real estate by outside investors. Supporters of such plans later targeted the operators of the XIT Ranch, decrying its foreign investors and absentee management. But a time limit on redemption was not the common rule among the array of land policies enacted through the years. The ranch operators protested loudly and effectively, even offering to return the acreage to the state at the same price it was then offering school lands at the time—$2.00 an acre.[3]

When Gov. Oran M. Roberts urged the Sixteenth Legislature in 1879 to implement the terms of the 1876 constitution regarding the building of a new capitol, flaws in land distribution practices were becoming obvious to at least some officials. Early bounty grants for service during the Texas Revolution or issued during the republic period offered a "league and labor"—4,605.5 acres. Later land allotments, however, provided certificates authorizing the bearer to claim between 320 and 1,280 acres. The 1876 constitution continued a guarantee of 160-acre homesteads to every Texan who wanted one. This lasted until 1898, when the Texas supreme court declared the public domain to be exhausted in *Hogue v. Baker*. In 1876 the state authorized a $150-per-year payment to indigent veterans of the Texas Revolution. When this payment became a strain on the treasury, the 1879 legislature replaced it with a law granting these veterans certificates to claim from 640 to 1,280 acres of unappropriated land. Texas passed a statute in 1881 that provided land to all disabled Confederate veterans or their widows. Both actions drew further attention to the problem of dwindling land surpluses and the limitations of policies that seemed to be allowing the accumulation of more and more formerly public land into the hands of fewer and fewer people.[4]

On July 14, 1879, legislators approved Roberts's proposed "Fifty-cent Act." Half of the proceeds for public land sales were designated for the state's permanent school fund. Despite a 640-acre limit on land purchased under the act, speculators, land agents, and entrepreneurs found ways around the restrictions. Before the law's repeal in 1883, some 3.2 million acres of public land fell into private hands. Land speculators and large livestock operations took much of it. The XIT was thus not the only big cattle outfit to benefit from generous land policies. The fifty-four West Texas and Panhandle counties included in the Fifty-cent Act soon became home to a select few "Land & Cattle" companies. The "imperial ranch" was the big cattle operation financed, and often overseen, from distant headquarters and often dependent on foreign investment. Eastern and foreign money controlled vast swaths of the West. Although men in saddles on cattle ranges in Texas and Montana provide a familiar icon, the offices and boardrooms in Chicago and London from where ranch managers and foremen received their orders present an often misunderstood or overlooked aspect of the American West and the "classical" period of the cattle business often depicted by popular media. And for investors who put their time or money into a huge livestock operation, their actions did not represent simply a series of financial transactions; they represented a cultural performance establishing themselves as a participant in the mad dash of imperial capitalism then sweeping the globe.[5]

A few Texans saw folly in Texas's land policies of the late 1870s and early 1880s, recognizing that the state could not sustain the pace at which it was giving up its lands to private ownership. The commissioner of the General Land Office in the state at the time, William C. Walsh, carefully managed land transactions until a new administration led by Gov. John Ireland began rolling back Governor Roberts's policies. Ireland, in his inaugural address to the Eighteenth Legislature on January 9, 1883, in a candid and detailed speech covering past, present, and future Texas, said about land policies in the state:

> I think I see away down the corridors of time this splendid territory teeming with millions. No more public lands; no more cheap homes—poverty and squalid want gathering fast and thick around the inhabitants, when some one of them will gather up the fragments of our history and read to the gazing and mind-famished multitudes how this generation had in its power and keeping a fund that should have gathered like a snowball as time rolled on, and how, if we had been true to ourselves, to posterity, to *them*, they could have educated all their children, paid all their taxes, reared school houses, built roads and bridges—and then I see them turn with deep mutterings from the wicked folly that crazed our people from 1865 to 1882.[6]

The governor earned the nickname "Oxcart John" for his steady opposition to land grants and subsidies for railroad companies building in the state. Ireland opposed giving away the state's resources to those whose greater interests rested elsewhere. He stubbornly insisted that builders contracted for the construction of the state's new capitol complete the building using primarily Texas materials. No fan of the project, Ireland undoubtedly used his determined leadership to bring a successful outcome for both the state and the building's contractors. The governor envisioned a Texas for Texans and felt the new capitol should reflect that. Long debated, the equity of the bargain, to the satisfaction of few, remains unanswered.[7]

Legislation in 1883 repealed the Confederate soldiers grant, and the indigent veterans grants ended in 1887. When the Chicago syndicate offered to build the new capitol in exchange for the land set aside for that purpose, they likely did not fully understand the terms of the contract or realize that the state's changing policies hindered their efforts to sell the land profitably. Legislating a minimum price essentially established the maximum price as well. Why would anyone pay $2.00 an acre when similar land was available at $0.50 per acre?[8]

Certainly, the state could and did find benefit in the commercial appropriation of portions of its lands. In northwest Texas—the Panhandle—the commercial exploitation and privatization of the region by large cattle-ranching enterprises redefined the image of the state. Cattle ranching reshaped the state's legacy from its foundational heritage of Southern monoculture into the place where the West begins. Although Texas can claim a long association with cattle husbandry, in the latter half of the nineteenth century the beef business changed from a parochial craft that supplied a primarily local clientele into a globalized commodity industry. The men who came to own the XIT fit right into a network of political and financial power in Texas and elsewhere, embracing the Gilded Age policies then guiding industry in the United States and commerce around the world.[9]

Few delegates defining future laws at Texas's constitutional convention in the fall of 1875 likely imagined that their decisions would result in the development of a huge ranch in the Texas Panhandle—or a single grand building in Austin. Continued use of what most still thought to be a nearly limitless body of unappropriated Texas land was a popular idea among the delegates. Unfortunately, most misunderstood the resources and extent of these lands and overestimated the capabilities of a small government to manage them.[10] The subsequent rush of large livestock operations into northwest Texas, including the establishment and operation of the XIT Ranch, demonstrated that.[11]

It is likely, too, that the framers of the constitution did not expect that the land eventually set aside would wind up in the hands of Illinois capitalists far more interested in the bottom line of their balance sheet than the benefits their actions would bring to Texans. Convention delegates saw the opportunity as a last chance to exploit the last bits of the nation's yet unclaimed reaches. Led by John V. Farwell, a wealthy dry goods merchant in Chicago, the Capitol Syndicate formed with the original intent of subdividing and selling the huge land tract to individuals and groups eager to establish farms, towns, and ranches in Texas's undeveloped regions. Instead, they found there to be little demand for the land set aside as the Capitol Reservation. The very policies that created it hindered its profitability. The creation and operation of the XIT Ranch highlights the political and economic connections that directed the country's cattle business and Texas's role in it. The real story behind the creation of the legendary ranch begins with the 1879–80 survey undertaken to identify the bounds of the new reservation and the subsequent acquisition of the capitol project contract by Farwell and his associates.[12]

The convention delegates did not specify an exact location for the reservation, and their actions may have been little more than a way to assuage representatives from the state's western regions and their desire for further development, particularly through rail access. The U.S. Army's expulsion of the Comanches and Kiowas from the remote Panhandle, considered little more than a desolate wasteland by many at the time, made it more attractive. Mexican shepherds, merchants, former buffalo hunters, and a few brave farmers moved in to eke out a scant living from the unforgiving, although not unusable, plains of northwest Texas. Cattlemen, too, soon ventured there. More people came to the region by the time lawmakers ordered a survey of the reserve. Some held apparent legal claims to portions of what would later be within the area defined as part of the capitol project. Cattle ranchers locating there were not interested in sharing the Panhandle's meager resources with others.[13]

For years, trail drivers, exchanging drinks and stories with buffalo hunters and traders in cow town saloons, had looked forward to exploiting the great stands of grama and buffalo grass spanning Texas's Panhandle country. A commonly told story has Charles Goodnight, his cattle operation in southern Colorado crushed by the Panic of 1873, starting over again back in Texas. He scraped together enough financial backing to put together a herd in Colorado. Still leery of Indian raids but attuned to the land qualities around him, Goodnight cautiously drifted his new herd south. According to biographers, when the legendary Ranger, trail driver, and cowman struck the Canadian River and followed it into Texas, he found large bands of sheep along its banks and in the nearby hills. Small "plazas" of one or a few Mexican families subsisted up and down the river, including at the site of the soon-to-be founded town of Tascosa. A few whites, too, managed sheep and small cattle herds there or operated other businesses along the river's tributaries. Goodnight, as the story is told, having heard of another site farther south, negotiated with the *mayordomo* of the *pastores* on the Canadian. He offered to take his cattle south to the Palo Duro Canyon as long as the *pastores* never brought sheep to his range there. Goodnight later often consulted with the XIT operators and supplied the ranch's first purebred Hereford bulls.[14]

Sheep or not, the old trail driver passed on a claim to what might have been some of the best grazing ground in the southwest United States. Perhaps he anticipated the milder climate of the Palo Duro or a slight advantage in tree covering and shelter. Many say Goodnight settled there to depend on the steep canyon walls as natural fencing. Goodnight may have known exactly where he was going, possibly after consulting with a pair of ambitious North Texas land speculators.[15]

Two enterprising sometime lawyers had operated in the area for some time. Well known and with offices in the North Texas towns of Denison and Sherman, Jules "Jot" Gunter and William Benjamin "Ben" Munson advertised themselves as "Dealers in Real Estate." Munson had visited the Panhandle as early as 1874. The local paper in Denison welcomed his safe return in one issue. "W. B. Munson has returned from a two week tour in the extreme West," wrote the editor for the *Daily News* on May 5, 1875. He continued, opining, "Verily, Munson is a great traveler; he will be extremely fortunate if he doesn't get his hair lifted some of these times." Eight months later, the Texas constitutional convention memorialized the U.S. Congress for continued frontier protection in an effort to make sure that Munson and other developers in the Panhandle were not attacked by Indians.[16]

The Indian problem on the Texas frontier effectively ended with Quanah Parker's surrender in June 1875, but many people had seen the Indians subdued before and remained skeptical of the safety one could expect in that part of the state. Small bands of renegade Indians occasionally escaped the reservations over the next few years to raid into the Panhandle, but their slight numbers caused few problems. A detachment of Texas Rangers led by George Washington Arrington, to the chagrin of army leaders at Fort Elliot, pursued renegades across northwest Texas, reportedly rooting reluctant Indians out of their Panhandle hideouts into early 1880.[17]

If people were not too anxious to find out what the Panhandle was really like—at least not yet—it worked to the advantage of operators like Gunter and Munson. A forbidding image of the region served the interests of the primary beneficiaries of Gunter and Munson's efforts, too. As their numbers grew, cattlemen discouraged settler entry into the Panhandle. The so-called Fence Cutting War of 1883–84 represented the culmination of these actions. With the Indian danger under control and buffalo nearly gone, large cattle interests moved quickly to secure their claim to the northwestern Texas plains. It was Gunter and Munson who brought Goodnight back to Texas and helped provide him and his partner Adair with secure title to more than 200,000 acres of prime grazing lands.[18]

Munson had "read" the law for Oran M. Roberts in the future Texas governor's Gilmer office before coming to Sherman in the early 1870s. He and Gunter, another one-time law apprentice to Roberts, met soon after Munson's arrival in Sherman. Booming growth in the area soon convinced them that their legal backgrounds served a better purpose in the land business than with practicing law. When residents in Sherman failed to show interest in a plan to draw the Missouri, Kansas & Texas Railway—the "Katy"—to town, a group of men including Gunter and Munson founded Denison almost overnight and offered bonuses to the Katy men to build their North Texas yards and branch line hubs there, thereby taking an important step toward cementing their position in Texas history and their contributions to the growth and prosperity of nineteenth-century Texas. In their efforts, however, little attention focused on "actual settlers."[19]

According to a local historian, the relationship between Gunter and Munson made for "a most unusual law firm." "There has never been, nor will there ever be, another law firm like this one," Neilson Rogers told a Sherman, Texas, reporter in 2001. An old photograph showed that beneath the firm's letterhead listing the men's names in bold appeared the words "Attorneys at Law and Dealers in Real Estate." A sidebar reminded customers of the complete services they offered: "Lands Listed, Patents Secured, Titles Investigated, Taxes Paid." "During its 10 years of existence," Rogers continued, "this law firm surveyed so much of West Texas that it gained the reputation of the only law firm which could find vacant land in West Texas. At the same time, the firm was buying land certificates for as little as $25 each and selling the land for $1 per acre."[20]

The business of locating land was not new, but circumstances in Texas in the 1870s made it an especially lucrative venture there. Gunter and Munson became among the best known of these enterprises. Successful in Grayson, Cooke, Denton, Wise, Clay, and Wichita counties, the partners sought new horizons in the Panhandle. More than six thousand land grants recorded in the General Land Office attest to the success of the Gunter and Munson partnership. The pair preferred railroads as clients, but they also dealt in bounty lands, veteran grants, and the other land scrip Texas had issued throughout its history. Gunter and Munson maintained a cadre of men locating grantees, surveying land, and filing patent claims for title to grants and school lands.[21]

Many practices by individuals, companies, and politicians accompanying the disposal of Texas's public land in the 1880s would not draw favorable review from observers today. By illegal and legal methods, many exploited weaknesses in Texas's land policies to put personal ambition before state goals or actual settlers. Thomas Lloyd Miller is one of the few historians to look critically at Texas's land policies over time. "The average Texas citizen, in matters concerning land," Miller wrote, "was not . . . above reproach." Even the most honest of men, he continued, could not resist any opportunity, legal or illegal, to get more land. Clever entrepreneurs could easily exploit Texas land policy, riddled with loopholes, to their own advantage. As the last great tracts of the southwest frontier, West Texas and the Panhandle became popular places in Texas to find free or almost free land. A huge land fraud scheme in Texas, uncovered in 1877, led to arrests throughout the country on charges of forging land records and arson.[22] Outright fraud was probably unnecessary in the Panhandle, though. The law did not bar the activities of most Texas land agents. Distributed from Spanish times, even a small portion of outstanding land certificates, if claimed, represented an extensive portion of the public lands. Many remained outstanding and with few restrictions on them.[23]

Operators like Gunter and Munson found the holders of unused land scrip and purchased their certificates, often for pennies to the acre. Surveyors mapped choice parcels of unclaimed land, usually with adequate water, wood, or, perhaps, surface mineral resources, matching these to a land certificate. With state patent laws satisfied and legal title to thousands of acres, focusing primarily on cattle interests, Gunter and Munson bundled large contiguous parcels in West Texas and the Panhandle and sold them to wealthy investors. Grantees often turned out to be widows or other assignees of the original bearer, a trend indicated in Texas Land Office records beginning in the mid-1870s. The old soldiers were dying. Too often the only thing left to their widows was a discolored and worn land certificate recognizing service at San Jacinto or during the "Siege of Bexar." Acting first as agents for scrip holders, the land men provided the necessary survey notes to district land offices and then filed sales transfers of the parcels to the speculators, who then filed for the patent approving the land title.[24]

Cash-strapped rail companies were more than eager participants in Texas's land selloff. Railroad land grants, no matter where the line operated (if it ever did), could be selected from any of the state's vast expanse of unappropriated public lands. Agents purchased hundreds of land certificates from the railroads throughout the western reaches of Texas in the 1870s and early 1880s. In the Panhandle, many were from the International & Great Northern Railroad Company, the Houston & Texas Central, the Texas & New Orleans, the Gulf, Colorado & Santa Fe Railway Company, and others.[25] Although some of these agents retained lands for their own purposes, most went to parties interested in the bourgeoning

Panhandle cattle industry. By the time Goodnight located his ranch at the top of the Palo Duro Canyon in 1877, this was the prevailing method for securing land.[26] Railroad land grants required that, for each section claimed for the railroad, an alternate section designated as school land be surveyed for the state. Proceeds from sale of these lands financed the state's public education programs. The state saved money by requiring the railroad or its assignee to survey the state's parcels. Purchasing railroad grants at low prices, Gunter and Munson often were able to buy adjacent school lands, benefiting from the Fifty-cent Act, despite lawmakers' public intention that those lands be sold to actual settlers. Gunter and Munson profited greatly by supplying large tracts of prime grazing land to cattle interests. Eastern or foreign capitalists eager to be part of the then booming cattle industry, as well as to own a piece of the already mythical West, financed many of the cattle operations. According to Munson's privately published biography, the pair made money "going and coming."[27]

Little reluctance existed for other men eager for huge profits in the cattle business and anxious to push their way into the Canadian River region. Gunter and Munson also served as land agents for a pair of successful traders from Dodge City, Kansas. Albert E. Reynolds and William McDole (W.M.D.) Lee formed the Lee and Reynolds Freight Company to fulfill the demands of an expanding government presence on the near southwestern frontier after the Civil War. As the military established forts in Indian Territory and Texas, the company contracted to supply all the needs of remote outposts at Fort Sill, Camp Supply, and Fort Elliott. As the Indians in the Texas Panhandle were subdued and driven out, buffalo hunters swept in to pursue the small, but still profitable, bison herds remaining in the region. Lee and Reynolds quickly moved in to service their business.[28]

The buffalo trade in the Panhandle became so lucrative that Lee and Reynolds established a satellite headquarters not far from Fort Elliott. First called "Hidetown," the outpost became Mobeetie, the first town founded in the Texas Panhandle. Chasing neither Indians nor bison presented long-term opportunity in any one place. The army was mostly successful at its job, and garrisons were shrinking in that part of the country. The buffalo were no match for the throngs of white hunters stalking them across the prairies. With business declining and their bank accounts full of cash, the partners decided to go their separate ways. Lee, who had settled in Mobeetie, had accumulated a substantial herd of cattle from his business dealings. With no prospects there, and settlers entering at a quicker pace, he moved his herd west, eventually finding his way to Romero Canyon in today's Hartley County.[29]

Liking what he found, Lee sent word to Reynolds, inquiring whether his old partner wanted to get into the cattle business. Receiving a positive response, Lee then moved to purchase land along Trujillo Creek, an important Canadian River tributary in today's Oldham County. There the partners established the LE Ranch. A rift in the two friends' business relationship developed in 1879. Already threatened by the state's intentions regarding the Capitol Reservation, with Gunter and Munson in the lead, Lee and Reynolds scrambled to secure separate claims to land about to be divided by a partnership gone bad. Reynolds's unwillingness to sell his portion of the LE angered Lee. The men never renewed their friendship but continued to operate independent ranches for some time. Both outfits were eventually nearly enclosed by the fences surrounding the XIT, and both Lee and Reynolds later had extensive interaction with the principals of the XIT. In 1888, the LS—Lee's portion in the split—traded about 71,000 acres for about 106,000 acres of XIT range. Lee also became a major partner with John Farwell, his brother Charles, and other associates in a plan to build deepwater harbors on the Texas coast. Reynolds brought in a brother as a partner to operate the LE Ranch, much of which bordered Capitol Reservation lands. While negotiating an "exchange of land," Abner Taylor once wrote Reynolds that "matters on the other side of the water" would delay the deal.[30]

Even prior to the creation of the Capitol Reservation, the Texas Panhandle was being divided among the "cattle barons." Some soon found out that the cattle business was not all it promised. They did not give up readily, however. Cattle and Texas land consolidated into fewer hands. The state's land policies attracted more Gilded Age entrepreneurs who took advantage of vast tracts of cheap land. Besides Lee and Reynolds, other large-scale neighbors like the Prairie and Hansford cattle companies soon joined Goodnight. More foreign principals appeared when the Matador, Espuela, and Francklyn Land and Cattle Company commenced operations. The advent of the imperial ranch on the arid reaches of the Great Plains and Rocky Mountain front coincided with the European scramble for empire then under way in the Middle East and interior Africa. The increase in European investment, British in particular, cannot be looked on simply as the result of optimistic reports of the opportunities for adventure in the American West.

Foreign investors viewed it as an opportunity to make a lot of money. Thousands of Europeans invested in foreign ventures around the world. And though it was romantic to claim that you had a cattle ranch in Texas or Colorado or Wyoming, few of these beef barons ever saw anything of ranching except for the stockholders' reports.[31]

Legislators ordered that the three million acres set aside for the Capitol Reservation be selected from the most northwestern counties of the state, all of which were included in the Fifty-cent Act. The legislature provided for a survey of all suitable land in the region and ordered the precise identification of the reservation boundaries. The governor led a five-person board to oversee the project, including the construction of the capitol building. To pay for the survey work, the legislature added fifty thousand acres to the reserve. Governor Roberts ordered that bid proposals on the work be solicited throughout the state. The advertisement drew numerous responses. Officials of the Capitol board accepted Joseph T. "J.T." Munson's bid of $7,440. The governor and board selected Nimrod L. Norton of Salado to oversee the work as the state's superintendent.[32]

Capitol Reservation surveyor Munson's younger brother was Ben Munson, of Gunter and Munson. The Munson brothers had been and would be—but currently were not—business partners. J.T., a lifelong bachelor, roomed in the fine house built by his brother in Denison. He is listed as the patentee in nearly two hundred land office abstracts. Strict penalties intended to prevent collusion inhibited government surveyors' ability to profit from the knowledge gained during their activities. It does seem curious that in an open bidding process, even in 1879, the brother of one of the state's most active speculators was selected to delineate the area in which his brother was at that moment most active. It probably did not hurt that Ben Munson studied law under the eye of the person heading the capitol project—Governor Roberts.[33]

J.T. Munson acknowledged acceptance of his contract in a letter to Governor Roberts on July 17, 1879. Outlining his immediate plans from his home in Denison, the surveyor wrote that he intended to travel to Fort Elliott, where he would meet part of his survey crew. He planned to rendezvous with the rest in Tascosa, a rough and tumble town with a well-earned reputation. They would begin working in Oldham County on the north side of the Canadian River, the surveyor told Roberts. Munson thanked the governor for offering the service of Texas Rangers, "though I anticipate no danger."[34]

Munson began the survey before Norton's arrival. The announcement of the capitol project launched a scramble among Panhandle land speculators and other interested parties. Reports from Norton, responsible for oversight of the Capitol Reservation survey, indicate his frustration with land speculators operating as agents for cattle interests. Correspondence from Norton and others suggests that Gunter and Munson attempted to influence the survey's outcome. Unfortunately, a fire in the old capitol at Austin in November 1881 destroyed most of the records of the state commission in charge of the survey. Questions remain unanswered regarding the early stages of the capitol project. Many likely will remain so.[35]

The Capitol Reservation stretched from the northwest corner of Texas, at a point last officially surveyed and marked in 1859, two hundred miles south along or parallel to the New Mexico territorial border. It reached an average of twenty-five miles in width. The Texas survey crews measured their progress in Spanish leagues, the square of which represents 4,428 acres. The project statutorily required visible markers to be erected at two corners of each league, but the surveyors were hard pressed at times to find rock or lumber on the bleak plain sufficient to fulfill their obligation. Doing their best to follow the governor's admonishment "that no land absolutely worthless such as rock or sand, barren of grass should be surveyed," the surveyors also struggled against harsh conditions.[36]

A late start and severe drought delayed the work. Munson's crew found the Panhandle environment challenging. By early September, "sickness having [reduced] the survey party below a fair working capacity," Norton allowed Munson to abandon the work until the spring of 1880. Norton tried to relieve Governor Roberts of any anxiety that Munson could not finish the job by the statutory deadline of September 1880. "There is . . . no reason to fear the fulfillment of his contract," Norton wrote. "He will simply come better prepared to operate in an isolated & [illegible] country." In beginning the survey prior to Norton's arrival, Munson may have stepped out of line. Suspicion marked the superintendent's tone when he wrote Roberts of his intention to inspect the areas surveyed prior to his joining Munson, using "two competent men [employed] at my own expense [to] accompany me over the entire work." He suggested the possibility that he might not return until December with a full account of "other reasons [for allowing Munson to leave,] which I will explain when I see you." The governor wrote back to inform Norton of his disinterest in further investigation. "I have received your letter . . . about your going back up north," the governor began. "If you have seen enough to regard the information that you have correct, I should think you could make your report upon it." What "other reasons" Norton wished to relay remain left to inquiry and speculation. It is not clear when Norton next saw the governor, but he was back home in Salado on December 1, far from what was, reportedly, a hard Panhandle winter.[37]

Norton saw for himself the many new arrivals in what lawmakers in Austin recently regarded a dangerous frontier. Indeed, it remained a dangerous place, especially if you were a Mexican shepherd or a hardworking "nester" trying to raise a few cattle and a small hay crop. Growing numbers of big cattle outfits in the area enforced their own rules on land policy. A livestock association formed in 1880 and hired such gunmen as Pat Garrett to stop "rustling." Owners and managers of the region's largest ranches sometimes implicated small cattle owners with less means or even sheep raisers in cattle thefts. The Denison *Daily News,* in early 1880, reported:

> The stock interests are rapidly increasing here [in northwest Texas]. Cattle largely preponderate. Sheep are confined mostly to Hartley, Oldham, and Deaf Smith. There are in these three counties about 150,000 sheep, distributed among some eighteen owners, none of whom own any lands, and all of them will have to move out soon unless they buy ranch sites, as the cattle men are rapidly buying up the desirable ranch sites that are for sale—in fact they already own most of them. The sheep men are, with two or three exceptions, Mexicans.[38]

The cattle interests had the money, power, and influence to do it. "The old notion among herd owners that free grass and water is their natural heritage, is fast vanishing," the *Daily News* article concluded. Commissioner Walsh, also a member of the Capitol board, did not share Governor Roberts's zeal when it came to parting with the state's resources. Walsh recognized the limits of Texas's land policies and clearly understood their shortcomings. Responding to Norton's reports, he expressed his concern in a letter to the governor: "The enclosed letter of Col. Norton only confirms my fear that interested parties, in collusion with Dist[rict] Surveyors would cover all the best land in the reserve and *date their entries back.*"[39]

Norton sent the governor several letters in the days prior to Walsh's letter. In one, he wrote, mysteriously, "for reasons that can be satisfactorily explained [later]," he had some information that "would in all probability save the state money." Norton trusted the governor to "regard this information as strictly confidential" and reminded him, "I only report facts as I find them without expressing any opinion." Norton himself received an equally mysterious letter from Edward Montgomery, the mail superintendent for the line from Tascosa to Fort Bascom, New Mexico Territory. In it, the postal agent suggested his willingness to produce witnesses to "the land grab or rather water grab of G&M." This and other correspondence suggesting illicit collusion among district surveyors and the partnership of Gunter and Munson troubled Norton—at least for the moment.[40]

Surveyor Munson may have felt pressure from officials after they received Norton's reports. Expressing both his frustration and gratitude, he wrote the governor:

> Is it desired by the Board . . . that I should now furnish to your Honorable Board maps and field notes of the surveys thus far made? Will the state pay me pro rata for the work done as soon as land can be sold for that purpose, in case I report field notes and plats at once . . . ? I find that the cost of the work is going to exceed my estimates very considerable. I should be very grateful should your board decide to pay pro rata as soon as sales are made.[41]

A resurvey of the Capitol Reservation was performed in 1886 and acknowledged errors in Munson's survey. Nothing ever revealed those errors to have been nefarious. Later correspondence indicates that Norton and Munson maintained a friendly working relationship. The tone of Munson's letter, however, signals his irritation at inquiries regarding his work. Rather than involving a question of his honor, this may stem simply from his own realization that he had badly underestimated the job. It is not the last time he informed the board that his initial bid was low. The timing of the letter may be coincidental, but that it comes simultaneous to questions raised about the survey seems more than just coincidence.[42]

Munson did not hide his loyalties when he spoke to at least one newspaper about what he thought of the prospects for the Panhandle after harsh conditions and low supplies drove him from his work there in 1879. "The *Denison Herald* has interviewed Mr. J. T. Munson who has just returned from making the survey in the Panhandle country where the 3,050,000 acres of land set aside for the construction of a state capitol are located. He says the country is not suited to agricultural products, because of the scarcity of water. The survey is not yet completed and will not be resumed until May next."[43]

His assessment differed considerably from Norton's later reports promoting the colonization potential of several areas within the reservation he felt well suited to agriculture. Munson may have simply been being honest, but it is easy to judge his attitude as reflective of his brother's interest in discouraging settlers in order to provide an opportunity for wealthier investors.[44]

Still pursuing his suspicions about Panhandle land claims, that winter Norton met Frank Sperling in Mobeetie or Dallas while the latter was in the custody of U.S. marshals. The Sperling brothers had opened a general store near Trujillo in 1878, before Lee and Reynolds's arrival at the same place soon after. The Sperling store did not fit with Lee and Reynolds's plans for the area. At least one account has Lee and Reynolds purchasing land from the Sperlings. The former pair may have been handed some, perhaps unwelcome, assistance in securing their claim to the area. Frank Sperling wrote Norton in February 1880 remarking on the "exposure of the Marshal and his gang" and the trader's unjust treatment by them just prior to that exposure.[45]

Deputy U.S. marshal Walter Johnson and four other men arrived in Mobeetie in the early fall of 1879. The group carried arrest warrants signed by a federal revenue commissioner in Dallas, but these contained no specific names or charges. Johnson's reputation in North Texas for his actions against the production and sale of illegal liquor was well known. Apparently, he was bringing that reputation to the Panhandle, and soon charges of selling stolen government munitions and illegal dealing in tobacco and liquor were made against several men and businesses, including Lee and Reynolds and Charles Goodnight.[46] After rounding up a few men in Mobeetie and from nearby Fort Elliott, Johnson and his men rode west to Tascosa and Trujillo, where Sperling and his brother Charles were arrested and charged with "not cancelling the grangers stamp on a whisky barrel."[47]

Johnson's group, returning to Dallas with ten or eleven prisoners, including the Sperlings and two soldiers, were overtaken by a posse led by Mobeetie officials. A federal versus state authority standoff ensued. By the end of December, charges against the men brought to Dallas were dropped and the men released. "You can imagine better than anyone down in the state, how much we were injured . . . [with] our business . . . [left] to the mercy of strangers," Frank Sperling wrote Norton, referring to his arrest and confinement. Wheeler County officials brought charges that Johnson and his men perpetrated fraud; the marshals apparently were paid on the number of warrant arrestees they took in. A Wheeler County court convicted Johnson of unlawful arrest and fined him $500.[48]

What injury had been done to the Sperlings' business during their weeks in custody is not detailed in Frank Sperling's letter to Norton. He did add that they "overcame it & prospects are favorable to a good trade in the future." Sperling, however, seemed to have a different motive for his letter than lamenting his recent arrest. "The immigration to this country," he wrote, "would increase considerable, if the land question was somewhat near favorable to settlers; but in the contrary it appears as if this waste country was held by a few speculators, who are determined to drive every settler from this land." The storekeeper continued "that Gunter & M has sold [much land] to Lee & Reynolds of Ft. Elliott, who said they would drive off everybody next spring to give room to their cattle." Although at least one newspaper suggested that Lee and Reynolds were among Deputy Johnson's initial targets, testimony in the case indicated that another deputy had filled out a warrant while at Lee's office in Mobeetie. Most of those arrested were mentioned in the testimony regarding when the warrants were completed. The Sperlings' names do not appear. It remains a mystery as to whose name appeared on the warrant filled out in Lee's office. Lee and Reynolds operated a store in Mobeetie not unlike the Sperlings' in Trujillo. Might Lee, just then attempting to obtain land in the Canadian River valley, have suggested to an inquiring deputy a suspect who might be an obstacle to his plans? "I have my doubt to the legality of G&M's patents," Sperling continued, "[and] beg you to inform me wether this party holds legal patents [and] have the right to move settlers from the land."[49]

Munson and Norton returned in the spring of 1880 to finish the job of surveying. A drought continued unabated, a condition well known among the handful of people actually familiar with the area. Munson's correspondence indicates a change in his attitude regarding the Texas Ranger escort provided by the state. Rather than tendering his thanks for an unneeded benefit, the surveyor seemed anxious. "Safety for those who shall do the work, in my opinion," Munson wrote Governor Roberts, "makes an urgent necessity for the escort asked." It was not Comanches and Kiowas he feared, but a growing number of powerful cattle interests securing their claims to the region.[50]

It is not clear that Roberts or anyone else ever acted on Norton's suspicions. In December 1879, Norton wrote a lengthy assessment of the legal situation regarding the Capitol Reservation—as he saw it. Without naming anyone, the superintendent assailed the efforts of the "surveyors" that would make it possible for "all the water & choice locations to fall to the share of individuals & all the least desirable lands without water to fall to the state." Norton's official correspondence clearly references Gunter and Munson and, by implication, Lee and Reynolds. He referred to questionable "square surveys" and cites "the Act of January 30, 1854," of which there were several, including "An Act to encourage the construction of railroads in Texas" and "An Act to establish a System of Schools." Norton encouraged Governor Roberts to make "null & void" claims to "the entire Canadian River front on both sides," allowing the land to "revert to the state from the simple fact that it [surveyors' practice of making such claims] is plainly & probably & definitely opposed both to the letter and spirit of a statute which admits of only one construction." Governor Roberts responded to Norton's suggestion that men with legal experience be sent to audit new claims at the district land office: "We have sent a good attorney to Jacksboro and other places to examine the book file &c in the Land offices."[51]

Norton delivered a detailed report of the survey and the land characteristics to the Capitol Commission board in January 1881. No further questions regarding the survey arose at the time. The surveyed leagues numbered from 1 to 739, although league 646 is not, inexplicably, listed. The Commission excluded fourteen leagues as inferior land. Another thirty were excluded as beyond the limits of the reservation. Mathematically, this represents 3,028,752 acres, a 21,248-acre discrepancy from the statutory requirement of 3,050,000 acres and a substantial amount of land. The Capitol Syndicate subsequently made various land swaps with neighboring ranches and later received a small parcel of valuable land in Harris County, but its members in 1888 agreed to close the deal with Texas, acknowledging that company records showed they were 23,743 acres short. Norton's notes offer detailed characteristics for the most representative leagues. The report does not indicate the characteristics for land found inferior. The last evidence of Norton's suspicions regarding the Capitol Reservation was his recommendation that Henry Kimball, a Tascosa blacksmith and "friend & supporter of the land of the state," who "has the confidence of all the parties [and] is perfectly familiar with the Spanish language," be appointed as a notary public. Norton then turned his attention to his duties as one of two commissioners to oversee the construction of the new capitol.[52]

In November 1880, the Capitol board received the first bids for purchasing the 50,000 acres set aside as payment for the survey. This first call solicited only three responses. A letter from Gunter and Munson addressed to Governor Roberts and the board withdrew the bid they offered on behalf of Lee and Reynolds, possibly reflecting the trouble between the former partners. The board then rejected the two remaining bids and readvertised the survey acreage. In the next round, Lee, under the Lee & Reynolds letterhead, submitted one of two bids received. His rival offered $0.50 an acre on a portion of the reserve and $0.555 on the remainder. Lee's bid, presented on December 10, offered $0.53 per acre on most of the land but $0.55 on a smaller portion. Another bid from Lee, dated February 1, 1881, came with a guarantee from Lucien and Lyman Scott of Leavenworth, Kansas. Bankers, the brothers partnered with Lee in the LS Ranch after Lee and Reynolds split. The state accepted their offer of $0.555 per acre. The law set the minimum selling price of land at $0.50 per acre, but the 50,000 acres represented choice grazing and well-watered sections—among the finest of the Capitol Reservation. Similar lands elsewhere in Texas sold for $2.00 an acre.[53]

The reports of questionable land practices along the Canadian River remain mysterious. A map of the Capitol Reservation demonstrates peculiarities. Substantial sections of the upper portion of the Canadian River valley to Tascosa, as well as several of its major tributaries on either bank, belonged to others. Eleven leagues in an angular area carved out near where the river drops from New Mexico into Texas mark the 50,000 acres set aside for the survey work. Nearly the entire Punta De Agua, a major tributary, also was in private hands at the time. In addition to the eleven leagues sold to finance the Capitol Reservation survey, a substantial portion of these riparian areas belonged to Lee. Later land exchanges between the XIT and other Panhandle ranching interests, along with lawsuits that redrew lines, obscure the originally declared boundaries. A careful examination of maps and other evidence suggests that the XIT's three million acres was not, as legend imagines, the largest continuously fenced ranch. A small gap in the ranch's boundary appears to separate the northern half of the ranch from the south. The evidence leaves one believing that Norton was only partly successful in his efforts to pursue Governor Roberts's instruction to "secure the best land for the State." Norton's final report makes no mention of any concerns he had expressed earlier. Although the men who built the capitol for three million Panhandle acres later spent time investigating historic land laws and earlier surveys, they showed little concern or suspicion that the land they received in return for building the capitol was less than called for in the bargain.[54]

Someone likely informed Gunter and Munson, acting on behalf of Lee and Reynolds, of the suspicions among government officials. Wishing therefore to avoid any hint of impropriety in subsequent transactions with the state, the partners withdrew their association in the bid for the survey acreage. Publicly, this allowed the state to distance itself from an association with Gunter and Munson's land speculation practices. The state, nevertheless, faced a fait accompli: the LE, LS, and other ranches were, after all, already there, and powerful men controlled them. Rather than face lawsuits and political conflict, might a bargain have been struck to maintain an illusion that the grand capitol could be built for the $1.5 million originally projected? What explains Lee's amended bid on the 50,000 acres of what is clearly among the best land offered throughout the Capitol Reservation? Other than the sale price of the land, $27,750—half of that earmarked for the public education fund, and the leagues sold—the official record is sketchy regarding the purchase. The first official report of the Capitol Commission board is silent on the question. Lee's bid is in the board's records. An 1887 map of Oldham County clearly identifies as Lee's property the same eleven leagues listed in the board's first report.[55]

In one of the many legal challenges fought by the Syndicate, the State of Texas, in 1923, acted against the Syndicate to recover 57,836 acres. Courts favored the state after finding fault with Munson's survey. Certainly, the errors were not the fault of the capitol contractors who received the land. Indeed, they paid taxes on those 57,836 acres for nearly forty years and by then had greatly reduced their Panhandle holdings. It appears that any conflicting claims at the time of the survey were resolved without affecting the subsequent agreement with the Chicago men, either with the state or with surrounding residents. No evidence of legal actions regarding previous claims to Capitol Reservation lands has been found. Perhaps when you have more land than most can imagine, a few thousand acres does not garner much attention.[56]

Gunter and Munson continued to operate successfully in the Panhandle until disbanding their partnership in 1885. As part of Munson's share in the dissolution of the partnership, he received the T-Anchor Ranch, just to the east of the Capitol

Reservation and north of Charles Goodnight's ranch. Founded in 1878, the ranch had been among the first to establish there. Munson sold most of the land and cattle soon after the partnership broke up.[57]

With the survey complete, the state held a contest for the new capitol's design. The Capitol board eventually selected Elijah E. Myers, a Detroit architect and designer of the recently completed Michigan capitol in Lansing. In making the selection, the board passed over a plan proposed by one of Texas's then best-known architects as well as that of the one woman who had submitted a proposal. Myers later also completed the preliminary architecture for Colorado's capitol building. The state's superintendents for the capitol project began locating construction material for the building and advertising for bids on the project from contractors.[58]

The design reflected the theme of the golden age of capitol building design. It reflected the tradition of the national capitol, particularly after Myers exchanged his original tower design for the trademark dome that eventually would top the building. Post–Civil War capitols, many in the West, carried forward as a symbol of democracy certain characteristics—the classic columns, reaching porticos, and awe-inspiring rotunda. Historian William Seale has called the capitols built from 1865 to 1900 "beacons on the landscape," broadcasting that there stood the house of the people. Done in essentially the Renaissance Revival style established by Thomas U. Walter in the 1850s, if the design lacked originality it did not lack in bold and pronounced expressions that Myers had developed in watching the Illinois capitol go up and, of course, in his most recent triumph with the Michigan capitol.[59]

Unquestionably, the state, members of the Capitol Commission board, and the board's superintendents placed tremendous burdens upon Myers. As shall be seen, Myers developed a strained relationship with the board, eventually resulting in his abandonment of the project. At this stage, however, he was its darling. After his unquestioned agreement to their modification requests, Myers accepted an additional $12,000 fee and an invitation to Austin to finalize the designs. In July 1881, building commissioners Norton and Joseph Lee, a respected Texas lawyer, former judge, legislator, and public servant, announced the state's intentions to seek bids "for supplying all material and completing every class of work required in the construction of a new State Capitol at Austin, Texas." The classic design of the building included enough room to accommodate the legislative,

judicial, and executive bodies of the state and apparatus for "light, heating, venti-
lating, plumbing, drainage, sewerage, elevators, and other appliances and conve-
niences of a complete modern State Capitol." The final construction specifications
are extensively detailed in the 280 line items delineated in the original contract.
Land parcels were to be transferred as the construction progressed through thirty-
five benchmarks.[60]

On November 9, 1881, while the Capitol Commission board met to consider
the plans and proposals thus far received, a poorly installed stovepipe ignited
documents in a storage room of the decrepit statehouse first occupied in 1854 and
kindly called "the Old Stone Capitol." Board members first attempted to extin-
guish the growing blaze, then tried to retrieve state documents that appeared in
the greatest peril. Austin firefighters arrived to what at first appeared to be light
damage and a controllable fire, but fire hydrants nearby failed. Firefighters found
themselves unable to contain the flames. By day's end, only a smoldering ruin
remained. A great many of the state's important records were lost to the blaze,
including documents regarding the capitol project. The fire delayed the construction bid deadline to January 1, 1882. Even so, only two bids appeared. One, from
Texas contractor A. A. Burck, who went on to play a different role in the project,
failed to attract the board members' confidence. Mattheas Schnell from Rock
Island, Illinois, submitted the winning bid.[61]

Initially, most officials felt the state could make do with what they had. Governor Roberts called a special session of the legislature in April 1882. He proposed three solutions for the continued housing of government agencies. One, the
supreme court and treasury buildings could be moved, intact, to the east side of
Capitol Square and used as temporary quarters until a new capitol could be completed; two, a temporary capitol could be built, salvaging the ruins of the burned
capitol and material from the supreme court and treasury buildings, or; three,
existing buildings could be purchased throughout the city, refurbished for appropriate use, then resold upon completion of a new capitol. The legislature handed
the decision back to the board in May, but not for the last time. After weighing
the alternatives, members appropriated $45,000 to build the temporary capitol on
an unused portion of the capitol complex. Requests for proposals were promptly
issued, and seven were received. The design selected was that of local architect
Frederick Ruffini, a protégé of the former building superintendent, Jasper Preston. J. B. Smith won the building contract and began construction on May 30.[62]

Work progressed rapidly on the temporary building. D. J. Duhamel, the Commission's superintendent who eventually replaced Preston, reported the mid-June completion of foundation excavation, measurements, and construction layout. In September, with the temporary structure well under way, disaster struck in the form of an autumn Texas storm. On September 8, Duhamel wrote the board "to report to you an accident which has occurred to the Temporary Capitol in so much as parts of the north and west walls have fallen." The storm brought questions about the stability of the structure. No significant delays stalled construction of the "very cheap affair," however, and newspapers announced major finishing work on the temporary statehouse near an end in early January. Dedicated on January 1, 1883, it was occupied in March, just in time for spring storms. During one, legislators withdrew from their deliberations to move across the street to watch the wind blow down their chambers. Some were disappointed when the building withstood the fury, as it would continue to in various capacities until succumbing to the fate of its predecessor in an 1899 fire.[63]

Chicago businessman Charles Farwell, a leading Illinois Republican politician and former congressman, learned of the capitol land deal under way in Texas through friends in Washington. Men everywhere knew about the great cattle empires growing in the West and the vast acres of grazing lands seemingly free for the taking in places like Texas. Later, back in Chicago and speaking with his merchant brother, John, the interest of his always-sensible brother surprised Charles. At a Republican Party meeting, Farwell heard of others interested—namely, political and business associates Abner Taylor and Amos Babcock.[64]

Ambitious in Illinois politics, Taylor was a respected contractor in Chicago, recognized for his contributions to the city's recovery after the disastrous Great Fire in 1871. It is not clear when Taylor earned the Southern honorary title "Colonel." Babcock, too, could boast of his own influence in both state and national politics. He may have been an architect, but the entry for his profession on his death certificate describes him as a "man of leisure." These two had already corralled Schnell, who, having previously raised the $250,000 bond and prepared the Texas capitol bid, was initially content to take his chances going forward with the project on his own. Schnell was a builder, but regarding the ownership of more land than some can imagine he had little clue. He must have come to his senses. According to Lewis Nordyke, one chronicler of the XIT Ranch, just prior to Christmas in 1881 Taylor, Babcock, and the Farwells struck a deal with Schnell.

On paper, Schnell continued as the sole bidder on the project. The agreement between the men then called for three-quarters interest in the project to be sold to the silent partners, should Schnell's bid be accepted. Burck and Schnell submitted their bids, along with their $20,000 bonds, on December 31, and the Texas commissioners opened and examined them on January 1. The Capitol board selected Schnell's bid. Schnell and the two commissioners, Joseph Lee and Norton, signed a contract on January 10, which the board accepted on January 18. A notarized bond of $250,000 dated January 31 appears in the Commission report signed by Schnell along with Taylor, Babcock, and the Farwell brothers. That date coincides with a telegram sent to Governor Roberts, the board, Norton, and Lee in which J. M. Beardsley, an influential Illinois lawyer with strong ties to the Republican Party there, informed them that "Schnells bond [is] signed by men worth two million dollars. It will be there and work commenced on time."[65]

Commissioners Lee and Norton turned the first shovels of earth for a groundbreaking ceremony on February 1, 1882. No real work began until February 20. Governor Roberts and the board accepted Schnell's bond on February 7. A letter from Illinois governor Shelby M. Cullom, penned February 1, offered glowing praise for Schnell and the others. About Taylor, Babcock, and the Farwells, Cullom offered that he "had known each of these gentlemen for many years. They are wealthy men and I feel sure are worth all together from two to three million dollars." Cullom also sent a telegram the day that the bond was accepted. The board recognized Taylor, Babcock, and the Farwells as the owners of an undivided three-quarter share of the project on February 11.[66]

The project team, under the auspices of "Taylor, Babcock, and Co." (TBC), accepted the contract on May 9. Despite their absence from the company moniker, the Farwells were equal, probably majority, owners. Charles Farwell's involvement in Illinois Republican politics almost certainly led the other men to minimize public attention to his involvement in the deal. Texans preferred not to draw attention to their larger dealings with "Yankees." Schnell disappears from the story after June 19. Mystery still shrouds TBC's assumption of the contract. As is the case for many aspects of this story, unanswered questions remain. The ledgers for the capitol account in the XIT Papers list a $13,900 payment to Schnell on May 9 and a $2,500 payment to an associate on June 6. Two separate payments of $7,200 and $5,300 between April 15 and May 18 appear for J. M. Beardsley. His role in earning $12,500 from them is unclear. Unraveling the origins of this

project is tricky. The influence, and profits, of the capitol project spread widely—
for better or worse.[67]

Within a month of TBC assuming full ownership of the building contract,
Babcock made his way to the wilds of northwest Texas. Political favors granting
him a military escort ensured a safe journey across the Texas frontier, and his
arrival in Tascosa, the notorious Panhandle town just off the eastern boundary of
Capitol Reservation lands, signaled a big change for that town and the hundreds
of square miles around it.

In a long review of the Capitol Reservation land transaction from the *Clipper*
in Colorado City, Texas, in the spring of 1886, the author reflected on the concerns that Governor Ireland had voiced in his message three years before:

> The enterprise . . . will in time undoubtedly become one of the very great
> proportions, and the children of the present day will criticize fifty years
> hence the wisdom of their fathers in getting so little for so much. The
> state house will not grow, but the value of these lands will. . . . But a few
> moments' business reflection will put a different face upon the matter. . . .
> it is enough to know that when this trade was made these state house
> builders paid more than \$1 per acre for land that could have been bought
> at that time for fifty cents.[68]

In time, as the *Clipper* predicted, the value of the land increased. Eventually
the bargain proved profitable for the Farwell family heirs, but it failed to produce
the great wealth that many had earlier predicted would come from the deal. The
ranch brought prestige and affluence to a few of those associated with it, too, but
nothing that elevated either owners or associates to heights reached by a Rocke-
feller or Carnegie. The XIT Ranch's operators, despite its size, struggled throughout its existence to sustain its operation. None of the principals in the operation
gained the title of "cattle baron." The Farwells and their associates gambled on the
hope that the Capitol Reservation would extend an already substantial business.
Instead it became an albatross around their necks.

༂

Capitol Capital

The November 1881 fire that took down the old capitol represented only a marginal delay for the effort to build the new permanent state structure. While Myers took the state's modification requests back to Detroit to complete the working plans for the building, representatives of the Capitol board fanned out to begin the selection of construction material for the project. Land commissioner William C. Walsh traveled to Detroit and Lansing and "derived much valuable information." Lee and Norton sought out quarries, examined metal and wood samples, and procured testing of various stone, lime, and cement from the Smithsonian Institution and the federal arsenal at Rock Island, Illinois. The most important search, however, was for a suitable quarry from which they could obtain the limestone for the capitol walls. From the beginning, Texans envisioned a structure truly representative of Texas. Obviously, choosing a non-Texan as their architect signaled a willingness to go beyond Texas for material and expertise, if necessary. Governor Roberts led commissioners to approach this issue pragmatically. Nevertheless, the state felt confident that most of the material and expertise required to build the capitol could be acquired in Texas. Although there is certainly room for discussion, the overwhelming initial choice of stone for the buildings was limestone, if for no other reason than its nearby abundance.[1]

An initial list of fifteen potential quarry sites eventually expanded to eighteen. Samples of some of the material were sent to the Smithsonian for analysis. Reporting their regret that they could thoroughly test only one sample, the scientific institute reported chemical evaluations on sample "No. 2." The Smithsonian called the sample "remarkably pure limestone" that would be of excellent use "in the construction of the foundation of your State House." But there was a caveat: "Care should be taken to protect the portion beneath the ground from the action of the water." The report concluded that "in the absence of better materials [it] can be very advantageously employed for superstructures." This sample came from what would become the Oatmanville quarry, just on the outskirts of Austin. The question of the stone used for the building superstructure plagued the project for some time to come. Stonework was not yet, though, a source of conflict. Lee and Norton were also testing the various limes and cements to be used and generally reported there to be "abundant and cheap" resources available nearby. Competent experts, like army general and engineer Quincy A. Gillmore, also tested the material. Regarding a sample from San Antonio, the general wrote, "Your Roman cement takes a very high rank among cements of its name and kind, being superior in quality to some imported Portland cements offered from time to time in this market." Kentucky cement identified by Taylor would eventually serve as the primary bonding agent used in the project.[2]

Signing a contract among parties does not guarantee the success of the contracted project. The state and the Chicago men spent much of the next three years defining among themselves what it was they all expected to get through their agreement and how they were going to go about getting it. This chapter examines events and actions revolving around the Capitol project from 1882 to 1885. Although focusing on developments regarding construction on the building, it also examines the formative activities undertaken regarding the future ranch.

On June 20, 1882, TBC assigned the entire capitol building project to Abner Taylor as the principal contractor, "the more effectually and properly to carry out the provisions" of the contract. The Syndicate was trying to minimize resentment that a non-Texas firm was to be responsible for construction of the capitol. Hoping to mitigate this issue, the partners agreed to place their construction business interests solely in Taylor's name. Apparently they felt that the fewer non-Texas principals associated with the project, the less resistance there would be to their activities. This was no more than a political ploy, and Taylor realized little additional business influence in the partnership because of it. This is the first substantial contract modification, other than ownership, undertaken by the parties since the board accepted Schnell's bid. It would not be the last. Two main changes for the June 20 contract were a request to change the size of the individual foundation stones and to change the stone selection from the "No. 4" stone to the "No. 2."

A clarification of the foundation excavation specifications slightly delayed later conflict that developed regarding the foundation itself. More important, however, this marks the end of TBC's investigation into the terms of the deal in which they found themselves. Working out the details of their business relationship, TBC chose Taylor, a clearly competent and ambitious man, to manage the project. At the time, this was probably an easy decision. Exactly who was in charge later plagued Syndicate operations. In 1882, and for some time to come, however, the partners seemed to work well with one another, with Taylor as the nominal chief of operations.[3]

Activity on the new capitol picked up after Taylor assumed the principal contractor position. Obtaining a set of plans by which he and his men could work became the first order of business. The building plans became an object of concern throughout much of the project. Technology has made duplication a simple process today. In 1882, an office built on the construction site housed a small army of draughtsmen working on developing and tracing the working construction plans from Myers's designs. Writing for Taylor, Reginald DeKoven, a Chicago aide, on July 7 complained to Lee and Norton that Taylor had instructed Burck on April 19 "to call upon you for detail drawings and plans" and that "we could not proceed much further without them." By this time, the state's building commissioners were usually observing at the construction office, as was the state's superintendent, E. J. Duhamel. W. D. Clark replaced Duhamel in October 1882, after criticism over the collapse at the temporary capitol.[4]

Exceptions to the on-site observation stipulation took place, of course, since the commissioners also had duties elsewhere. TBC was often helpful to the state when these occasions arose. Taylor often requested special passes on the various railroads he used during his travels, typically asking for the perquisite while negotiating lower shipping rates. Commissioner Norton planned to go to Detroit to consult with Myers and to look at the Michigan statehouse. Taylor, then negotiating with Missouri Pacific Railroad general manager H. M. Hoxie about shipping rates and cooperation on building rail lines to assist in the construction, requested a pass for Norton to travel to St. Louis. Taylor wrote to another railroad representative that "Norton wishes to come North in a few days" and asked if, since Hoxie had borne the man to St. Louis, he might also "fix him the balance of the way."[5]

John T. Dickinson became the secretary of the Capitol board in November 1881. He worked well with Taylor and for much of the project served as the primary conduit to Taylor for communication with the board. Among the first documented exchanges in this relationship, on August 11, Taylor apologized for not earlier acknowledging receipt of several important documents. On August 15, Taylor thanked Dickinson for the reports on the stone tested for use in the project. Dickinson became a critical link to the state for TBC and, perhaps, they felt his work worth rewarding beyond his service to the state. Correspondence in 1884 indicates that TBC was helpful to Dickinson's needs, too. Babcock wrote to an associate in Illinois: "I wish you would select a good buggy horse for the party I mentioned in Austin Texas. He wants a horse 6 to 8 years old. fair size and good style. fair roadster. Not particular about speed. Price $200. Ike do your best in making the selection for reasons I mentioned to you here. Ship horse to John T. Dickinson in Austin Texas . . . bill to Taylor Babcock & Co. here . . . write me a full description."[6]

Taylor followed up with Dickinson several days later, informing the board's secretary that Babcock's friend had found "a very fine mare" and Taylor supposed she would arrive any day. He went on to propose that Dickinson could likely find a better buggy in Austin, and that he should let Taylor know his thoughts. Correspondence between TBC and state officials is occasionally present in both the Commission and TBC records, though Commission records reveal nothing of this matter. Ethical oversight of gifts and other considerations to influential individuals politically was yet to reach the extent seen today. This bit of correspondence does not strongly indict either Babcock or Dickinson. The mention of price suggests that Babcock was passing along Dickinson's requirements for a fine northern-bred horse. Nevertheless, evidence exists that influence peddling at some level took place throughout the execution of the capitol contracts, beginning with the initial survey (see chapter 2).[7]

By August 1882, the excavation atop Capitol Square was nearly complete and Taylor advertised for bids to undertake the foundation work. The excavation of the site etched a 61,000 square foot divot out of a single, solid piece of bedrock. The completed capitol eventually rested on a 2.25-acre footprint. The city of Austin began to feel the stress of the project in May when blasting began. Local newspapers reported growing danger at the capitol site, warning that "large pieces of rock fall among private residences in that part of the city." A voice for the city would continue to rise, first over the safety of the temporary capitol project after the accident there, then concerning the "frog and snake pond" that grew during the excavation and construction of the foundation. Rail right-of-way through the city to haul stone to the construction site would cause more conflict.[8]

Excavation contractor Ed Creary was not a favorite of Taylor. Gustav Wilke won the foundation bid awarded on August 31. Wilke would later go on to be a trusted associate in the project and was assigned as chief contractor by TBC for the duration of the project. For now, the foundation work would entail any correction necessary to the excavated site, such as concrete work, as well as the quarrying of the limestone, the water table, sewerage, and the foundation itself. In early September, Creary received a terse letter informing him of his loss of the foundation contract. "We received a much lower proposal," Taylor informed Creary, "and expect to award the contract on said proposal."[9]

Taylor had already determined that the quarry site initially selected by the board, represented by sample No. 4, despite complete testing on sample No. 2, would not provide the quantity of rock necessary. The board acknowledged this in August. This marked the beginning of difficulties regarding the various stone used in construction. Unsatisfied with the selections stipulated in the contract, Taylor went on to invest another $16,000 in dispatching his own experts to locate and secure quarries capable of supplying high-quality stone in enough quantities. The issue hindered progress on the building until 1886. Taylor, still waiting on a complete set of working plans, passed time contacting railroad officials to negotiate haul rates and a road from the Oatmanville quarry site.[10]

With excavation complete, to Taylor's thinking, TBC was due a land allotment. The contractor submitted papers to claim the first land certificate, 1.5 percent of the three million acres. "Under the terms of the contract," Taylor wrote to commissioners Lee and Norton on August 15, "all the payments and work has been done." Another letter, apparently to an Austin banker, accompanied the foregoing message, summarizing a payment of $5,574.50 for Creary. Taylor posted again the next day elaborating to Burck his instructions to the bank: he should "furnish the bank with W. K. Finbaugh & Co. claim of amount due them. . . . Also get from Creary his receipted pay roll and file with the Commission." The temporary capitol collapsed within a month of this claim, and the consequences of that incident occupied the commissioners' attention. No further action took place until April 1883. TBC apparently had rocky relations with Creary, although Taylor sought to justify TBC accounts fully through further attempts to obtain vouchers and receipts from Creary. Perhaps highlighting the dearth of expertise in projects of this scale, company ledgers for TBC show that Creary was later assigned other projects, including clearing one of the quarry sites and work on the railroad bed from the quarry.[11]

There is little correspondence to reflect Taylor's probable frustration with the state's inaction on his request to transfer the first land allotment. In the autumn of 1882, he filled his time with rail rate negotiations and land and investment inquiries. Several exchanges with Myers took place, one in which he proposed that Myers delay a trip so that Taylor might "be able to go south with you when you go." The board asked Myers to review the temporary capitol debacle. He replied by letter with lengthy recommendations on September 21. Draughtsmen worked in both Detroit and Austin to complete copies of the capitol plans. Myers, at first, made frequent trips to Austin to inspect progress there. His report on the temporary capitol does not make it clear that he visited that fall. A set of complete plans for use by the contractor was delivered in October. Myers may have been on hand to approve them. Already, Myers was revealing habits of excuses and delays that would later drive a wedge between him and the board. Babcock's presence in Austin in October "to secure railroad right-of-way" is well known. Taylor reported his "health poor" during this time and his expectation that "Col Babcock will go to Austin in my place."[12]

Taylor spent much of this downtime fielding the many inquiries regarding land. He began floating potential sales arrangements, possibly in hopes of taking advantage of the unprecedented Texas land boom of the Roberts administration. "We would not care to sell any part of our Texas land for less than $2.50 per acre," he wrote Abner Morgan of New York. Taylor never offered the land for prices the state offered for similar parcels it continued to hold in West Texas and the Panhandle, however. TBC, nevertheless, would be a target for the next governor, John Ireland, who sought to roll back the liberal land policies encouraged during the Roberts years. Unfortunately for Taylor and his partners, Ireland would use the capitol deal to influence public opinion against those policies. Unwittingly, though, the governor probably improved the TBC position. Not all the public opinion in Texas was going to change an airtight contract. Later, Taylor simply had to be patient while Ireland ranted about the inequities of the contract. Perhaps anticipating a looming need for capital, Taylor also floated the idea that the partners seek investors in England.[13]

When Ireland took office January 16, 1883, the temporary capitol was nearly ready for occupancy. North up the hill, foundation preparation had continued through the winter as the solid stone was prepared for the basement walls and sewerage routes were set. Equipment and materials were at the site by January 1. TBC continued to work toward securing right-of-way to build a trunk line to the site. In December, Taylor, who had continued in his sick bed and was restricted to Chicago throughout the fall, wrote to reassure Myers. The biggest hurdle to progress, he told the architect, was the Austin city government. "There has been no progress in the matter of obtaining the right of way, but Wilke is at work down there opening a quarry and preparing the foundation and Col. Babcock is still there and I think will obtain the right of way soon. I have not heard a word about the Commissioners." Presumably, this last comment indirectly references the just-completed election and the turnover in board membership. Surprisingly, little discussion of the political events of any period are common among TBC correspondents, although there is an aura of political maneuvering throughout much of the records of the Commission and the XIT Papers. The city, protective of its main thoroughfare, Congress Avenue, granted right-of-way up East Avenue, then west seven blocks along Mesquite Street. Later, private landowners forced bitter negotiations for right-of-way from Oatmanville and the Burnet County quarries. A note to Taylor's foreman, G. W. Turner, in August 1883 typifies the nature and difficulties faced in these efforts: "Your favor of the 23rd at hand. I think you had better pay Mrs. Glasscock the $100 for right of way as it will not pay to fight."[14]

There were other obstacles to securing the means to get material to the building site. Taylor wrote an Austin lawyer, A. J. Peeler, to request his services in defending the group from a suit for damages brought by an Austin citizen. Taylor told his foreman in Austin that "Mr. L. Schlinger has commenced suit for damages to lot 1, block 143 [directly east of Capitol Square]. I sent the papers to Mr. A. J. Peeler and attorney, and asked him to look after the matter. Please call and see him and give him any information you can." That property was just north of Mesquite Street, where the spur of the rail line ran. Damages from blasting during excavation on the building site were reported. It is not known what Schlinger claimed as his loss.[15]

Instead of London, Taylor wound up in Austin continuing negotiations on railroad right-of-way, construction, and hauling rates. It was now clear to him that the circumstances of a new administration in Austin required a ground-level view and assessment of the project and politics. The main issue was the new governor's rumored dissatisfaction with the plan to use limestone in the new capitol's superstructure. Ireland felt that more attractive and durable granite available close by was more representative of Texas. The proximity of any materials to be used was important. Railroads, despite grants from the State of Texas for something over 32 million acres of public lands, were not in a generous mood when it came to negotiating haul rates and other forms of cooperation on the statehouse project. Taylor began serious negotiations and bidding on material for the railroad he intended to build from the quarry. Frugality was in his nature. While he sought partners in constructing a trunk line from the Oatmanville quarry, he offered potential incentives to those willing to help the most. Seeking to minimize TBC's dependence on the Missouri Pacific, Taylor sought to curry favor from someone who might be able to lure competition from other carriers:

> I am trying to make an arrangement with H. M. Hoxie to haul our material for the state house at Austin, Texas. We will have about 20,000 cars of stone. . . . our freight bill will be from $300,000 to $500,000. The quarry . . . [is] about 5 miles from the I. & G.N.R.R. a new road will have to be constructed that distance. We propose to grade and bridge a line and have Mr. Hoxie tie and rail it. this would open up a very valuable stone quarry and the only known one in Texas today. Mr. Hoxie is willing to [assist in building a spur to Missouri Pacific tracks] but his rate for doing the business is too high.
>
> Mr. Farwell thinks you can assist us in obtaining a fair rate and fair treatment. If you can do this you will render us and the parties who own the Railroads a great service as we will then give them all the business.[16]

Taylor continued seeking bids to construct a locomotive that would haul up to twenty-five tons of stone at a time. He settled finally on Baldwin Locomotive Works of Philadelphia, although correspondence regarding the same machine took place with "Messrs. Burnham Parry Williams & Co." Taylor gave notice to Baldwin Locomotive on August 15 that "we telegraphed you today accepting your proposal of Aug 6/83." Taylor ordered a November 15 delivery. On September 17, he wrote Burnham, Parry et al. that "you can mark that Locomotive 'Lone Star' instead of A. Taylor as you suggested." On November 14, Taylor inquired of

Baldwin, "When will the Engine you are making for us be shipped." Still later, he again wrote Burnham and company, enclosing a check for $7,350 and his apologies and an excuse for not paying for the engine sooner.[17]

Taylor heard that the Houston & Texas Central Railway had unused iron rails and sought to buy them from the company rather than have new rails cast and shipped from northern foundries. He was searching for any way to save the Syndicate money. He wrote John V. Farwell, who was still seeking investors in London, to express the hope that his partner would soon find "a hole large enough to get through," referring to what was becoming an increasing burden—cash flow. The Syndicate finally settled on the Missouri Pacific to perform the actual work of laying the track. The road would intersect with International & Great Northern tracks in Austin, cross the city on their tracks, then switch to company tracks again on East Street and up to the capitol site, the route approved by Austin's city officials. TBC also arranged to purchase from and haul material for the road via the St. Louis company. "Mr. Hoxie wants the Oatmanville Road organized into a company," he wrote his superintendent in early September. "You had better call it the Austin and Oatmanville Railroad," Taylor concluded the message. By November the materials were present and preparations completed on the roadbed. Taylor seemed anxious writing Hoxie on November 9: "I was in St. Louis yesterday to see you, but did not find you at home. The road bed to the quarry is now ready for the rails. and we have about two thousand car loads of stone ready for shipment and are very desirous to commence laying it at an early day. Please advise me when you can lay the track and be ready to commence hauling stone. You have not sent me a copy of that contract yet."[18]

A decision about the type of cement to use in the capitol foundation and a dispute over the concrete depth presented continued delays, too. Nevertheless, begun in May, foundation concrete was poured and curing by November. Sewerage proved yet another obstacle of frustration late in the year. The original plan called for sewer lines placed and foundation poured around them. The board was demanding that Taylor install the specific numbers of connections and pipes called for in the plans, which was not useful to the construction as it was progressing. He displayed his frustration at the various parties meddling in his business. An associate of Myers, William Richardson, had directed the drilling of several test holes in the excavated site earlier in the project. TBC intended to do the same thing and Taylor had discussed it with Myers. Richardson, in Austin, apparently represented himself as Myers's agent to the board's commissioners and convinced them to order the testing. Taylor resented the circumvention of his own authority. "I intend," he wrote in an angry letter to Norton, "to eradicate Wm Richardson influence from that Board before I proceed much further with this building."[19]

Taylor felt that he worked hard to follow the contract and deliver the best possible work—at the least possible cost to TBC. The demands of the Capitol board and commissioners often tested his patience. The position of the board on sewerage issues raised Taylor's ire. He wrote Secretary Dickinson a long letter on December 19: "Your communication of the 7th . . . is before me. And I wish to take exceptions to the report of the Commissioners and the action of the Board to matters in my communication [regarding sewerage connections in initial plans]. The position taken by the Commissioners that the contract compels me to put in these connections I am confident cannot be maintained."[20]

Still frustrated by the board, he wrote again on December 31: "I fail to find anything [in the contract specifications] that would compel me to put in sewerage not shown on the plans." Obviously, a deficiency existed in either the construction or the plan. Taylor likely was motivated, as he was often, by cost concerns. Just then, he was expecting to gain possession of another land installment for completing the second stage of the project's benchmarks. A hint of what, or who, might have been part of the problem came a few days prior in a letter Taylor sent Myers. "I returned from Austin yesterday and want to see you," he wrote, sounding something like a school principal. "I want to have a long talk with you about matters at Austin," he went on. "I think your letter done you great damage there." Although Texas officials frustrated Taylor, they were becoming more frustrated with Myers's unresponsiveness to their inquiries and requests to see him.[21]

Myers did show up in Austin in January 1884. His timing was poor. The legislature was just commencing a called session to address the state's worsening fence-cutting controversy. Board members, especially the governor, had their attentions there and gave Myers little notice. The board had recently announced the hiring of Gen. R. L. Walker of Richmond, Virginia, to succeed the former superintendent, W. D. Clark. Clark, recommended for the job by Myers, may have been the source of the beginning of the sewerage dispute. He had called attention to deficiencies in the sewer plan in October, but Myers was able to provide the board an acceptable explanation. It apparently was not acceptable to Clark. He resigned on December 7. It is not clear whether Clark or Myers created the trouble for Taylor, but these events help provide an explanation for Taylor's later exchanges with Dickinson—and, possibly, later disputes Myers had with the board. Walker would not arrive to fill the superintendent vacancy until February. Still, from TBC's perspective, Myers's appearance in Austin worked to their advantage. The architect declared the concrete work the best he had seen. This, apparently, was enough to prompt the board to grant the second installment of Capitol lands, another 45,000 acres, for which Taylor applied February 1, 1884. The board approved the conveyance in April, withholding 7,500 acres from the allotment until the sewerage issue was resolved.[22]

As 1883 ended, excavation for the water table at the capitol and preparation for the laying of the basement walls was under way. An artesian well, drilled through the bedrock of Capitol Square several years earlier, was cleared and initially routed to supply built-in cisterns. The original design called for this deep-spring water-power to operate the structure's elevators. Other technology changed this plan, but the spring was made accessible and continues to operate on the grounds today. Workmen completed the trunk line from Oatmanville and up to the summit of Capitol Square by March 1884. The "Lone Star" hauled the first dressed lime-stone excavated for the superstructure up to the job site. The new building super-intendent, General Walker, immediately rejected it for use on the outer capitol walls because it did not meet the color consistency of the contract: "Whilst I am sure this stone will make a . . . satisfactory foundation and basement," the general informed board members, "color . . . will render its use [for exterior cut stonework] impracticable." Despite Taylor's assurances to Farwell in the summer of 1883 that the "stone question is settled," the resulting controversy took over a year to resolve.[23]

Governor Ireland came into office determined to make changes in Texas land policy and in the course of the capitol project. He immediately began public lob-bying for a change in the superstructure specifications. Ireland's preference was for black or red granite from quarries operating near Burnet, northwest of Austin. Opening the 1884 legislature, the governor lamented, "It is greatly regrettable that the contract did not provide for the use of granite, as there is no doubt of its great superiority to the material called for, and is quite as accessible." Its accessibility was a matter of much debate, but an untapped reserve of "town mountain" gran-ite was offered the state free of charge as early as 1882. "Railroad communication has been established with the town of Burnet," commissioners Norton and Lee wrote in the Commission's first biennial report. "Propositions to supply [the granite] free of cost, have been repeatedly made. Having no authority to entertain a question already settled by the law and the contract, we have been unable to give any assurance of their acceptance. The contract, when concluded, was the best for the State which could have been made. The means of transportation, since secured, could not then be anticipated."[24]

That Norton held a stake in the proposed quarry seemed not to bother the governor. Ireland was not one to have anything as trivial as the law or contract stand in his way. Walker, of course, worked for the governor. Most employees follow the direction of their leadership, but there is no evidence the governor influenced Walker to reject the stone. Taylor, undoubtedly, was discouraged. With sixty tons of quarried and cut stone on his hands, he did not spend much time protesting Walker's decision. He did write to the general, "Recommendation for your son received, and I will do everything I can to find him a place and think I will be able to do so." There are no signs that this offer was anything more than a friendly gesture. Taylor had the utmost respect for Walker. He also contacted an apparent friend of Walker's in Richmond to offer the opportunity of bidding on a "granite" contract. He wrote to Myers, "Give [Cutshaw and associates] all the information you can, as they are Genl Walkers friends." Again, the actions of individuals in the past cannot really be viewed fairly through our modern lens, although perhaps corruption in plain sight is a better option than corruption out of sight. Instead, he sought other stone resources around the country, not just for the superstructure but for the basement and water table, too. Specifications called for varied stonework in the different phases of the construction. They used some cut and dressed stone at each stage, along with "rubble" stone in the foundation, basement, and water table. Several feet beyond the foundation and basement edges, like the outer wall of a medieval moat, the water table was an additional wall intended to strengthen the foundation and reduce erosion effects from seepage at the base of the structure.[25]

Granite rubble was already being hauled up from Burnet in large wagons, and Myers had specified several black marble columns at the entrance of the building to come from sources there. Taylor, having already thoroughly investigated known stone resources, was well aware of the Granite Mountain site several miles south of Burnet at Marble Falls. Building commissioner Norton was a shareholder in the property and undoubtedly referred it to Taylor. Despite the presence of the Austin & Northwestern at Burnet, Taylor was not anxious to build another rail spur more than three times longer than that he had just undertaken for the Oatmanville road. To some measure, Taylor seemed to ignore Ireland's objections to limestone and the rejection of the first stone. He was already petitioning to use granite from Missouri on the water table. In April, TBC sent out eleven proposal requests to companies around the country for bids to put up the capitol walls. None were sent to Texas. In responses to inquiries from those offered the opportunity to bid, Taylor named the source of the stone as the Oatmanville quarry each time. As late as April 1885 he informed a prospective bidder, "Our Stone quarry is about ten miles from Austin."[26]

Taylor initially gained approval for use of the Missouri stone in the water table and basement. After initially informing the Missouri source of his intentions to use their stone, Taylor suddenly reversed himself and agreed to use the Granite Mountain stone. Wagons brought the rough-cut stone to Burnet, where any necessary cutting or dressing took place. Once it was prepared, wagons or the narrow-gauge Austin & Northwestern carried the stone on to Austin. By September, Taylor was calling on the state for the third land installment, marking the "walls, exterior and interior . . . completed within ten feet of the top of the first floor line." Work on the remainder of the building's lowest level continued to completion in November. From correspondence, it does not seem that Taylor was opposed to the use of granite in the building's superstructure. He wrote Dickinson, Myers, and Babcock on several occasions throughout the remainder of the year suggesting steps should "the State [have] any thought of trying to have the State House built of granite." The state, led by Walker's experienced supervision, was also requesting changes in the foundation supporting the building's dome and questioning structural specification in the basement's ironwork. Questions to Myers, from both the Syndicate and the state, increased, and responses became less frequent and helpful.[27]

It certainly must have been obvious to Taylor that Ireland was determined to have his way. Even the citizens of Burnet seemed assured of the use of the nearby stone, it being reported in February newspapers that workers from the Austin & Northwestern "immediately went to work locating the road . . . to the granite quarries. . . . Our citizens are wild over the good and glorious news." Taylor proceeded as if that were not the case, although he sent both Amos C. Babcock and Gus Wilke to Detroit to meet with Myers regarding various changes in the building. Wilke was responsible for the Oatmanville quarry, was of great assistance on building the railroad, and had recently been awarded the TBC contract for the capitol's interior walls. Identifying the cost impact of changing to granite from a structural and logistical viewpoint was their primary consideration. Walsh, reporting before that year's legislative session, used the plan and estimates worked out by them in announcing a cost increase of $613,865. Both houses of the legislature sent the report to committee, but both houses adjourned without taking final action on their preference in the matter. The board debated the question into the spring. Taylor, however, realizing that his continued desire to use the Oatmanville stone for the exterior walls was hopeless, located a limestone quarry in Bedford, Indiana. In May he wrote the commissioners:

> I have come to the conclusion that you will not receive the Oatmanville limestone in sufficient quantities to construct the building, and believing it will not be possible to procure stone in Texas that will be acceptable to you, I submit a specimen of limestone from the Bedford quarry, Indiana. . . . This stone has been used in the construction of many fine buildings, among them the cotton exchange in New Orleans, the city hall, Chicago; and the statehouse in Georgia is contracted to be constructed of it.[28]

The commissioners sent this "specimen" to Superintendent Walsh for his opinion. Walsh pronounced the Bedford sample "superior in every respect to the sample from the Oatmanville quarries." Upon this report, on May 6, the commissioners wrote TBC of their tentative approval of the stone. They reported their findings to the governor and other board members the same day: "While we are as solicitous as any one to construct the exterior walls of our capitol building of native stone, we do not believe it expedient for the best interests of the State to sacrifice to this solicitude a matter of more vital importance, viz: the construction of the building as soon as practicable, of the very best material, even though it should come from another State."[29]

Ireland's lengthy reply, drenched in cordiality and diplomatic backhanding, hints at what Taylor would face if he continued his reluctance to accept Ireland's position:

> I have no doubt . . . there may be stone obtained at Oatmanville equal to the sample called for in the specification . . . but whether in sufficient

quantity is a question that I cannot determine. . . . Under the contract, the State is not required to answer such questions; but it has reserved the right to inspect and determine the suitability of all material. . . . I hope . . . you . . . inform Colonel Taylor that you admit into the building any stone that comes up to the sample called for, even if it comes from Oatmanville. . . . I have to say that the State is anxious to have the house built according to contract; but upon its failure because of a want of stone of the quality called for, I have to suggest—in which I suppose you and the Capitol Board will concur—that permission will be given the contractor to make the building of red Burnet granite, with such modifications of the style of architecture as would allow the use of granite.[30]

Ireland knew Taylor would not continue quarrying stone from Oatmanville without assurances of its acceptance. Taylor responded in an even longer letter. He reviewed the obstacles he faced throughout the project and highlighted the efforts to which he had gone out of his way to please the state. With rational logic, he laid out a scenario in which he delivered enough acceptable-quality stone from one quarry to build half of the walls. In that case, Taylor proposed he could then go to another quarry and obtain stone equal to the specified sample, but still unmatched to the shade and consistency of that used for the first half of the building, nevertheless acceptable to the specifications. Most people have experienced attempts at matching paint in a room where wall repairs were made. One can get close, but never quite right. Taylor described the same thing happening at the capitol. He needed a single source for all the stone to be used. He told the board this and once again provided more evidence of the Indiana stone's quality. The commissioners decided to have the stone tested. Positive reports and acknowledgment that nothing contractually prohibited its use compelled them to recommend that the board accept Taylor's proposal to use the Bedford limestone. After meeting throughout June on the stone issue, as well as regarding changes to the ironwork specifications, Taylor proposed a contract modification that accepted the use of the Indiana limestone. The board approved it on July 1 over the protests of two of the five members, including Governor Ireland. When it sent the new modifications to Chicago for Syndicate approval, Taylor surprisingly returned them unsigned, on July 16, claiming the Syndicate's costs would significantly increase should they accept the new terms. Taylor countered with three proposals he did find acceptable. One proposed to use the Burnet granite. Final details on a contract were quickly worked out.[31]

In exchange for red Texas granite, the new contract called for some significant concessions to the contractor. Gone were the east and west porticoes of the building, although the north portico was enhanced. The dome construction was modified (not the first or last time); steel, cheaper than iron at the time, was substituted in several instances; several finishing specifications were eliminated for the basement; and limestone wainscoting was replaced by wood. The contract extended the time allotted for finishing the building from January 1, 1888, to January 1, 1890. A contract was drawn in which the state acknowledged the "free" use of the Granite Mountain stone. The state was to use all its influence in retaining right-of-way for a sixteen-mile rail line between the quarry and Burnet. The state also agreed to furnish up to five hundred convicts to work on the railroad and in the quarries. The most significant concession, however, emerged from the state's agreement to lease the entire three million acres of the Capitol Reservation to TBC immediately. Signed July 25, more than three years after groundbreaking on the project, the changed contract removed several obstacles to progress for both the building and the land. Although virtually no work atop the hill of Capitol Square took place again until January 5, 1886, few future changes requested by either the state or contractor represented significant delays in the project.[32]

The cornerstone of the building, to great fanfare, was laid on March 2, 1885, forty-nine years after Texas's independence from Mexico. Taylor wrote apologies for his absence to the chairman of the cornerstone celebration: "Regret my duties to my state prevent me from being present to participate in laying the cornerstone of the most magnificent State House on this continent being erected in one of the grandest states where destinies are wielded in a manner that must be commended by the long line of heroes who bought her liberty with their blood."[33]

A list of the items left for posterity inside the dressed cornerstone shows among the contents "the roll of the Austin Hook and Ladder Company No. 1," "Brief statistical account of the Swede Ev. Lutheran congregation in Austin with photo of church," "Old Texas Treasury notes," "Confederate notes," "Photograph of Jeff Davis," "Ode to Texas by a young lady," "Roll of membership of Innocent's Abroad by W. H. Stacy," "History of the gavel used in laying the cornerstone," and "Tooth powders by Dr. Stodard." The state, however, refused to pay for the finely crafted piece. Contractor Wilke declined the offer of $400 for his work on the elaborately cut, dressed, and polished granite block. The cost was $1,545.[34]

Although Taylor would continue to insist into the summer that a change to Texas granite was just too costly, the resignation of Commissioner Norton on March 9 signaled headway in the granite controversy. To this point, Norton's partnership in the Slaughter survey at Granite Mountain had not been an impediment, despite the use of stone for the water table walls from there already. More intensive development of the location's stone resources, however, might have brought questions about Norton's involvement with the group supplying material to the capitol project. Norton had worked on the project for a long time, and it might have just been time to go. Still, three months reduced chances of associating Norton with any accusations of profiteering, even though he and his partners offered the actual stone to the state free of charge. M. H. McLaurin, a former superintendent of the temporary capitol construction, quickly replaced Norton. Norton's role in the story does continue, however; John V. Farwell later informed him that his assistance was needed helping officials who were resurveying the Capitol lands. Farwell also wanted the former commissioner to provide his observations on the property to British investors and offer his opinion on the water situation of the land. Norton became the postmaster of Granite, using an office established at the quarry site.[35]

The language of business, found in ledgers and balance sheets, is not always grasped by all the parties involved in an operation. The Chicago men were professional businessmen, and the Syndicate maintained its accounts obsessively. Those working for them were not always as disciplined as Taylor and the rest liked. The Chicago office was continually demanding the receipts and accounts of its Austin contractors and sometimes suffered weeks frustrated at the lack of reports of any kind from Ed Creary, A. A. Burck, or G. W. Turner. "Are you *dead*?" Taylor inquired of Turner. "If you are not dead," he continued, hopefully, "will you take the time to write and tell us how the work is progressing." Taylor sent a terse telegram to Turner in October 1883: "Have you sent your report why do you not answer our letters." Even when their reports were received, it got no easier for the employees. "Your statement of Oct 22nd," Taylor opened a letter to Turner, "does not agree with the bank account." He ordered Turner to address the discrepancy and closed by demanding he hunt down receipts for payments to Creary, the building site excavator in the early days of the project.[36]

In Austin, although work immediately began on opening the Granite Mountain quarry, Taylor and the rest of the Syndicate men quickly lost interest in the building in Austin in favor of efforts toward the ranch. Although Taylor continued to take a direct role in the capitol project up to the end, the Syndicate sublet the job to Gustav Wilke, who agreed to take it over for $2.3 million. A full review of the fiscal twists of the capitol project and a full financial accounting of it remains undone, a challenge to researchers in its complexity. In any case, the board accepted the transfer to Wilke, his bond was retained, and the contract was duly amended.[37]

The Syndicate sought convict labor on the project as early as 1883. The amended contract included an agreement with the state penitentiary board spelling out the terms of the prisoners' assignment. Numerous public protests rose over this arrangement. In particular, the Granite Cutters' International Association of America sharply denounced the plan. Wilke, a German-born Chicagoan, matched his employers in his efforts to keep costs under control. He had already antagonized organized labor by hiring workers on the project at three-quarters the rate union leaders had targeted for work on the capitol. Throughout the project, labor unions boycotted the construction. When the convicts began quarrying and cutting granite, the boycott resulted in a shortage of qualified stonemasons to train and oversee the prisoners' work. Unable to retain local expertise at wages the contractor was willing to pay, the Syndicate sought to import master stoneworkers from Scotland. Local and nationwide stoneworker unions protested the immigrant labor. A federal law restricting immigrant labor had recently gone into effect, and federal agents greeted eighty-six Scottish masons destined for Austin as they disembarked in New York. Several of the men returned immediately to Scotland, after discussing the issue with labor representatives also there to greet them. The majority, however, eventually got to Texas. Their problems did not end, though, nor did the company's. Wilke, in the name of Taylor, Babcock, and the Farwells, was able to delay legal proceedings. Initially Wilke incurred fines totaling about $64,000 for violating federal laws, but political pressure delayed execution of the penalty through the completion of the capitol. Wilke wound up paying a modest settlement of $8,000 to conclude the case in 1893.[38]

The Capitol board appears to have stayed out of the employment practices of their contractor. In many ways, however, they were responsible for them. The limitations of the original contract and the conditions it placed on land conveyances encouraged the contractors to find cost-saving measures whenever possible. The allowance for convict labor in the amended contract represented a huge cost savings for the Syndicate, ostensibly offsetting the cost of using the Texas granite. The state made no effort whatsoever to encourage the company to hire locally or to bargain with labor groups. Further, the quarries were not the only aspect of the project to utilize prison labor. Faced with the prospect that much of the ironwork contracted to go in the building would come from northern or European foundries, the board supported the selection of the state penitentiary at Rusk for some of the work. TBC readily agreed to the choice, particularly when the state agreed to urge lower hauling rates from the railroad shipping the material to the building site.[39]

By the time fruitful progress once again became recognizable at the summit of Capitol Square, architect Myers had had enough. Always agreeable in the early days of the project, the designing architect was sorely pressed by the demands of the board under Ireland's leadership, along with his numerous other projects. His troubles surfaced with the resignation of Superintendent Clark, Myers's own choice for the job. Clark almost certainly was a victim of the architect's growing disinterest in his Texas project. The appointment of General Walker as the board's superintendent hastened Myers's divorce from the project. The general, as has been discussed, was a formidable overseer of the work. His opinions weighed mightily on the board's decisions. Walker identified many flaws in the original design and requested many changes, most of them fully acceptable to the contractor. Design changes, however, contractually needed the consent and approval of the designing architect—Myers. That became more and more of a problem.

TBC supported the architect as much as it could, and even covered for him. At one point, while seeking bids for stonework, probably addressing rumors of Texas's dissatisfaction with Myers, Taylor assured a potential bidder for the work, Robert Greenlee, that "Mr Myers is still the architect of the building and I think will continue so until it is completed." On several occasions, TBC found itself mediating differences between the Capitol board and the Detroit architect. Animosity also built between Wilke and Myers. Taylor diplomatically scolded Myers, encouraged Myers, but was frustrated by Myers.

Superintendent Clark suffered from Myers's scapegoating. Wilke also seemed to be a target for blame when Myers faced questions from the board. Taylor, earlier in the year, declared to Myers his support for Wilke. In a long dress-down to Myers in July, the contractor alluded to usurping forces apparently at work in Austin:

> Yours of July 14th to Mr. Farwell in relation to the work done by Mr. Wilke . . . was forwarded to me at Austin. . . . I learned that Gov Ireland, Secty Dickinson and Supt Clark each had a similar letter. I am very much surprised to learn this, and am confident if you had reflected you would not have written these letters, as I know you would not intentionally wrong anyone. . . .
>
> With your knowledge of us, you must know we would not let a contract to any person of the magnitude of the contract Wilke has until we knew all about him. . . .
>
> . . . I know why this attack is made, what it is made for, and the parties who are doing it, and I will do you the justice to say that you are not one of them. . . .
>
> I want to say to you and through you to the parties who are instigative that it must *stop,* and it *must stop now.* I have known of their scheme for some time. . . . but I fear the parties have taken my silence for ignorance, they had better understand that . . . any further attempts will justify me in striking back.
>
> . . . I shall stand by [Wilke] and a fight on him is a fight on me.[40]

Taylor may have known the parties, but their names are not in the records. One might suspect that the previously mentioned William Richardson remained a source of intrigue at the Texas capital. Taylor again directed advice and protection to Myers during the granite controversy. Walker and the commissioners long sought Myers's assistance on requested changes to the iron framing in the capitol basement and the structural support for the majestic dome. Taylor wrote Babcock, in Austin, on February 27, 1885, "[Myers] is here today and has wired a dispatch to his son in Detroit to be sent to Dickinson withdrawing his letter." A copy of the wired withdrawal request accompanies this letter. The parties exchanged more letters, however. On March 18, the board wrote to Myers regarding strengthening the carrying capacity of iron beams supporting basement stairways and landings and questioned the design for a wall that apparently had no support structure whatsoever. The 1886 commissioner's report called Myers's reply of March 31 "irrelevant and evasive," prompting the board to post further requests to him on April 6 and 11.[41]

Myers had long since collected and spent any compensation from his work on the Texas capitol. To some extent, the board and commissioners sympathized with him, but the contract was clear about his role in approving changes in the construction. Myers had too many other concerns, and the board knew it. A short window for delivery of plans in a competition for the design of Colorado's new capitol presented Myers a July 1885 deadline. He once again applied as the Treasury Department's supervising architect in the new Cleveland administration, but the president retained the former appointee. He was also completing the Douglas County courthouse in Omaha and bidding on another courthouse in Ohio. Myers avoided demands from the Capitol board to appear in Austin by July 1 when his son offered the excuse that continued illness prevented his father's travel. Unhappy with continued delays caused by Myers, the board asked the Texas attorney general to investigate a breach of contract suit. The Texans appeared ready to move on. Beginning with the amended contract of July 25, 1885, steps that eliminated the designing architect from a role in decision making allowed the commissioners and the contractor to approve and make future design changes.[42]

TBC, too, seems to have been frustrated with the whole affair. Although friendly, a note from Taylor to his Michigan neighbor on August 11 lacked collegial warmth:

> Your former of Aug 10th at hand. We changed the material for the Texas State House to granite to be built in accordance with the plans and perfections sent down by you. In making this change we had to eliminate some things from the interior in order to reduce the expense so as to pay us in part for the change. I enclose a copy of the contract by which the aforesaid change is made. I shall be at all times glad to give you any information you may require in the matter.[43]

The Capitol board received an August 16 notice from Myers that he accepted the design changes on the building and would appear in Austin in October to address the board's concerns. A brief visit due to "pressing professional engagements" allowed him to address only a few of the board's questions. The pressing engagements were his obligations to the State of Colorado, which had selected his plan and demanded more and more of his attention. With continued excuses and delays as responses to their questions, in January 1886 the board renewed calls for Attorney General John T. Templeton to prepare legal action against Myers. By that time, Myers had renewed his finger pointing, with Wilke as his main target. TBC continued to favor Wilke, and Myers's protests drew no favors from Chicago. Templeton asked for advice again six months later. It seems the board simply decided that they no longer needed the architect's services and chose to ignore him. The state never acted against Myers. His design for the Austin capitol, along with those of the Michigan and Colorado statehouses, is the work of a talented individual. Many other buildings around the country demonstrate that as well. Unfortunately, a reputation for low-ball estimates, missed deadlines, and inattentiveness was catching up to him. Colorado soon chose the same course as Texas and determined that his services were of little value beyond his initial concept and design. As one chronicler of the man described him, Myers "was a talented, dishonest, hard-working, spiteful, clever, unbalanced, self-assured, self-destructive hypochondriac whose story must be pieced together from fragments." His career and reputation slowly dimmed until his death in 1909.[44]

William Benjamin "Ben" Munson. Panhandle-Plains Historical Museum (catalog #2287-2_001).

Jules "Jot" Gunter. Panhandle-Plains Historical Museum (catalog #174-1_001).

The "Old Stone Capitol" as it burns, looking north from the corner of 11th and Congress in Austin, November 9, 1881 (misidentified November 7, 1881). Low water pressure on the scene limited Austin firefighters' chances in extinguishing what at first appeared to be only a minor blaze. Only a few of Texas's important government papers escaped the blaze. Many of the early records of the commission overseeing the capitol project were lost. Austin History Center, Austin Public Library (photo #C00231).

Granite for the capitol, 1884. The use of the red Texas granite in the capitol's construction resolved a nearly two-year standoff between Governor Ireland and TBC's Abner Taylor. The amended capitol contract gave the Capitol Syndicate fuller control of the Capitol Reservation and allowed for the immediate creation of Capitol Freehold Land and Investment Company, thus leading to the establishment of what soon was being called the XIT Ranch. Austin History Center, Austin Public Library (AR-X-016-E106_01).

Scottish granite cutters. Taylor drew legal challenges from the federal government and the national granite cutter's union when he contracted with granite cutters in Scotland. Many of those workers were turned back before reaching Texas, but others worked on the capitol project. Taylor later paid fines for violating laws prohibiting the importation of foreign workers. Scores of African American Texas convicts also labored at the Burnet location, where the stone was milled and shaped for final use. Austin History Center, Austin Public Library (photo #C00194).

Taylor (center) and Gus Wilke (second from right), TBC's onsite contractor. Austin History Center, Austin Public Library (photo #PICA-16647).

Abner Taylor. Panhandle-Plains Historical Museum (catalog #409-13_001).

Charles B. Farwell. Photo Archives, Montana Historical Society (catalog #Lot 006 B10 F2 09).

Ready for a grand ball. The Marquess of Tweeddale was the first and longtime chair of Capitol Freehold's board of directors. Lady (Susan Elizabeth) Clementine Waring (née Hay) as Valentina; William Montagu Hay, 10th Marquess of Tweeddale, as St Bris (Les Huguenots), 1897. © National Portrait Gallery, London (catalog #Ax41134).

Sir Henry Seton-Karr, 1904. Sir Henry served on Capitol Freehold's first board. Among its British members he was, perhaps, the most ardent supporter of the company's cattle operations. He visited the Texas ranch at least twice and reported back a positive and enthusiastic outlook to the board and stockholders. © National Portrait Gallery, London (catalog #x35057).

Matthew White Ridley, 1st Viscount Ridley, 1897. Although Ridley was not on Capitol Freehold's board of directors when the company formed, he became its vice-chair after the contract with the Syndicate was renegotiated in 1892. Ridley served as home secretary for the British government from 1895 to 1900. © National Portrait Gallery, London (catalog #x35031).

Quintin Hogg, about 1900. After earning a fortune in the tea and sugar trade, Hogg turned his attention to Christian philanthropy. A trust in his name continues to support London's University of Westminster. A Farwell confidant, Hogg served as one of the trustees for Capitol Freehold debenture holders. © National Portrait Gallery, London (catalog #P1700[83c]).

A devout Presbyterian, John V. Farwell supported evangelist Dwight L. Moody and helped Moody establish the Young Men's Christian Association in Chicago. Farwell sought to have Sundays on the ranch reserved for religious purpose. Barbecue Campbell, himself a Christian devotee, finally convinced his boss that cattle did not care if it was Sunday. Still, if Farwell visited the ranch, a Sunday meant that work stopped long enough for Farwell to address the spiritual needs of the employees. Farwell sits before his congregation. This photo probably was made in the mid-1890s, possibly later. Longtime ranch manager A. G. Boyce is pictured just over Farwell's right shoulder. Nita Stewart Haley Memorial Library (catalog #J. Evetts Haley Collection I-30.52).

Farwell sits with Boyce and another Texas associate, "Uncle" Henry Stevens, a former Bandera County sheriff and cattle drover who assisted in Capitol Freehold land sales. This photo, likely taken in the mid-1890s, reveals that Farwell could be persuaded on occasion to partake of liquor. Nita Stewart Haley Memorial Library (catalog #J. Evetts Haley Collection I-35-51).

Texas accepted its capitol in 1888, nearly three years ahead of schedule. Capitol Hill in Austin today little resembles this idyllic scene from 1892. Austin History Center, Austin Public Library (photo #C01632).

~~

Cattle Convention

Historian Jimmy Skaggs wrote, "The [western] cattle ranch as a business endeavor was . . . significant not for the magnitude of its livestock production, but for its control of the land, an appreciating asset."[1] The circumstances of the gigantic land acquisition of the Capitol Syndicate—John V. Farwell, Charles B. Farwell, Abner Taylor, and Amos Babcock—forced the group to focus on cattle ranching instead of real estate and "colonization." The Syndicate's planning began to evolve as these men realized the limitations of the bargain they made with Texas, in terms of both taking possession of the land and the character of the land itself. Finding the property in slight demand by Texas settlers, the Syndicate deferred their plans for colonization of the acreage in lieu of joining the several other cattle conglomerates operating around them. With limited experience in the livestock business, the group used its extensive political and financial connections to mold the Capitol Reservation into the XIT Ranch. The creation of the XIT, and its success, depended on the Syndicate's ability to secure the support of powerful individuals and organizations around the country.

Texas stands out in a greater world of cattle, but it does not stand above the many other pieces of the western cattle business. By 1884, the beef business in the United States rivaled many other Gilded Age industrial behemoths like railroads, mining, and steel companies in production and marketing. The men who controlled the soon-to-be-great XIT fit comfortably among the cattle capitalists who defined the industry, a powerful network of investors, politicians, cattle breeders, cattle raisers, cattle buyers, packinghouses, and railroads. The first national cattlemen's convention, in November 1884, revealed the grievances of the country's cattle business as well as the friction between cattle raisers of varying means and styles who came from vastly different regions of the country. But it also defined the business for the Syndicate as it developed the XIT Ranch.[2]

Attempts by the Syndicate to sell the Capitol Reservation land began almost immediately. In 1882, through TBC, the Syndicate optimistically, perhaps naively, asked between $2.00 and $2.50 per acre to sell the entire three-million-acre parcel. A great deal of correspondence changed hands as each of the Syndicate members sought buyers. Some of those they contacted took liberty with their information and began representing themselves as authorized agents for the Syndicate. One person enlisted to help find investors received sharp criticism and dismissal by Taylor: "If your dispatch of the 18th about the sale of lands is true, you have violated your pledge, and we decline to have any further communication with you." The blended chain of command that had both Farwells, Taylor, and Babcock making independent inquiries and efforts led to problems, then and later. After other aborted negotiations, Babcock and Charles B. Farwell got together and suggested that John V. Farwell be the only agent of the company authorized "to dispose of the lands." They further suggested immediately selling 500,000 acres at $2.00 an acre while they heavily advertised the entire tract in British newspapers.[3]

After two years of effort, the Syndicate realized that, for the time being, they stood little chance of earning even $2.00 per acre on any but the best of the land. Texas was selling its public lands for far less and leasing vast tracts, too. The ensuing surge in public land sales following the Fifty-cent Act in 1879 resulted in widespread, often fraudulent, speculation before its repeal in 1883. The Fifty-cent Act hurt the Syndicate, too. Sales were not likely at $2.00 an acre when better land could be purchased for less, sometimes far less. Except from large cattle interests, several of which already operated in and around the Capitol Reservation, demand for most of northwest Texas remained light despite dwindling reserves of arable Texas public land. There were plenty of nibbles, but nothing that would seem close to recouping the costs that were beginning to add up on the capitol project. Furthermore, as subsequent relations between Texas officials and the capitol contractors demonstrated, the authority of the Syndicate to bargain for the sale of the lands at the time was questionable. Pressed by the situation, the Syndicate began investigating and discussing the formation of a "cattle company" and a "scheme for stocking and fencing our entire tract."[4]

A somewhat curious offshoot of the Syndicate trying to sell land is that plenty of people thought the members might want to buy more land. Edwin S. Graham, the founder of Graham, Texas, and an agent for the Texas Emigration and Land Company, contacted TBC early in 1883. Taylor's replies to inquiries such as this grew succinct. "Your favor of Jany 3rd at hand," Taylor curtly responded. "We have all the Texas lands we can handle at present, and do not wish to purchase anymore."[5] Edwin S. Graham, along with his brother, Gustavus A. Graham, had also sunk the first gas well in Texas—accidently, while searching for underground saltwater sources for the local salt plant they operated. No great petroleum or gas reserves ever turned up on the XIT, much to the disappointment of future heirs to the XIT legacy. Perhaps Taylor should have entertained Graham's offer.[6]

Governor Ireland, backed by his commissioner of the General Land Office, William C. Walsh, and the rest of the Capitol board tasked with oversight on the project refused to allow possession of the land prior to completion of contracted benchmarks. Delays postponed meeting those goals, severely limiting the Syndicate's ability to market the land in any legitimate way. Taylor, replying for TBC, wrote to a prospective investor in Germany about the issue: "There was an Associated Press Dispatch in the newspapers a few days ago that the State House Capitol Board at Austin Texas had decided that we were not entitled to the immediate possession of the Capitol Lands. But only entitled to possession as we took our patents. This report, like many others in relation to this land, was mistaken. The Capitol Board has taken no action and none is contemplated."[7]

Ireland and Walsh had decided on that exact course. The Syndicate's failure to obtain legal possession of the land in bulk continued to be a problem until the completion of the capitol in 1888. Doling out the allotted land slowly as the statehouse project milestones were met, while frustrating to the Syndicate, benefitted the state in more ways than satisfying its building preferences. The lack of patents on the land prevented it from going on the market while Ireland and the state attempted to impose some control on remaining Texas public lands. Taylor's compromise with Ireland did, however, allow the Syndicate to lease the entire three million acres. Texas agreed to accept a capitol somewhat smaller than called for in the original design for the change to granite, reducing the final cost by about $500,000, to a total of $3.7 million. Now free to utilize the entire Capitol Reservation, but limited by the patent issue, the Syndicate had little choice but to enter the cattle business.[8]

By May 1885, the Syndicate held the patents on nearly 400,000 acres of the Capitol Reservation. The lease on the remainder called for $0.06 per acre annually. Texas issued patents to the company as it met benchmarks in Austin. When Texas land commissioner Walsh began charging the Syndicate for issuing those patents, Taylor strongly protested. Walsh told Taylor he would issue the documents at $15 per league. "Please take notice that these fees are demanded by you," Taylor pointed out, "and they are paid under protest," he stressed. "I rely upon my rights," the contractor insisted, "to have State Lands transferred to me free of charge and this money refunded." Although Governor Ireland later sought to rescind this fee, the Syndicate ultimately paid more than $10,000 for official Texas land patents. A clause in the lease made the Syndicate liable for the payments only should they fail to complete the building. It excluded portions of the land previously patented. Taylor placed a bond of $50,000 for this contract modification. The change allowed the company to continue fencing, "artificial water" projects, and other improvements it considered critical. The Syndicate determined that cattle ranching provided their best chance at profiting from the property at the time. Identifying the best location to begin cultivating several experimental crops also became a priority.[9] (See the map in chapter 5.)

Crop cultivation began on the northern boundary in the Buffalo Springs pasture before cattle began to arrive. By 1888, active farming operations were under way at six locations on the sprawling ranch: one west of Buffalo Springs, another established at Farwell Park, two more near the New Mexico border in the Middle-Water and Minneosa pastures, and two near the southern boundary of the ranch at Spring Lake and the Yellow Houses. These early efforts impressed some potential investors courted by the Syndicate in Great Britain, and so John V. Farwell, negotiating with suitors in London, soon made a bargain that created the Capitol Freehold Land and Investment Company, Limited. Cash immediately began to reach the Americans. Taylor and the Farwells were named directors in the new company along with several notable and well-connected British lords, members of Parliament, and sundry gentlemen. By fall, advertisements for investment in the company appeared in British newspapers.[10]

Taylor and Farwell's work in England bore fruit only after they began communicating with E. L. Sheldon of London. Sheldon visited the western United States, possibly even the Panhandle, in late 1882 and contacted the Chicago men to discuss forming a "cattle company" in early 1883. Nothing came of the talks at the time, but contact with Sheldon resumed in early 1884. The parties exchanged coded messages, but the careful Chicago men sensed deceit. "Your favor of April 19th received and we are very much astonished at its contents," began a five-page dispatch to Sheldon. The letter reviewed the conditions and actions under which the parties had negotiated and expressed offense at Sheldon's accusation that they were refusing to work with him because they had a better offer. "This is not done for the reason you assign," wrote Taylor for the group. "We have no offer and have entered into no arrangement." The contractor closed with finality: "We have no confidence in your being able to do anything from the fact that you furnish no evidence of your ability to do so."[11]

The Chicago men did put Sheldon in touch with John Stuart and Company, a Manchester group that engaged their attention in the winter of 1883. But Taylor quickly found fault with their efforts as well. "We shall withdraw all proposals," Taylor wrote them. "It is too good an enterprise to be hawked in such a manner." While still working with Stuart, another London group seemed poised to gain the Chicagoans' attention—if only the Syndicate could gain theirs. Taylor wrote to John W. Maugham in June 1884. "We cabled you on the 9th and directed the cable according to your instructions," Taylor wrote in his familiar hand and often blunt style. "Word came back that they could not find you. . . . We fear you must be dead. If so of course you will not answer. But if you are still in the land of the living, we would be pleased to hear from you."[12]

Confident a resolution to their impasse with the State of Texas could be reached on the capitol question, the Syndicate's focus on developments in the Panhandle grew sharper. Excitement built as activities regarding the land intensified. The Illinois men's confidence in a solution to both their cash supply problems and the capitol question was so high that by the winter of 1884 they enlisted Burton H. "Barbecue" Campbell, a Kansas stock grower, to begin purchasing cattle for delivery on the property the summer of 1885. Campbell got his nickname from the brand he used on his cattle, Bar BQ, a horizontal "bar" beneath a capital BQ. John V. Farwell had invested in Campbell's cattle interests in the Cherokee Strip of Indian Territory, and Campbell once contracted with Abner Taylor to market his "stock farm" in Kansas. When the company could not reach an investment agreement with him, Campbell was instead hired to manage the ranch operations. The Syndicate set a goal of 60,000 head for the upcoming year. Even Taylor and Farwell, while in London, negotiated more cattle purchases.

Fortunately, contracts for even more cattle went unfulfilled in 1885, sparing the Chicago men thousands and thousands of more losses in what turned out to be a preview of the Big Die-Up of the following winter.[13]

It is not clear whether either Stuart or Maugham played a role, but a "Memorandum of Association" announcing the creation of the Capitol Freehold Land and Investment Company, registered in England on June 25, 1885, predated an amended Texas capitol contract by one month. Unlike in many western ranches, the British stockholders in Capitol Freehold were not particularly active in operations in the Panhandle, although the London group occasionally sent agents to inspect the place. English investment, however, raised further resentment in Texas toward the Illinois capitalists. The original Syndicate partners leased the ranch and cattle back from Capitol Freehold in 1889 upon completion of the capitol in Austin. This arrangement later provided needed cover against Texas policies that paralleled nationwide movements toward land reforms designed to limit corporate and foreign ownership of large tracts of what had been the public domain. The Americans, in fact, always maintained operational management. John V. Farwell, either directly or indirectly, steered the Syndicate's actions, and his business acumen cannot be overestimated. Financial leverage can be very effective in expressing one's opinion, however, and the British voice was seldom silent. Capitol Freehold intended to raise big money fast and provide a generous return over time. For most outside investors, however, the rewards would be spare, often just the knowledge that you once had invested in one of the American West's great ranches. At the first stockholder's meeting in October, the chair, the Marquess of Tweeddale, announced that $2,000,000 in debentures already offered had drawn $1,460,000 in purchases.[14]

The timing of the arrangement between the Capitol Syndicate and its British partners was fortuitous and typical of those made by many other similar operations. By the mid-1880s, foreign principals partly or wholly owned many livestock operations in the western United States. Future XIT neighbors and competitors included Francklyn Land and Cattle Company, financed with money from the Cunard Steamship fortune; the Espuela Land and Cattle Company, known as the "Spur" Ranch; and the Matador Land and Cattle Company. These three were among the most notable "big" ranches in Texas, but the same model dominated the cattle business across the West.[15] Taylor and the Farwells served on an illustrious international board of directors. The new company offered debentures in denominations of £50 to £1,000, paying 5 and 7 percent annual interest to the public. A London newspaper excitedly announced the great potential for investors' return on their investments, noting that the "land is valued at $3.75 an acre, making the whole tract worth $11,250,000."[16]

The Chicago men, in their decision to enter the cattle business, joined a new order of cattle ranching far different than the trail enterprises that blazed the path of the western range cattle business. While the Syndicate skirmished with Texas officials and trolled financial centers for potential investors in a cattle operation, the concerns of their competitors in the business shaped the enterprise into which they had plunged. Wealthy cattle ranchers formed powerful organizations and held well-attended conventions beginning in the mid-1880s. State legislatures and Congress heard cattlemen's voices. Their concerns peaked in 1884 with the establishment of the Bureau of Animal Industry (BAI), a subagency of the Department of Agriculture. Some of the most prominent names in the cattle industry called on beef interests throughout the country to "organize a Cattle Association" that sought "to secure advantages and recognition . . . accorded railroad and manufacturing companies." Cattlemen from across the country gathered for their first convention at St. Louis's Exposition Center on November 17, 1884. Representatives from thirty-one states and territories and from the District of Columbia met for five days to discuss "the questions of paramount importance affecting the great interests which [they] represent."[17]

Robert D. Hunter, one-half of the Hunter-Evans cattle conglomerate and one of many attendees the Syndicate members would later engage during their cattle operations, opened the convention at about 11:20 that Monday morning. Hunter was one of several prominent individuals and organizations that had called for the gathering earlier that month at a meeting in Chicago. Hunter summoned Charles C. Rainwater, a St. Louis resident with large interests in Texas cattle operations, to the podium as the temporary chairman of the body. After Rainwater's brief introductory remarks, the convention wasted no time getting down to business. Until the organization of the body and its members' credentials were decided, no work could take place. What initially appeared to be acceptance of state/territorial representation quickly drew dissent as delegates, still milling about the floor in disorder, began to realize what they were deciding. One newspaper's headline for a report on the first days of the meeting proclaimed that the convention was "much fun, but little work."[18]

Represented by sixteen separate livestock associations, Texas sent, by far, the most individual delegates to the convention. Judge Joseph M. Carey—a pioneering Wyoming lawyer, future U.S. senator, and Wyoming governor—spoke for his territory's interests, rising on the second day to say, "The Wyoming Stock Growers' Association represents more cattle, more wealth, and has a larger membership I believe, than any other association represented upon this floor." Carey may have overstated reality on one or two points; although the 47 percent of the attendees who were from Texas did not speak as one body, the Lone Star State's cattle interests spoke loudly. Already the hoped-for unity of organization showed signs of the differences in regional interests that would make that difficult.[19]

Several delegates proposed that the body would be better represented by the various associations present. New Mexico delegate W. T. Thornton announced that, although he believed the convention was meant to be national in its scope of interest, the particular purpose then was to "advance the interests" of the arid regions of the country. Thornton questioned a process that "gives to the State of Rhode Island, which probably has one man and a hundred head of cattle represented here, the same authority and the same power in the convention that comes from the entire State of Texas." A New York delegate offered a modification that would maintain state and territorial representation. Colorado delegates argued for representation by each association. L. R. Rhodes of Colorado outlined the main issues the many western delegates hoped would be addressed. "We don't propose to be drawn into any traps by any delegation from New York, Chicago, or anywhere else," Rhodes told the room. "I would ask the gentleman if he is interested in a National Trail? New York, that does not know a National Trail from a public highway, should not decide it for us. We are interested in the great question of epidemic diseases. . . . New York is not interested to any great extent [and] leasing the domain of Uncle Sam . . . is a question we want to discuss. New York has not any public domain . . . and she should have but very little to say in this matter."[20]

Indications were high that heated debate lay before the body, but Rainwater gaveled the house to order and reminded attendees to welcome the esteemed guests there and officially open the proceeding. The delegates settled on a motion to reconsider their earlier resolution. Then the mayor of St. Louis, William L. Ewing, rose to welcome the delegates. After brief remarks, he, in turn, introduced Missouri's governor, Thomas T. Crittenden.[21]

Governor Crittenden, promising that after the mayor's welcome he had "little left . . . to say or do," found he had quite a lot more to say. Delivering a supportive, knowledgeable, informative, and lengthy speech, he began by complimenting the attendees on their "extensive business association," referring to the many stock associations represented. Welcoming the attendees to "this Convention, the first in the life of this renowned cattle trade," the cattle business, he said, was "one of the great trunk-lines of business of the world." "You are statesmen as well as cattle kings," he told them, in coming together to learn "to feed the largest classes and numbers of humanity at the least cost to society, as well as at the greatest profit to the producer." Urging conventioneers to continue efforts toward improving their business, Crittenden called the American cattle trade a new "wonder of the world."

> This business has awakened into new life a new power—a new race of
> man—and made fruitful of resources . . . immense tracts of lands which
> have been given to desolation and waste. It has taken the frugal cowboy
> and made him a potential millionaire. It has made the 276,000 square
> miles of Texas the mightiest empire of possibilities in America, making
> the cattle trails of the past the forerunner and engineer's line of the railway
> of the present. . . . This business has not and is not only revolutionizing
> new States and new Territories, becoming in some, if not all, political, or
> dividing questions, but it is also making its mark, its impression, upon the
> meat markets of the world and the dividends of the trunk railways of our
> land.[22]

The governor also asked the delegates to consider the future of their business. Wisdom, he told them, came from preparing for the future. "A skilled general always prepares his pontoon bridges before reaching the streams," the governor said, martially. He told the crowd to look forward to a day when herds would be smaller. He urged them to exercise modern practices of management and feeding, a warning to the many western ranches still depending on foraging cattle to, primarily, maintain themselves. "A few years ago Kansas and Missouri were immense grazing fields—today they are surveyed and fenced farms," he said. "What is true of them may within a few years be equally true of Texas, Montana, and Wyoming." In closing, Crittenden called feeding humanity the greatest of all issues before a deliberative body, telling them, "I know of no trade or calling which demands and commands a greater love of liberty and union than this great one of yours." For those still present and awake, it must have been an encouraging salute to the progress they hoped to make for their businesses over the next few days.[23]

Gen. William Tecumseh Sherman, in town "by the merest accident," followed Crittenden. The general had retired from the army earlier that year. He lived in St. Louis and made appearances at dinners, banquets, and conventions. Speaking to the group, the "old traveler and soldier" lamented "the fate of the buffalo" but offered his admiration and good wishes for the health, happiness, and prosperity of the gathering, "whether proprietors or simply men who range around in . . . 'roundups,' or what we used to call in old California *rodeos*." Uncharacteristically, the general spoke only briefly, perhaps sympathizing with the group after the governor's long presentation or perhaps anticipating criticism from a Missouri newspaper editor a few weeks later. The writer objected to Sherman's accusations against Jefferson Davis and suggested that he "rest on his military record" and pursue other activities to "supplement his soldier fame" rather than write or speak. After the dignitaries finished, a motion for adjournment was made but failed to be seconded when delegates insisted that the question of membership be addressed promptly. The process took up most of the convention's first two days, though much other business was transacted among the attendees, no doubt.[24]

The final decision of the body on representation called for one voting representative from each association and from each state and territory not represented by a stock association. The convention's first day ended with the various groups submitting their selections for committee members. An official list of convention delegates and membership appeared on the third day. A brief debate on people omitted preceded its acceptance. A committee of three members escorted the body's president-elect, Gov. John L. Routt of Colorado, to the convention chair.[25]

After Routt's opening remarks, debate commenced regarding the work of the new organization's Committee on Resolutions in its preparation of the group's constitution. Some delegates desired a strong message to the committee regarding the full convention's seemingly foremost goal—a federally funded and maintained national livestock trail. Early discussion of the issue seemed focused on how best to express support for the plan rather than on any strong dissent to the proposal. Opposition did exist, however.[26]

Granville Stuart, known as "Mr. Montana," a pioneering Montana beef man and cofounder of the famous DHS Ranch in north-central Montana, rose to object to wording that characterized Texas as the prime breeding ground of the country and the northern ranges as simply "maturing" regions. "The strip of country on both sides of the Rocky Mountains, from Texas to the British possessions, is as much breeding grounds for cattle as the great State of Texas," Stuart reasoned, speaking against government aid for a Texas problem. "Let them ship to the East, as we of Montana have had to do." Stuart claimed that the Montana delegates as a whole opposed extension of a national trail to Montana. Stuart, noting that Texans had always been welcomed in Montana with "the hand of fellowship," reminded delegates that the Texans' concern was what to do with their surplus cattle. "We, in Montana, are . . . overstocked [and] thousands of cattle have been shipped to market," he said, warning of further price erosions ahead for their industry.[27]

The Montana delegation proved, as did many of the non-Texas western delegations, that opposition was less about the movement of beeves than the details of the trail and its government subsidization. "Bring their cattle to Montana the good old fashioned way," Stuart admonished, "as everybody else had got their cattle there," ignoring the obvious irony of the statement—they wanted the trail to keep doing it "the old fashioned way." The chair dismissed a series of motions regarding the trail for lack of a second. Joseph A. Carroll of Denton, Texas, a former district judge who had presided over Panhandle courts during the region's early days, spoke for the resolutions committee and introduced the proposition supporting the trail to the full convention. A lengthy debate led by the protests of a Missouri delegate delayed proceedings, but the convention eventually voted it to be "the sense of the Convention that there should be established and maintained a National trail," thus setting the western cattlemen's agenda as the group's greatest priority—at least for those with ties to Texas. The idea of a national trail for livestock was a demand from mostly Texas cattlemen for an outlet that bypassed the quarantines nearly all of states north of Texas were imposing against splenic fever. Texans hoped for free travel for their surplus stock, away from overgrazed Texas to somewhere the grass still grew. In 1885, however, overgrazed pasturage hindered the industry throughout the western grazing regions.[28]

Texas cattle raisers waged a long battle against northern stock growers' fears of epidemic disease. Splenic fever (bovine babesiosis)—also known as Texas or

Spanish fever, or cattle plague—was a tick-borne protozoan infection that caused grotesque deaths to cattle and had been a concern for the business at least since the end of the Civil War. Although the parasite left southern cattle such as longhorns—"coasters," as the cowboys came to call them—seemingly unscathed, it could be devastating to cattle in other regions, especially other breeds like the European purebred varieties increasingly being imported and raised in Missouri, Iowa, Kansas, and Nebraska as well as in the Texas Panhandle and the other western grazing regions. A mystery until 1893, the parasite infected cattle through the bite of ticks found on the southern coastal plains from South Carolina to Texas. Until then, almost everyone associated with the range cattle industry had a theory as to Texas fever's cause. Many thought dormant spores peculiar to Texas grasses might be the cause, or maybe poison soil; some thought it a "scurvy" type of disease brought on by long drives and inadequate food, water, and rest.[29]

Iberian-blooded longhorn cattle, with nearly three hundred years of adaptation in the region, had developed a resistance to the worst effects of splenic fever, though the longhorns were not immune to the effects entirely. Calves were infected but were aided in resisting the parasite by antibodies passed from mothers during gestation and an additional booster from their mother's milk after their birth. The carrier ticks, primarily *Rhipicephalus (Boophilus) annulatus,* are sensitive to climate and do not survive long outside of their native region. Quarantines prohibiting Texas cattle were lifted in the winter months. Victor A. Norgaard, a BAI scientist, demonstrated an effective "dip" in 1897. King Ranch manager Robert J. Kleberg is credited with building the first dipping vat in Texas. Effectively eradicated in the 1940s, in the United States today the disease is found only in a few remote areas along Texas's southwestern border with Mexico. The disease did not really present many problems for the beef business until after the Civil War, though. Many know the story—or think they do. An abundance of Texas cattle and a huge increase in the demand for beef in an industrializing nation led to the great cattle trails north from Texas to railheads in Kansas. The cattle trail defines America's story of its "Old West." The role a microscopic organism played in the story is less known.[30]

The cattle trail—not a single trail but a weave of ever-changing paths of convenience and necessity—wound its way north out of Texas long before the Civil War. Cattle fever may have been recognized as early as the 1790s when North Carolina banned cattle from South Carolina between April and November.

Cattle brought by American settlers to Texas in 1824 presented similar symptoms. Until midcentury the cattle business remained primarily local or regional. Pork dominated the public meat marketplace. Ohio feeders bought Texas cattle regularly as early as 1846, though. Texas cattle fed California miners in the 1850s, led there by either brave or crazy drovers. Texas cattlemen trailed their herds to Montana and Wyoming after the Civil War. The Texans, at first, competed with the "native" herds of the western part of the territories where road ranches and Oregon-bred cattle had provided the stock to feed the booming mining and timber region. In both territories, however, the cattle interests consolidated into powerful organizations that helped reshape their industry.[31]

Even before the Civil War, Missourians noticed that when their cattle mixed with Texas cattle coming up the trail during the summer months the Missouri cattle soon began to die while the Texas livestock seemed fine. Until the Civil War the cattle trail from Texas to Missouri was well used, if increasingly inconvenient. The cattle business grew. Settlers moved west. Booming expansion, hastened, perhaps, by the Civil War, brought more opportunities for contact between Texas trail herds and new settlers and entrepreneurs pushing onto the plains to start farms or ranches of their own. Knowing little else about the disease except that it showed up when Texas cattle did, Missouri authorized the first quarantines on southern cattle in 1854. Kansas and other states and territories soon followed with quarantines of their own. Courts repeatedly sided with Texas cattle owners, but by 1884 demands for disease prevention and regulation of livestock transportation convinced Congress to create the BAI. Nearly every state and territory north of Texas imposed regional and seasonal quarantines (sometimes these were of the Winchester variety). Charles Goodnight led Panhandle cattlemen in enforcing the embargo of southern cattle. The XIT's first manager, Barbecue Campbell, resisted joining the cattlemen's association that Goodnight led. Lingering animosity from the period may have led to periodic accusations regarding the presence of Texas fever in cattle purchased by the XIT.[32]

Although states and territories enacted different restrictions, federal authorities eventually recognized a line drawn roughly diagonally across Texas from the Big Bend region of the Rio Grande where the boundaries of Presidio and then–Pecos County converged, exiting Texas between Wichita and Wilbarger County in the north, then on to the northeast corner of the Indian Territory where it turned east and extended across the Gulf states. Generally, the quarantine area was recognized as the area south and east of the lines forming about the junction of the 100th meridian and the Texas and Pacific Railway. Despite lying above this line, Texas beef raisers in the Panhandle suffered the consequences by association. The real damage to northern cattle herds from tick-borne fever is arguable. Established to stop the disease, quarantines also benefitted northern cattle prices by limiting Texas cattle's ability to enter the marketplace. Although this was essentially a constitutional question, on which courts generally sided with Texas and other southern stock growers—interstate commerce is a federal prerogative—the establishment of the BAI reflected growing support for improved standards for health and safety for people and animals. Quarantines generally banned importation of southern cattle between March and October. Quarantine laws exempted southern cattle certified to have spent at least ninety days outside the quarantined zone. The line bisected Texas into two nearly equal segments, and the large cattle interests north and west of that line took their own steps to restrict southern Texas cattle. Still, despite the restrictions, Texas cattle driven from all parts of the state made their way north.[33]

At the convention, Texas delegates succeeded in excluding specific mention of Texas fever from their discussions of livestock diseases, primarily foot-and-mouth disease and pleuro-pneumonia, the latter of which, although a separate disease, seems to have been a euphemism for what many believed was Texas fever. Pleuro-pneumonia, primarily found in newer breeds of cattle increasingly being imported from Europe, contributed to livestock trade disputes between Great Britain and the United States. The British were sensitive to imported livestock after another "cattle plague," rinderpest (or steppe murrain), devastated British and western European cattle in the late 1860s. A fear of disease-induced beef shortages in England led, at least partially, to the rise in British investment in the North American cattle business during the late 1870s and early 1880s. Pleuro-pneumonia was mostly a concern to ranchers stocking the newer purebred cattle from eastern breeders. Many of the Texas delegation—and others in the quarantine zones—disputed whether splenic fever existed at all. Bad water, poisonous plants, any number of reasons could account for death among cattle, they said. George Findlay, later the XIT Ranch's business manager, defended the Syndicate's position regarding lawsuits in 1890 to an associate: "Murrain & other diseases presents symptoms very similar to Splenic fever & it would require an expert & postmortem examination to decide what the disease was."[34]

The convention delegates discussed other concerns as well. Until 1874, the presence of Comanche, Kiowa, and Cheyenne peoples with previous claims to the area limited cattle raising west and northwest of the quarantine line. The Red River War in 1874–75 and the final destruction of the southern plain's bison herd resolved "the Indian problem," opening West Texas and the Panhandle to cattle. Stock raisers and others coveted the western half of what became the state of Oklahoma, although these were mostly titular Indian lands. Lax regulation and sometimes fraudulent leases gave southern cattlemen a place to condition their cattle before sending them to market or for finishing in the corn-growing states or on the grass of the northern ranges. The actions inhibited the federal government's efforts at forcing pastoralism upon the region's Indians.[35]

The practice known as "double-wintering" became standard operating procedure for the country's largest cattle raisers. A conveyor belt of cattle production began with cheap coasters, mostly steers, brought in and wintered above the quarantine line on "free" grass, then driven to the nearest railhead and shipped on to Kansas City, St. Louis, or Chicago. As the free grass in the Panhandle disappeared after 1884, fewer southern Texas cattle made their way there. In "breeding up" their stock, Panhandle stock growers matched the southern longhorns with hybrid and purebred bulls. Eventually, ranches like the XIT bred most of their own cattle. The conveyor belt pattern continued, becoming more complex as these ranches simultaneously bred, bought, and sold cattle. Texas continued as the great supplier of cattle, but Granville Stuart was right, too. On both sides of the Rocky Mountains ranch operators bred fine cattle. Most calves born there would not fatten happily on pasture in Texas, Colorado, or Montana but increasingly in the Corn Belt feedlots of Nebraska, Iowa, and Kansas.[36]

The far reaches of west and northwest Texas in the early 1880s offered only temporary relief to the Texas cattlemen's rising problem of surplus cattle. Owners and well-heeled lessees, thanks to generous, loosely regulated land policies in Texas, soon laid claim to all of the Texas Panhandle grazing land. Enclosed by fences, the once "free" range disappeared, subdivided into pastures, farms, and towns. People began to realize the environmental quirks of northwestern Texas, too. The Panhandle suffered almost unending drought in much of the last two decades of the nineteenth century. Even the largest of the ranches in the region found their herds limited by the resources available to sustain them. The XIT and other ranches there experimented with several ventures that promised to bring rain. When those parched pastures failed to support XIT managers' livestock sales projections, the company determined to expand operation to "the northern ranges." Opposition on the northern plains, quarantines, settlement, and railroad development seemingly ended northbound cattle trailing operations out of Texas around 1885, the same time period the XIT became a reality. Texans, however, stubbornly resisted closing a disappearing northern trail. The XIT Ranch and others defied the end of the cattle trail.[37]

Delegates spent much of the convention in St. Louis discussing the national trail and not discussing Texas fever, but they also placed Indian relations and public lands high on their agenda of concerns. Several attendees expressed a seemingly enlightened and compassionate view of the Indian people. Consensus, however, formed around a resolution declaring that free-roaming Indians could not be tolerated and demanding that the government restrict Indians to their reservations. Often accused of stealing stock, Indians were viewed by some like wolves—predators needing elimination. Again, it was Montana's Granville Stuart, married to a Shoshone woman, who spoke the mind of many delegates: "The Indian . . . is a much abused individual and I will stand up for him, even if he does steal my horses once in a while." Stuart denounced "the atrocious policy of the United States" that encouraged American Indians to leave reservations on which "we pay taxes to feed and clothe [them]." It was a less than subtle jab at the corruption that plagued the Indian agencies regarding subsidies and annuity payments, grazing leases, and provision supply contracts. Stuart and many other stock growers favored allotment of Indian reservation land. Livestock interests stood to profit from a return of huge tracts of land to the public domain. In Montana, for the near future, allotment meant turning millions of acres over to livestock interests. Their calls prompted action two years and two months later when the Dawes Severalty Act went into effect February 8, 1887.[38]

On the northern plains, as on the plains of Texas and Colorado, cattle replaced the millions of bison that seemingly disappeared overnight from 1882 to 1883. The Assiniboines and the Crows held the oldest claims to much of the region. Crow people met William Clark at Pompey's Pillar, Montana Territory, in 1806. They signed their first treaty with the United States in 1825. The 1851 Fort Laramie Treaty identified the country between the Missouri and Yellowstone, from the Musselshell River, as land shared among the Arikaras, Assiniboines, and Crows. The treaty also recognized the area from the Powder River west to the Yellowstone headwaters as Crow land. These tribes, however, contended with aggressive Lakota Sioux. In the same treaty, the government recognized much of today's western South Dakota as Lakota territory. Joined by Gros Ventre people living among the Blackfeet Confederacy west of the Musselshell River, the Crows fought a losing war with the Lakotas in 1867. In the aftermath of the 1868 Fort Laramie Treaty, the Crows and other Indian peoples in the region ceded significant portions of their land to the United States in return for protection from Lakota expansion. The cessions included all the land between the Missouri and Yellowstone rivers, where the XIT would later locate its northern grazing range, and in the Powder River basin as well. The eventual containment of the Great Plains Indians provided a buffer zone on the fringes of settlement in which surplus Texas cattle could be made both closer to and more desirable in the marketplace.[39]

On the sixth and final day of the convention, delegates took up the discussion of public land leases. This again exposed the division among the attendees, particularly the split between large and small operators. The convention's objective of unifying the nation's cattle raisers appeared to be failing. A majority report introduced from the resolutions committee declared "that beef cattle can be more economically raised in the arid and elevated portions of the country . . . between the ninety-eighth meridian and the Sierra Nevada Mountains." The report recommended that the federal government exclude a huge portion of the inner West from "homestead and pre-emption laws" and offer land leases "for a term of years" to "the owners . . . holding them only by possession and sufferance, their property in constant peril from conflicting claims and unfavorable legislation." The report recommended a committee of seven to prepare a memorial to Congress. As with the trail resolution, supporters sought to emphasize the importance of the beef industry in the United States: "Whereas, The beef raised on these plains has become an important factor in our foreign trade, increasing in greater ratio than any other product, and will . . . become the most important article of food supplies sent from our shores . . . we believe it to be the duty of the government to aid this great industry in every way consistent with the general welfare."[40]

Others felt differently. The divide between the large and small beef operators, perhaps more so than the cattleman's infamous hatred for sheep operators, already had brought violence to the western cattle range. The "Fence-Cutting Wars" in the early 1880s in Texas revealed the split first. Ostensibly about keeping infected cattle from southern Texas out of northwest Texas, the violent outbreak also involved the fencing of public land, thus discouraging "nesters"—small-scale farm-beef operators—and "grangers"—farmers—from staking claims. All stock raisers feared rustling. Big operators claimed that prior use protected their ranges. Often backed by their stock associations, the largest outfits accused small operators of being or associating with cattle thieves and building their herds by nefarious means.[41]

Still a problematic practice today, rustling plagued the XIT and other large ranches. Earlier in 1884, Granville Stuart led a group of vigilantes—"Stranglers"—in pursuit of men accused of horse and cattle theft. Although shielded by anonymity at the time, members of Stuart's group included many of the same men who met in Miles City, Montana, during the spring of 1885 to establish the Montana Stockgrowers Association. Shot trying to fight or escape, most of the Stranglers' targets died where they were found. Pursuers hanged some, leaving the bodies twisting in the breeze, a sign posted identifying their crime as a warning.[42]

In Wyoming, the reach of the most powerful livestock association in the country touched every aspect of the territory's existence. Big livestock owners there were the de facto territorial government. Statehood brought little change. The lynching of a man and woman in 1889 near Sweetwater sparked angry challenges to the livestock association's hegemony. A huge publicity campaign encouraged by large cattle ranchers and the stock growers' association railed against the effects rustling was having on their herds. The animosity between large and small operators throughout the West culminated in the Johnson County War in Wyoming in 1892. Rather than an operation against conspiratorial cattle rustlers, the actions by some of the highest figures in the Wyoming Stock Growers' Association (WSGA), and by elected Wyoming officials, targeted small, honest land and cattle owners whom large operators viewed as usurpers of their prior claim to grazing areas.[43]

The Syndicate, before and later, associated with men implicated in that attack. A year after the Johnson County War, H. B. Ijams, longtime WSGA secretary, and George Findlay, the XIT's business manager in Chicago, corresponded regarding XIT steers stolen by a man named G. M. Kirlin, or Kirby. Ijams explained why he had not had the man prosecuted. Indicating that the WSGA remained shaken by the Johnson County War, "I was afraid of our prosecuting attorney," Ijams confessed. "He took the case here against the stockmen on that invasion last spring." The circumstances spooked the big cattle ranchers, but they could still unite against rustlers. Across the beef empire, such contacts and correspondence remained common. Ijams suggested that Findlay press the case in Texas, where Kirlin apparently resided and had stolen the livestock. Ijams asked for Findlay's help in contacting Hardin and Campbell, ranchers in north Wyoming, at their offices in Chicago, since Ijams had been unable to contact either at their ranch. Ijams told Findlay there were witnesses there who could help in Kirlin's prosecution in Wyoming. Many Syndicate documents attest to the intimate network linking the beef business.[44] Despite such help, the XIT continued to struggle with rustlers throughout its earliest years.

Barbecue Campbell, already in negotiations with the Syndicate about a role in their cattle company, was at the St. Louis convention representing the Cherokee Strip Live Stock Association. He likely heard the minority report on public land leases from the resolutions committee introduced by Colorado delegate S. S. Wallace, from the Las Animas County Stock Growers' Association. It called the measure before the convention biased "in the interests of wealthy cattle corporations and cattle owners [and] another way to . . . procure the right to fence the public domain." The dissent proclaimed that action on the resolution would repeal provisions of the homestead laws and "would work disastrously and prejudicially to the small owners." A lengthy debate followed, including several eloquent speeches from familiar names. Wyoming delegate A. T. Babbitt, general manager of Wyoming's Standard Cattle Company, spoke strongest in support of the majority report, perhaps best summarizing the stance of the room's "big" cattle interests:

It is alleged that this is a measure in the interests of the monopolists [and] a measure to supersede, checkmate and defeat the operations of the public land laws. It is nothing of the kind. It is a proposition to pay something for that which we now pay nothing. It is a proposition to bring some system—some order out of chaos. The gentleman from Colorado (Mr. Rhodes) makes the objection that the history of the cattle business has been sufficiently good; that we have all made money in the cattle business; why isn't that good enough? As long as ranges were available to people who wanted to invest their money the business was good; but in Texas they have reached their limit; they have reached their limit in the Northwest. Our ranges, the majority of them are too heavily stocked, and from this year forward, every head of cattle that is put on them is that much in excess of the grazing capacity of that Territory. The situation is serious and it is time when cattlemen should consider the situation and make a fair demand of Congress. If they don't ask something they will never get anything. We came from Wyoming objecting to the idea of a trail. Our objection has, to some extent, been misunderstood. We did not object to it on the ground of the liability of infection, or of cattle disease, because cattle driven from the South have never hurt us so far North, and we are not afraid of them. We have objected to the trail simply on the ground of safety of our investments. We have believed that if Government made an appropriation whereby a public highway for cattle was to be established, over which the immense herds of surplus cattle from Texas were to be invited to come and overwhelm us, that we were in danger of obliteration and extinction. Now we have said to our Texas friends you favor us in a measure which is very dear to us, and we will favor you with all earnestness and in good part in favor of every pet scheme from the South. We have made that proposition in good faith, and I say in behalf of my associates from the North—at least from Wyoming Territory Stock Growers' Association that we will carry out that in good faith. The idea is, if we can get a fair control of the ranges we desire to occupy, we will not object. We want their cattle. We have made our money on Texas cattle more than on any others.[45]

Trade-offs are expected in a successful organization. Opposition arguments were reasoned and garnered considerable support. A New Mexico delegate, seemingly on the fence regarding the issue, pressed on the body the reality of foreign investment in the western cattle business. He wanted the public range kept free and open to homesteaders and cattle ranchers alike, but he also desired protection from foreign corporations and overstocking of the range. Another delegate echoed concerns about foreign cattle companies and suggested a scheme whereby actual settlers, holders of 160-acre parcels controlling accessible water, were granted the right to claim or lease adjoining grazing lands. W. M. Stone, from the Southern Colorado Cattle Growers' Association, who had introduced the resolution, attempted mediation:

I think the gentleman who so earnestly antagonized the proposition . . . misunderstands the question, and misapprehends the motives of those who defend it. The very argument . . . urged against it can be urged in favor of it. . . . a great deal has been said about monopoly; a great deal has been said about the actual settler on the public domain. I am opposed to monopolies. All my days I have been in favor of the poor man and the settler. . . . Now in these later days, capital from . . . the British Empire has come on to those plains, and, by their large herds, have scattered and trampled out the rights of the settlers, and that state of affairs is becoming more intensified as the years roll round. It is in view of this that we offer the proposition, and ask the aid of the Federal Government to oppose its strong arm to prevent this monopoly of foreign capital, that is trampling down the rights of the actual settlers in these arid regions.[46]

Stone and others argued that leasing the public lands would strengthen American cattle ranchers against foreign operations by making access to grazing rights legally and financially secure. They claimed that a well-designed adjustment of homestead and preemption laws would allow "actual settlers" 160-acre homestead claims in the "Arid Regions" of the west and allow adjacent grazing lands to be leased according to the number of cattle the person held. Would title to 160-acre well-watered claims by someone who owned 25,000 head of cattle grant them exclusive leasing rights to 500,000 acres of public land? The arguments of supporters seem curious. It took twenty to forty acres per head to raise a beef in the country's arid regions. Supporters argued that the plan benefitted both large and small American cattle raisers. How this excluded large investors from finding someone willing to "prove" a claim and giving them thousands of dollars to buy cattle is not clear. Legendary cattleman Joseph G. McCoy, opposed to both a trail and the leasing of public lands, felt discussion of the land lease measure was a waste of the convention's time. He related the experiences of John Wesley Powell, who had long lobbied Congress to approve leases in the public arid regions. The introduction of such a bill, he was told by a congressional representative, represented political suicide.[47]

Representing Idaho Territory, Gen. James S. Brisbin offered his opinion in closing debates on the issue. "I hope this Convention will not exclude a measure which seems to be heartily supported by a large number of people who have come here for the purpose of securing its passage." Brisbin now told delegates in his approval of the resolution:

I think there are nearly 400 people here who would not have come to this convention if it had not been for the purpose of securing the passage of this land lease request. I am in favor of this land lease request. I am in favor of the land lease. Every herdsman to-day is a trespasser upon the public land, within the eye of the law; he is a criminal to a certain extent, and something should be done for his relief from that onus.[48]

"These arid plains," he had earlier written in what became a heavily cited classic, "so long considered worthless, are the natural meat-producing lands . . . and in a few years 30,000,000 people will draw their beef from them. All the figures I have seen published have rather understated than overestimated their capacity." Brisbin is the source of the oft-repeated claim that the "beef business cannot be overdone." That observation soon proved much more than optimistic.[49]

Delegates defeated a motion to send the reports to a special committee and a motion to accept the minority report. The majority report was approved. According to newspapers, the resolution passed with heavy support. Eager to support the plan after the majority backed their calls for the national trail, Texans, with little remaining public land of their own, overwhelmingly approved the measure.[50]

Conventioneers then resolved to ask Congress to put aside certain tracts of public land "*en route* to market" where "herds of cattle liable to communicate splenic fever" could be isolated until proved safe for the marketplace. They adopted a resolution urging "that all the covenants of the Government with the Indians should be most scrupulously and honestly carried out" and that the Indian groups named "should be rigidly limited to the limits of [their] reservations." Finally, a proposal urged Congress to strengthen the BAI inspection and quarantine rules by providing for competent and timely veterinary services from the agency. The convention adjourned *sine die* after voting its thanks to members, officers, and the citizens of St. Louis. Members also agreed to publication of the convention proceedings.[51]

The St. Louis convention called for a national organization unified for action. Its successes at achieving any of these goals, except those restricting Indians, were limited. The management of public land in the United States continued to be a flashpoint of conflict, often pitting cattlemen and other livestock operations against the government. Various livestock interests in the country enjoyed political leverage, but unity among this disparate group proved impossible for the moment.[52]

By 1885 every state and territory on the Great Plains imposed quarantines against Texas cattle at certain times of the year. The merits of a national trail met vocal public debate in newspapers throughout the country. The Texas legislature, rather than a committee of the cattlemen's association, adopted and championed calls for the cattle road. Senator Richard Coke, who as governor had led the conservative Democratic push to undo Reconstruction reforms in Texas, introduced a bill supporting the trail plan to the Senate in January 1885. Texas representative James F. Miller championed a similar measure in the House of Representatives. Loud opposition came from Kansas's governor, an outspoken critic of the plans. The Kansas legislature memorialized Congress against the proposals and further strengthened the state's quarantine law.[53]

Supporters pushed for the route. Running close to the eastern border of Colorado from Texas across the "no man's land" of the Oklahoma panhandle to Wyoming, it edged through the northern portion of the Capitol Reservation through what would be the XIT's Buffalo Springs pasture. Supporters hoped to sell the plan as a means of protecting settlers from wayward cattle herds and Texas fever while providing an outlet for supplying cattle to the northern plains. Backers argued that, like railroads, their industry had become critical to the nation's economy and deserved the same underwriting and subsidization that railroads and other prominent commercial operations were enjoying. Trail City, a forgotten Colorado town on the Kansas border, owed its brief existence to anticipation of the national trail's approval. The proposal was roundly panned as nothing more than a profit scheme by Texas cattlemen. Approved by committees in both houses of Congress, the plan failed full consideration. Objections from the railroads and states like Kansas, Colorado, and Nebraska defeated the measure. Even cattlemen in the territories—Wyoming, Montana, and Dakota—were not then anxious for more cattle.[54]

The next year, in Chicago, Granville Stuart once again denounced any government assistance to Texas cattle raisers. Montana's territorial governor, responding to pressure from cattlemen there, declared a quarantine on Texas cattle that summer, although it was filled with loopholes. The Wyoming territorial veterinarian reported cattle importation inspections through his agency from March 31,

1885, to March 31, 1887 at just under 80,000. Over half of those inspections were of Texas cattle. Nearly half were identified as cattle bound for Montana. Splenic fever was not mentioned in the veterinary report. Despite Montana's imposition of a quarantine and warnings in newspapers about the destructiveness of Texas fever, actual outbreaks there are not well documented. It seems highly unlikely the disease could have traveled easily to such a foreign climate. Moreover, many of the inbound Texas stock during the late 1800s came to Montana by trail, rather than rail, which was at least a two-month trip even if shipped by rail part of the way. Pleuro-pneumonia appeared, however, and gave Wyoming inspectors significant concern. Its presence in imported cattle, all from eastern states, resulted in the destruction of cattle found with this and a few other diseases.[55]

A similar national trail bill seemed to enjoy broader support in the next Congress. Once again, Senator Coke and Representative Miller sponsored the bills. The Senate bill passed in March and received a favorable report from the House Commerce Committee. After a lively debate led by John H. Reagan of Texas regarding the trail's route, the House voted. With the ayes and nays announced, the bill seemingly had passed, but then an Iowa congressman shrewdly announced, "No quorum." Another Texas member, Samuel W. T. Lantham, demanded that the vote be recorded. Inexplicably, Reagan then asked permission from the Speaker to withdraw the bill. This was the last official attempt to establish the national trail.[56]

Although Texas has long been first in the public mind as the country's chief producer of cattle, by the 1880s western expansion and heavy eastern and foreign investment in cattle raising were making feeding operations in Missouri, Kansas, Iowa, and Nebraska into a big business. For northern cattle raisers, the Texans had been more than a health threat to their cattle, they were competition. The territories of the northern ranges—the Dakotas, Wyoming, and Montana—where huge tracts of public land remained available for grazing livestock, represented a potential challenge to the preeminence of the Texas beef market. Additionally, shrewd campaigns by the "Big Four" packinghouses—Armour, Hammond, Morris, and Swift—encouraged changes in consumer tastes. Buyers wanted young, "fat" cattle, "finished" on northern grass or in Corn Belt farmer-feeder operations, spurning the common longhorns raised in Texas. Urged on by non-Texas cattle interests who hoped to grab a market edge on Texas raisers, the public became more convinced that the durable breed provided little better than "canning" grades of meat. Improved cattle in Texas, too, seemed to be at a disadvantage. Many proposed that the grasses in Texas on which cattle fed lacked the nutrients to provide the preferred grades of meat. Buyers claimed cattle raised on the northern Great Plains or seasoned in prairie feedlots experienced better rail service and suffered fewer losses during transport. Although Chicago buyers were not eager to buy cattle direct from Texas, they did not seem to mind purchasing those same steers raised on northern grass over two winters or fed for a season on corn and sorghum on midwestern farms. As the beef industry took shape through the 1870s and into the 1880s, Chicago became the capital of a new meat empire dominated by packers, commission houses, and railroad magnates. Many of the high gentry of the "land and cattle" companies made their homes there or frequented the city's fine hotels like the Drake and the Grand Pacific. Railroad lines that reached from Chicago filled with products reaped from the bounty of the country's western resources were the veins of that empire. The transportation of northern cattle to stockyards and slaughterhouses in St. Louis, Omaha, Kansas City, and, of course, Chicago presented fewer obstacles and shorter distances than the limited rail lines in and out of Texas's most productive grazing regions.[57]

As concerns about Texas fever and the growth of packinghouses and the nation's railroads made the outlook for cattle in Texas bleak, the changing structure of the cattle market influenced the development of the Montana cattle industry. Cattle ranching in the area had emerged on a small scale in the 1850s to feed the mining and lumber regions in the western part of the territory. After the Civil War, Nelson Story brought Texas herds into Montana Territory. By the early 1870s, cattlemen were driving herds onto soon-to-be and recently ceded tribal lands in the central part of the territory. The arrival of the Northern Pacific Railway in 1883 spread the large-scale development of open-range ranching across the territory's eastern plains, reshaping the geography of livestock production across the western United States. In eastbound rail cars at towns and sidings along the line, ranches shipped fat cattle to stockyards in Chicago, St. Paul, Omaha, Kansas City, and St. Louis and from there out into the growing global meat marketplace. This flow of capital and commodities increased as the Great Northern Railway built a line across the new state of Montana in the early 1890s.[58]

The export of "fat cattle" replaced local meat production. Processed for retail sale, the final product of the rich nutrients and good water offered there returned rebranded and repackaged by Armour or Swift. Local slaughter facilities became increasingly scarce despite valiant attempts to build them. Chicago and its ministries in St. Paul, Omaha, Kansas City, and St. Louis ruled the meat empire. Spoke-like cattle kingdoms literally fed the raw materials that its production depended on.

Each day, rail access became more critical to the cattle industry. In Texas, reliable rail service was slow to reach the Panhandle. Only in 1888 did the Fort Worth & Denver City (FW&DC) reach the XIT's Capitol Reservation, offering a north-south link to east-west lines in Colorado and on to more northern reaches in Wyoming. Even after the arrival of the FW&DC, the ranch, for some time, drove eastbound cattle to railheads in Liberal, Kansas, and Panhandle City, Texas. Other lines did not quickly reach ranch boundaries.[59]

Over the next few years, the operators of the XIT Ranch immersed themselves in the machinery of the cattle business. The operation teetered on disaster for its first years of operation, tested severely by the limitations on their purchase. The men who spoke most loudly at the St. Louis convention became the men the Syndicate associated with, and with whom they competed, negotiated, and cooperated. Most of them, beneath the cattle baron persona, knew that land, rather than the cattle on the land, was the secret. It would, however, take a series of environmental, political, and financial actions and events, even disasters, to move the XIT into the realm of legend and among the West's greatest beef outfits and, ultimately, real estate ventures.

∾

Changes in the Wind

By 1885, grasslands throughout the Great Plains were suffering extensively from overgrazing and drought. Markets reeled. There were too many cattle. Ernest Staples Osgood later wrote, "In the scramble for profit that had resulted from inflation and speculation, the business had extended far beyond the margin of safety." Millions of Texas longhorns made their journey to death in Kansas City, St. Louis, or Chicago, but the rangy Iberian mongrels were losing the eye of buyers attracted by swelling herds of northern European imports like the shorthorns (or Durhams), Herefords, and the most recent immigrants, Aberdeen-Angus cattle. Although the Fencing Wars of the early 1880s and the arrival of the XIT Ranch in the Panhandle in 1885 signaled the end of the open-range cattle business in Texas, they did not signal the end of the open range elsewhere; the result was even more competition. And though the push for a national cattle highway may have ended, the end for the long trail north arrived a decade later. As railroads extended west into the northern range lands, railroads in Texas reached beyond the ninety-eighth meridian only slowly. A transcontinental rail link spanned Texas by 1883, but it was 1888 before the Fort Worth & Denver City line reached the Panhandle of Texas. To complicate matters even further for Texas ranchers, the market center had coagulated in the nation's north. The prime cattle regions of the northern plains featured reliable rail service to the newest livestock facilities in South Omaha, St. Paul, and, of course, Chicago. Defying nature, competitors, and its own internal conflicts, the Capitol Syndicate entered the cattle business in Texas faced with monumental challenges.[1]

Ranching on both the southern and northern Great Plains had become a crowded industry with deep undercurrents of turmoil within its ranks. The limits of the western cattle industry had been revealed, if not yet completely understood. Prices too low could not support the production of too many cattle without the resources to sustain them. Twenty-five years passed before cattle prices again reached then all-time highs in 1884. When Ab Blocker put the XIT brand on the first steer in the summer of 1885, giving the ranch its name, Barbecue Campbell and the owners had already begun to realize the obstacles they faced in providing water and grass. The Syndicate scaled back their dreams of 300,000 head of fat cattle roaming their three million acres. Even with the ranch's efforts at improvements—fences, artificial water, and hay production—they could barely support what they had. A persistent drought combined with a winter filled with "blue-whistler northers" gave the southern plains a preview of the Big Die-Up winter coming throughout the plains in 1886–87. Prairie fires erupted in the heart of one storm and raged across pastures. This would not be the first or last fire to ravage XIT forage. Spring 1886 estimates showed that the ranch had lost nearly one-third of its previous year's purchases. Fortunately, contracts for an additional 45,000 head had not panned out, or losses would have been greater. On a broader scale, investors lost millions of dollars as winter storms turned cattle to drift before the wind, sometimes for hundreds of miles, before some obstacle—usually a barbed wire fence—stopped them to die from starvation or cold in rows and even piles. Company records indicate that after losses during "the Big White Ruin" there were just over 16,000 head of cattle on the ranch in the spring of 1886.[2]

As big as ranching was, and as important as Texas, Colorado, Wyoming, and Montana were in the western cattle business, small farms in the Midwest and elsewhere continued to produce the most meat sold in the marketplace. Only about 14 percent of domestic slaughter-cattle production came from big western range cattle operators during the 1880s. By 1900, that number had risen to 39 percent from eleven western states, but it fell back to only 30 percent by 1910. This pattern clearly shaped the evolving plans of the XIT owners. The Illinois men proposed subdividing the Capitol Reservation to better manage the huge tract. Initially, seven divisions defined the ranch's cattle operation: Buffalo Springs, Middle-Water, Ojo Bravo, Alamositas, Escarbada, Spring Lake, Yellow Houses. Another division, Rita Blanco, extended from Channing, or Rivers, as it was previously known, which became ranch headquarters in 1890. Each division foreman led his own crews for well drilling, fencing, planting, haying, and harvesting. Sub-divided into smaller pastures, each division employed its own cowhands, cooks, and wranglers in day-to-day livestock operations. Branded with XIT (later, just "long X"), calves born on the ranch also were stamped on their shoulders and jaws with brands for the division and birth year of the calf. Unique earmarks further identified XIT cattle. Eventually, each division was graded and specialized in a particular stage in the cattle-raising cycle. When the Pecos and Northern Texas Railway came through the ranch in 1898, management created an eighth division. The town of Bovina in Parmer County was built around a siding switch along the way where XIT bulls often congregated. For a short time, the town became the largest livestock shipping point in the country. The XIT had reorganized to oper-ate more efficiently in smaller units, more like small farms in the more established stock-raising areas of the country.[3]

Undeterred by the losses of 1885, the Syndicate ordered Campbell to buy more cattle, insisting, however, that he keep costs down. The British investors had already become fretful. Drought continued in the summer of 1886, too. Camp-bell fretted over water for his beeves. Taylor sought to provide it by drilling "arte-sian" wells. It was his persistent belief that deep wells of clear, flowing water lay beneath the land, and he hoped that the wells would turn the Capitol Reservation into a garden of bounty. Confident that it was there, Taylor misunderstood the region's primary water source, often ordering well drillers to continue drilling beyond water strikes discovered at depths of 75 to 300 feet. A decade and a half passed before government geologists discovered the Ogallala Aquifer. Effort was necessary to pull water from the aquifer's shallow, spongy core. Taylor hoped for deep, fast-flowing water that would, once tapped, bubble to the surface. He was disappointed. The massive underground lake, stretching north-to-south across much of the Great Plains, would have to do. Ranch operators later installed more than three hundred windmills and water tanks across the XIT, but these were not enough. Despite Campbell's objections about water shortages, the company purchased more than 52,000 cattle in 1886.[4]

The XIT was not unique. Thousands of cattle were bought and sold in Texas that year, and thousands, despite enhanced quarantine restrictions, made the trip north that year. It was dry in Texas. It was dry in Montana. The previous winter had not delivered much snow to the northern plains, and the grass was thin. Because it was worse in Texas and the Southwest, with grazing leases limited in

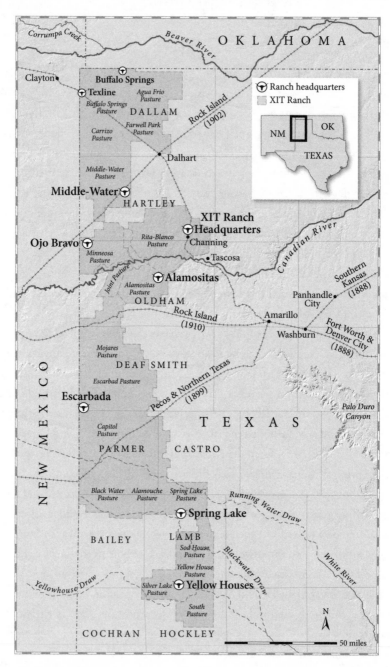

What became the XIT Ranch stretched south from the northwest corner of Texas to cover
nearly 4,600 square miles. A four-strand barbed wire fence enclosed the ranch by the end
of 1886. Seven division headquarters were initially established for the ranch, and in 1890 a
permanent ranch headquarters was established in Channing (Rivers). This map shows the year
the labeled railroads reached ranch boundaries. An eighth division was created in 1898 near
today's Bovina as the Pecos & Northern Texas built through the Capitol pasture.

Indian Territory, ranchmen crowded surplus cattle onto the stressed grasslands of the northern ranges late into that summer. Newly arrived "pilgrims" filled eastern Montana that fall. Many of these mostly Texas cattle came malnourished. Corn Belt feedlots were overstocked, too, and farmer-feeders sold cattle to eager western entrepreneurs. Cattle suffered the hardship of transport there, whether by rail or over the trail. Cattle are not without learned intelligence. Experience with bitter northern winters gave "natives" and earlier immigrants a better chance at survival. The new arrivals, apart from their nature, had not learned to forage beneath heavy snow. Many Montana ranches began winter feeding stock years earlier. Dozens of nesters with little experience with either cattle or winter on the northern Great Plains took advantage of the millions of acres of still "free" range there. If nothing else, the West has always offered people the hope of "next year." Low cattle prices were tempting, and everyone thought the market had to turn around soon. The first snowfall in eastern Montana that year came in September. More substantial snows began falling in November, when a blizzard began blowing across Montana and the Dakotas. The storm dumped 5–9 inches of snow on the ground. More snow fell through the end of the year, doubling normal precipitation in the region for the period.[5]

While northern stock growers familiar with the vagaries of the weather fretted about their overstocked ranges and a repeat of the winter of 1880–81, the Chicago operators of the XIT had concerns of their own, beyond the constant pressure from London to start making money. For months Campbell managed the steady stream of cattle filling the XIT's parched pastures. Fencing and the well-drilling projects continued, though not keeping pace with the arriving cattle. Campbell implemented a process whereby he received the cattle at the Yellow Houses in the southern part of the ranch, branded them, and then drifted them northward toward more reliable water, eventually balancing the cattle across the water and range in supportable numbers. J. Evetts Haley noted that the Syndicate trailed 15,000 head of cattle to the Dakotas in several bunches during the summer of 1886. Whether a printer's error or the author's, it is likely that Haley meant 1889, when J. W. Driskill agreed to manage 15,000 XIT steers along the Dakota-Wyoming border. Still, if Haley's date is correct, Campbell could have argued to owners that he needed to resell some of their contracts. Panhandle ranches often bought cattle elsewhere to sell to northern buyers. This "through cattle" type of transaction may have relieved the stressed ranch manager.[6]

The XIT and Campbell, however, were making few friends, and Chicago was hearing about it. Everyone, it seemed, had cattle to sell, and as many cattle as Barbecue had to buy, he could not buy from all those eager to sell. Campbell passed over the beeves of some of those with friends in high places, drawing protests and complaints. He also began drawing the ire of neighbors almost as soon as he arrived. The massive fencing operation, of course, was a travesty in the eyes of some cowpunchers and range bosses, even though their employers were doing the same thing. To be neighborly, Campbell agreed to allow cattle to be driven through his pastures to New Mexico or into the Neutral Strip, today's Oklahoma panhandle, with the understanding that they would pass through in a timely manner. During the ranch's first summer he found a Matador herd loitering at one of the rare small lakes on the ranch. Facing a long, dry drive, the trail boss refused to move on until there was a sign of rain. Campbell, with new cattle arriving and his own water concerns, threatened to use force to expel the herd from the XIT. Eventually the Matador man agreed to move his herd. His pace did not completely satisfy Campbell, but further conflict was avoided. Another time, some LS cowboys approached Campbell to obtain permission to look for strays in an XIT pasture. Campbell refused, telling the men that any of their cattle found on XIT range would be returned. The hated barbed wire enclosed the entire spread by the end of 1886. Range fires and challenging weather further shortened tempers. Contempt for the owners of the Capitol Reservation grew, and an epithet often prefixed any mention of the ranch.[7]

As men were completing the ranch's enclosure in Texas, snow continued to fall on the northern plains. In the second week of January 1887, a warm southwesterly wind—a chinook—began blowing across the snowbound plains in Montana. Livestock owners and managers were encouraged as grass was exposed and ice cleared from waterholes. Then, on January 28, the wind shifted and temperatures plunged while heavy snow began falling. By the next morning, the Big Die-Up had begun.[8]

The earlier chinook did not clear all the earlier snow, and the freezing temperatures turned what remained into a hard-crusted mass. New snow, 8–12 inches, piled heavily in the wind, filling coulees and draws and covering fences. Cattle instinctively turn away from the wind and in heavy snow begin to travel before it, to drift, in search of forage and shelter. The crusted base created two great problems for the cattle. It made foraging for grass difficult, for the beeves could not easily paw through it. And the frozen, broken snow tore at their legs. As the beasts waded through fresh, deepening snowdrifts, their hooves broke through the underlying thick crust of an earlier drift, trapping them and others that followed. If these cattle encountered a barrier they could not breech or sought shelter in a deep cut, they stayed there to freeze or starve. As many ranchers in Texas had discovered during the previous winter, fences intended to protect their cattle instead became deathtraps when the beeves became entangled in barbed wire buried beneath snow drifts.[9]

Subsequent blizzards came and even more chinooks followed, repeatedly pounding livestock and people alike. Mail went undelivered, freighters could not deliver to merchants, merchants could not deliver to customers, and rural customers could not get to towns. The Northern Pacific shut down when severe cold weather cracked rails. Montana merchant king and future U.S. senator Thomas C. Power was aboard a Northern Pacific train derailed by the weather that winter. The experiences of the 1880–81 winter, along with those of 1885–86 on the southern plains, had not been lost on the stock growers on the northern plains. Plenty of them harvested prairie hay for supplementing winter feeding. But the thaws and freezing collapsed storage barns and encased haystacks in thick frost and ice. There was no way to get the hay to the cattle or the cattle to the hay. Horses and mules floundered in the deep snow, and temperatures fell far below zero—reportedly as cold as 55 below from an official government report at Fort Assiniboine on Montana's north-central "High Line." A souvenir map from the Texas Sesquicentennial claims a temperature of 70 below in the Panhandle that winter, but one suspects subzero temperatures happened no more than a handful of times there—ever.[10] Official February averages in Montana, however, showed at well below zero throughout the territory. Veteran operators there tried to prepare, but many free-grass and nester operations seeking a livestock bonanza lost everything after gambling they could reap a bounty from the region.

The pulsating weather pattern broke a month later. Stockmen and homesteaders dug themselves out to assess their losses in early March. As the melting snow revealed thousands of dead cattle spread across the range, the magnitude of Charles Goodnight's admonishment about the cattle business was confirmed. Cattle losses reported in Montana from the Continental Divide eastward ranged from 10 to 90 percent. A cottage industry scavenging hides from the dead cattle boomed; the brisk business ruined the hide trade for years to come. The largest operations lost the most, numerically. Those owners, though, could often stand disaster the best. Many others lost everything.[11]

The winter did not spare Texas. C. C. Slaughter, just south of the XIT, lost 10,000 head of cattle. Panhandle stockgrowers found their beeves as far south as the Rio Grande that spring. Drift fences "went down like cobwebs" as storms drove livestock farther and farther. Questions arise regarding the winter's severity in Texas. Oldham County, in the heart of the XIT, say some, experienced its "mildest winter in recent memory." The XIT's neighbor in Texas, W. M. D. Lee and the Scott brothers' LS, operated on considerable range in Montana. Lee told a reporter that he intended restocking his Montana range from his southern stock as soon as possible. Losses in Montana were heavy, he said, but he had a large reserve from which to draw and the bad winter had not discouraged him. Another project in Texas prompted Lee to reverse course and sell his Montana operation the next year. Another chronicler of the LS wrote that good hands on the ranch in Texas minimized the fortunate owners' losses when bad weather struck.[12]

The Big Die-Up of the winter of 1886–87 accelerated transformations in the cattle business that had been emerging over the course of the early 1880s. The need to replace the livestock lost that winter eliminated much of the opposition to the importation of animals from the southern plains. As a result, a network of financial and political forces solidified their considerable power over the Montana cattle business. Wrangler and itinerant artist Charles M. Russell, responding to his absentee boss's request for information on how the cattle were faring, summarized that winter the best he knew how. Russell's sketched watercolor *Waiting for a Chinook* centers on a gaunt, brindle steer still willing to turn its horns down in the face of the circling wolves patiently awaiting the creature's end. The background divides between solid white broken only by the shadowy figures of other wolves and a darkening sky foretelling yet another storm. The Helena owner of the herd sought to make lemonade from the news and passed Russell's sketch, drawn on a paper box top, around to his friends. Someone wrote on it later, "The Last of 5000," referring to the Texas pilgrims the man had invested in apparently too late in the previous year. The drawing became the catalyst for Russell's transition from the low rung of the cattle-punching business to that of full-time sculpture, painter, writer, and pundit—today among the top two or three best-known western artists.[13]

Russell's boss was hardly alone. Plenty of cattle operators bought stock late in the season, lessening the pilgrim beeves' chances of surviving through spring. It had been a dry summer, but one stock raiser gave it a positive spin while acknowledging it. "I do not anticipate a hard winter," J. J. Kennedy, a Fort Benton cattle rancher, told a reporter from St. Paul's *Pioneer Press* in October 1886. "It has always been my experience that when we had a dry summer an open winter followed."[14]

The number of losses during the Big Die-Up remains somewhat controversial. In the first place, no one is sure how many beeves were on the northern ranges and how many people had been out there seeking to take advantage of low prices, confident that cattle production would recover from the weak market. There is also the matter of "book counts," the notoriously inaccurate cattle censuses on which many purchases of range operations were based. The cattle boom, like most other booms, drew its share of shifty characters, but with eastern and foreign buyers so eager to have a ranch it was difficult for the most honest of men to resist counting a few of their stock more than once. In fact, counting thousands and thousands of cattle sometimes spread across thousands of acres was an almost impossible task. Most large ranching operators settled on a method to estimate the extent of their herds on the range. Managers then kept herd books of sales and purchases, calving, and estimates of losses.[15]

The actual reports from that winter tell a mixed story. All the western and Montana newspapers reported extensively on the effects of the winter. In Fort Benton, the *River Press* reported from around Montana. The paper opened its coverage by discounting the report of a sheep owner who claimed a loss of 1,700 head to the winter, declaring the loss to be only about 500. One ranch foreman wrote that "as far as can be learned the losses of cattle will be light." Another told the paper that "the principle losses during the winter have been among cattle driven in last fall." A Mr. C. Wallace of Choteau said losses would be "less than fifteen per cent." "A prominent stock man residing at Miles City," the paper wrote, "sends word that reports of losses among cattle on the Yellowstone have been very much exaggerated." Bulls seem to have managed the weather particularly poorly, however, their loss being "very great," an assessment confirmed by a reputable stock inspector. One rancher, less optimistic than most correspondents, wrote that "it is a wonder that any cattle are left alive. The bulls have nearly all died." The foreman of the Benton & St. Louis Cattle Company told the paper, "There is hardly a bull left." Not all the losses were livestock. One cattle baron shared a report he had received from one of his range managers:

> Your letter of the 15th at hand. A chinook has struck us and the snow is going fast; some of the ridges are bare already. You need not be downhearted, as 15 per cent will cover the loss of the block herd. These are outside figures; some think the loss will be less.
>
> I have had the toes of both feet cut off [from frostbite], but my feet are healing rapidly and I hope to go to work this summer.
>
> There is, from all accounts, not as much snow on this side of the mountains as on the other, and the loss will not be as great. The coldest that it has been here is 46 below zero.
>
> I am in a pretty bad hole, I can tell you, although I will have feet enough to do a little riding. I will not be able to get out of bed for two weeks at the soonest.
>
> This is perfectly splendid weather, and if it keeps up this lick we will see green grass in a week or so, and then the cattle will begin to pick up and the loss of this winter will not be anything like what you expect.[16]

The cowhand's optimism must have been infectious, for the newspaper went on to editorialize on the past and contemplate the future:

> Later reports as to the condition of the stock from all over the ranges in this section are to the effect that the losses are not as great as was feared. Ridiculous estimates of from 50 to 75 per cent loss . . . have been reduced to fifteen to twenty-five per cent [and] losses are divided among many owners. The large owners are amply able to stand the loss as their profits in the past have been enormous, but the beginners and owners of small herds will feel it more severely. The larger companies, as a rule, are represented by men who are engaged in other pursuit and the investments in cattle are from the surplus growing out of their business. By reason of this fact there will be no distress, no failures, no panic and the stock business of Montana will continue to flourish as before. Such a winter as that of 1886–87 may not recur for half a century. The heavy snow fall is an assurance of a fine grass crop this year and the prospects are there will be more activity than

has been witnessed for years in this great industry, just as the hard winter of 1880–81 was followed by such a reaction.[17]

In addition, people tend to remember the last bad event as the worst. Indeed, the losses from the winter probably exceeded in numbers the previous winter on the southern plains and the 1880–81 winter on the northern ranges. It struck on a more widespread basis, with colder temperatures and more snow over a longer period. Still, at the Montana Stockgrowers meeting in April, despair did not seem to be the prevailing mood. Attendance seemed strong, although attendees represented only about a third of the membership. A reporter for the *Daily Yellowstone Journal* in Miles City, where the cattlemen were meeting, wrote, "H. R. Phillips, the genial and obese proprietor of the LU Bar . . . is not overly communicative, but from what little he said . . . he found everything satisfactory on his range, considering the severe winter." The reporter's description of the rancher may have addressed the cowman's reluctance to speak. Exactly eleven years later, perhaps the same commentator took note of Phillips upon his return to Miles City from Chicago, where he had wintered. The famous MacQueen House had burned down recently. Phillips "was much pleased," the reporter observed. "His comfort and happiness had been considered to the extent that the new hotel will have an extra wide porch." Few public acknowledgments at the meeting referenced the winter losses. Phillips was later among the closest associates of the XIT operators.[18]

Theodore Roosevelt's operation was wiped out by the winter tragedy. There for one of his last stock growers' meetings, he advised the group to avoid joining the railroad companies in opposing interstate commerce laws until learning more information. Attendees supported a resolution offering support to the Crow Indian agent, Maj. Henry E. Williamson, and backing proposals to assign Indian land allotments and the sale of surplus reservation acreage. Concerning the mistreatment of cattle during roundups, Granville Stuart proposed a resolution outlining the expected treatment of livestock. Moved by the winter's livestock losses, Stuart encouraged delegates to respect the cattle and horses that endured hardship in serving humans. In his autobiography, the old pioneer claimed the winter moved him to quit the cattle business a short time later. Stuart's address seemed one of the few public acknowledgments at the meeting of the winter losses. The organization's secretary, R. B. Harrison, the son of the next president of the United States, lamented the drought of the previous summer in his report. Other references to the winter's toll do not appear. A plan for the roundup was set on the convention's last day with no apparent references to the livestock losses. "Next year" optimism prevailed and, when grass grew thick across the northern plains well into summer, faith in the bounty of cattle returned. The Kansas City livestock firm of Towers & Gudgell, with interests from Texas to Montana, drove "10,000 Texas and 4,000 high-grade Colorado cattle to their Montana ranges" late that August. Many other large operations on the northern ranges did likewise.[19]

Still, things had changed. The next year's meeting saw less robust attendance, and the association's membership fell over the next three years, then recovered in 1890. Pioneer cattlemen in the region remained, many positioned to continue and even expand their operations. The former opposition to the importation of animals from the southern plains eased. Outside producers benefitted from the hard winter. Many local ranchers experienced disaster, but others found great opportunity. Many turned their hard-won knowledge, experience, and connections in the region into a new career as land and cattle brokers while a scramble erupted for control of what those washed out in the Big Die-Up left behind. Through their positions in the financial world, their political contacts in government, and their affiliation with Montana's Stockgrowers Association and Board of Stock Commissioners, an effective oligarchy controlled the territory's most productive grazing regions. When statehood came to Montana in November 1889, political issues and attention to western mining and timber regions left the cattle region's control primarily in those same hands into the early years of the twentieth century.[20]

The large ranches maintained close, even direct ties to the livestock commission houses that became the main intermediary to both packinghouses and railroads. Commission houses and their "men" became nearly as powerful as the railroad shipping agents, who determined just who would get the sometimes-limited cars available at shipping time. Their practices often marginalized small operators. Despite public denouncement of the "beef trust" from newspapers and populist politicians, this model dominated the cattle industry over the next two decades and molded the framework of the modern meat industry. In Montana, such men as John T. Murphy, Thomas Cruse, and Senator Power, already fortunate in other endeavors and with friends in the highest positions everywhere, consolidated their holdings into cattle, encouraged investors, and became even more powerful. Two other "barons" of the Montana cattle business, Conrad Kohrs and Pierre Wibaux, not without investors of their own, made their fortunes during this period as well.[21]

Theodore Roosevelt and his wealthy French neighbor, the Marquis de Mores, who both had appeared in the area in 1883, took heavy losses from the storms. Roosevelt, having lost half of his inherited wealth on his ranching adventure, decided to return to politics. He maintained a partnership in one of his two ranches, usually returning annually until the press of public service became too much. De Mores's dreams of a meat-processing hub in Medora, Dakota Territory, in competition with Chicago's Big Four, also ended with the storm. The packing plant he established there had ceased operations the summer of 1886, and despite the Marquis's seemingly deep pockets Medora itself was soon sputtering. The Marquis, who had not enjoyed the same welcome or popularity in the region as Roosevelt, reportedly died violently on a North African adventure a few years later.[22] His partners practically eliminated Granville Stuart from any control or participation on the DHS Ranch. The Pioneer Cattle Company, the DHS, sold out in 1891 when Conrad Kohrs took complete control of the operation.[23] E. S. "Zeke" Newman, with cattle interests in Nebraska, Colorado, and near the mouth of the Musselshell River in north-central Montana, branded more than 7,000 calves in Montana in 1886. That figure implies a herd of at least 21,000 cattle at the time. When Newman sold his N Bar Ranch—improvements, cattle, and range—to Montana gold king Thomas Cruse in 1889, his men could only gather 6,000 head to turn over. Cattle marketed in 1887 and 1888 likely account for some of the decrease, but it is not hard to imagine the Big Die-Up losses for Newman at 50 percent or more.[24]

H. S. Boice, a longtime hand in the northern livestock business whom Roosevelt had befriended, along with partner David Berry, a wealthy New York financier, soon controlled the range that the Roosevelt and De Mores cattle had roamed. Berry and Boice dominated the cattle business of the Little Missouri country spanning the border of Montana and what became North Dakota for nearly a decade before closing out in 1897. Boice became involved in other cattle operations but was hired to replace XIT Ranch manager Albert Gallatin (A.G.) Boyce in 1905. Another Frenchman, Pierre Wibaux, took advantage of Big Die-Up losses, too.[25] For some, it took time to feel the Big Die-Up's effect. Wibaux bought out the Vermont ownership of the Green Mountain Cattle Company in 1889—the outfit could never recover from its losses two years earlier. Wibaux intended to compete with Montana's biggest cattle operation, the N Bar N.[26]

Owned by St. Louis manufacturers William and Frederick Niedringhaus, famous for producing Granite Ironware cooking utensils and dishes, the N Bar N, or Home Land and Cattle Company, began in 1886 when the brothers bought 6,000 head of range cattle and range rights north of Glendive, Montana. Buying more cattle in New Mexico, they sent as many as 65,000 head north to range in Montana and across the international border on leased land in the Wood Mountains of what was then part of Canada's Northwest Territories. The immigrants arrived just in time for the bad winter. The N Bar N range stretched from the Dakota Territory border to the Judith River, between the "divide" that split the Missouri and Yellowstone tributaries, and across the Canadian border. Some reports put N Bar N cattle losses the winter of 1886–87 at 40,000. Other sources suggest 20,000.[27]

Despite their immense losses during the Big Die-Up, the Niedringhaus brothers doubled down on cattle. Although they parted with their Canadian range, the company acquired new foreign money and expanded in Montana, purchasing several other stock ranches, including rangeland along the Missouri River from the Hunter and Evans partnership, which found better luck in the cattle commission business and soon became one of the largest livestock commission houses in the Midwest. The Niedringhaus brothers later leased a ranch in the Texas Panhandle from White Deer Lands, the former Francklyn Land and Cattle Company, one of the first English-dominated imperial ranch companies in Texas. Charles G. Francklyn, with money from Cunard Steamship Line, had purchased 631,000 acres of land in the Panhandle in 1881 for $880,000, becoming among the first imperial ranchers entering the western beef bonanza. After the Niedringhaus brothers obtained it, the N Bar N bred and pastured cattle there, conditioning them for the trail north. It is doubtful any other Texas ranch ever held more cattle on its contiguous acres than the XIT in Texas when it was stocked with more than 120,000 beeves. It is equally hard to imagine that any other single, closely held company ever held the numbers that grazed on the N Bar N's Montana range during the 1890s. Historian Joe Frantz called the XIT "the world's largest ranch—in Montana." But though the XIT, at its greatest expansion, had far more beeves fattening on the Montana grasslands than in the Syndicate's Texas pastures, it is unlikely that it matched the Niedringhaus operation at its height there.[28]

As the most entrenched cattlemen assessed the winter of 1886–87, many chose to modestly restock or not restock at all, instead marketing claims they held on reliable water sources and on tentative cattlemen's claims to a still-huge tract of public land. The winter's pattern took some and left some—large and small. It was a pretty simple formula. Those who had money, influence, determination, and—usually—land stayed; lacking most of those qualifications meant doom. Renewed migration of southern stock began almost before the snow melted from the prairies as an even more powerful oligarchy consolidated control of the northern ranges. A cyclone of transactions swept the northern ranges as an entrenched elite sought to reenergize the beef bonanza with new and better blood. The storm revealed a new cattle empire on the Great Plains, ruled from Chicago and its ministries in St. Paul, Omaha, Kansas City, and St. Louis.

Somewhat curiously, falling cattle prices did not rebound after the harsh winters between 1885 and 1887. The response from northern cattlemen—at least those who survived the winters with either intact herds, substantial bank accounts, or firm land titles—was predictable: sell more cattle to make up for the lower prices. The cattle had to come from somewhere, though. Some problems are resolved when a greater problem arises. When ranchers held more cattle than they knew what to do with, Texas fever was a problem. Quarantines became the problem in 1887 when farmer-feeders and northern grazing operations needed stock. In the several years after the Big Die-Up, northern cattle-raising regions sought to ease restrictions on the importation of southern cattle.[29]

Cattle prices indicate that eliminating quarantines was not the solution to increasing production and prices for operations such as the XIT. Prices had peaked in 1869 at just over $25 per head but mostly declined through the 1870s. They again began to gain in the early 1880s, spurred by European investment, peaking at just over $25 in 1884 before beginning a steep drop-off in price that held until late in the century. There appears to be no corresponding fall in production until 1891. Production fell steadily before rising again at the end of the century. Cattle production figures for 1890 remained unmatched until 1902. Prices did not again reach their 1884 levels until the XIT had nearly phased out its ranching operation after 1910. Unlike the years following the bad winters of the mid-1880s, a noticeable drop in cattle production did come after the winter of 1906–7, remembered by many in Montana as comparable or surpassing the Big Die-Up in its ferocity. The big ranches operated from snowstorm to snowstorm until they could go on no more. Big cattle had survived on the margins of viability for decades. The winter of 1907 marked the end of one boom and the beginning of another: the homesteader had come in earnest.[30]

As revealed above, in Texas the XIT did not always garner favor from its neighbors. XIT managers allied with Goodnight, who fought to distinguish the Panhandle region from other parts of the state through the Panhandle-Plains Cattlemen's Association. Goodnight moved to strenuously enforce the quarantines, and the XIT joined him. Throughout the years from 1885 to 1890, however, the Syndicate fought off various accusations that the ranch's huge purchases of southern cattle frequently carried Texas fever into the Panhandle, infecting local cattle. These were part of the shadow of suspicion that drove Campbell to leave the XIT and return to Kansas in 1887.

Campbell retained the services of his brother, M. C. Campbell, to assist in purchasing the enormous numbers of cattle the company continued to stock. Amid rumors of poor management, unscrupulous employees, gambling, drinking, and women on the ranch, M.C. and Barbecue may have been engaged in purchasing inferior cattle for the ranch, inflating their numbers and grades, and skimming off Syndicate money for their own enrichment. The elder Campbell also faced accusations of bringing in fever-infected cattle and harboring rustlers. The company, too, was interested in finding the cause of continuing low income from its ranch. In the spring of 1887, the Syndicate enlisted Avery L. Matlock, a Montague County lawyer and former legislator, to investigate complaints. A supporter of the Syndicate in the 1883 Texas legislature, Matlock and an associate in 1885 received a loan from the company "for which they feel great obligation." Almost immediately upon his arrival at the ranch, Matlock spotted several men of notoriety familiar to him from his law career. He confronted Campbell and accused him of harboring criminals. One of the men, Campbell's range boss, Bill Ney, disputed Matlock's claim to have once saved the cowboy from a lynch mob. Ney accused Matlock of bearing a grudge from a time when Ney testified against men the lawyer was defending. Campbell defended Ney, and Matlock relented for the time being. But antagonism between Matlock and Ney did not fade. Through the summer, Matlock rode the ranch from south to north gathering evidence, seemingly relentlessly pursuing Campbell's job. George Findlay, a trusted associate and protégé of John V. Farwell, accompanied Matlock. Among the demands of Findlay's employers was for him to provide an accurate count of cattle on the ranch. His efforts "to point at and count" every bovine brought both glee and frustration to the cowboys. He quickly realized the futility of the effort and approved more traditional methods for the job. Campbell agreed that he would be responsible for a reliable count by the time they finished receiving and marketing cattle that fall.[31]

The best-known accounts of the XIT—by Cordelia S. Duke, J. Evetts Haley, and Lewis Nordyke—add mystery to the story with divergent accounts of actions involving Campbell. Duke largely echoed Haley, who offered little defense of Campbell's management of the ranch. Nordyke, more sympathetic to Barbecue, offered a letter from Campbell defending himself. The papers of Matlock, however, apparently collected and transcribed by Haley sometime during the 1920s and 1930s, shed light on the affair. During his investigation, Matlock contacted at least twenty-two persons to document Campbell's mismanagement of the ranch. He reported his finding to George F. Westover, the Syndicate's legal counsel in Chicago. Some of Matlock's respondents addressed their correspondence to Findlay. This could reflect distrust of Matlock, or it simply may indicate that the investigation was jointly conducted by Matlock and Findlay.[32]

Matlock and Findlay divided the task of investigating the XIT, Findlay focusing on business matters and Matlock looking for criminality. It was at this point that Findlay made his acquaintance with A. G. Boyce. The two formed a friendly, respectful bond that established a foundation of the ranch's success for the next eighteen years. Boyce had been to the ranch many times. In June 1887 he brought a herd of Snyder brothers' cattle onto the XIT. At the time he was a partner in and manager of the Snyder ranch, but losses by that outfit found him amenable to a change. Campbell, spooked by the fallout from Matlock's investigation and whatever news Findlay took back on his return to Chicago, approached Boyce to take charge as range boss of the XIT. Barbecue had approached Boyce the previous year, but the latter found the timing of the offer much more convenient now. Boyce asked Campbell if he could have some time to put things in order at his home in Georgetown, Texas. Campbell agreed, telling Boyce that he had not yet talked with Chicago regarding the position. While Boyce returned to Georgetown, conditions at the ranch deteriorated for both cattle and Campbell.[33]

When Boyce arrived back to the ranch's headquarters at Yellow Houses in mid-July, Campbell was nowhere to be found. A brief letter arrived the following day. "Sorry I did not see you," Campbell wrote from the Texas & Pacific Railroad depot in Colorado City. "Mr. Ney will give you my ideas about work, calf-branding, and to prepare drive beeves. Train coming," Campbell abruptly concluded. Ney held a letter from Campbell as well, which Boyce also read. To Boyce's recollection, the substance of Ney's letter instructed the men to get the calves branded and beeves prepared for market. Boyce began to undertake those operations but soon discovered that new cattle were arriving faster than they could be handled and watered. Apparently, to complete his agreement to count the ranch's cattle, Campbell ordered the year's new arrivals held at the Yellow Houses. Boyce soon discovered that mud plugged some water wells and many had not been completed. He ordered work be commenced on well maintenance and that several thousand head of cattle be drifted north, despite Campbell's orders. Returning to Yellow Houses, Boyce found a new letter from Campbell. Campbell began the missive, "Friend Boyce." He had been hasty in his earlier letter, Campbell wrote, apologetically. He reiterated what he had written in Ney's letter, emphasizing its points as the "two important things to do." He also wanted some bulls moved from one pasture to another and suggested riders be dispatched to ensure that a herd of "very wild" cattle be held together at a windmill and "kept from traveling." Campbell wrote, "I shall return in a few weeks" but added little more useful information than Boyce had already discovered for himself. "The mail is ready and I must stop," Campbell closed. Addressed from the Mansion Hotel in Fort Worth on July 9, Boyce read it on July 25.[34]

Campbell, apparently, was on his way to Chicago, where he settled with the Syndicate and returned to his home in Wichita, Kansas. That, at least, is the account in Nordyke's book. The letter Nordyke attributes from Campbell to the Syndicate offered high praise for Boyce, declaring he had made a "partial arrangement" promising him a salary of $2,500 a year as Campbell's range boss. Campbell's letter does not suggest his resignation. Possibly, a resolution of their differences could not be reached upon his arrival in Chicago. Instead, Matlock was located by telegram and instructed to return to and take charge of the ranch. His arrival did not meet with the approval of employees hired during the reign of the former manager. Upon hearing that Matlock was taking over the ranch, Ney and several of his men departed. According to Haley, Ney returned with ten men and threatened Matlock. Backed by Boyce and others, however, Matlock stood up to the sometime outlaw whom the lawyer himself once called "a very good cowman." Soon, Haley wrote, "the population of New Mexico was slightly increased."[35]

Matlock was not done. Leaving the southern section of the ranch in Boyce's hands, he made his way to Buffalo Springs. The lawyer fired half of the ranch employees there, many on suspicion of rustling or horse theft but others for gambling, drinking, or otherwise breaking ranch rules, which included the carrying of "six-shooters." To some of the punchers, Matlock's acts seemed arbitrary at times.[36] In his reports, Matlock angrily denounced Campbell's management of the ranch, describing a litany of actions that called into question both the man's competence and his allegiance. "I deem it the first and most important duty of a man in charge of any business," Matlock stated early in his first report, "to call about himself honest and capable help." The lawyer claimed the ranch had become "the stopping place and rendezvous for a large number of bad men and criminals."[37]

In a March 1888 report to Westover, Matlock continued to rail against Campbell, calling him a conspirator "in defrauding the Company." The Texas lawyer detailed the method by which the Campbells passed younger cattle for older cattle, overcounted, or graded the animals higher than warranted. He calculated that the two might have netted $1.75 per head on the cattle, well beyond a typical buyer's commission of $0.50. "Now I have got another little matter," Matlock added, "that shows either collusion, neglect, irregularity, fraud or all of these things combined." According to Matlock, on one purchase of bulls for the ranch, not only were they priced higher than their grade warranted, but seventy-five of those purchased were never actually delivered to the ranch. Matlock told Westover that he "was about to get my hands relieved of considerable work . . . and I can put more time in on the B.H. and M.C. matter." It is not clear that the Syndicate devoted any more time to the matter after their ranch manager left. Nordyke wrote that Taylor, who had been in Europe through much of the investigation, returned to claim Matlock's reports on Campbell were untrue. In any case, rather than Matlock, Taylor, his role in the capitol project critical now, became the ranch general manager in Chicago, and Boyce was promoted to manager of the Texas ranch on January 1, 1888.[38]

As for Barbecue Campbell, although he left the XIT under adverse circumstances, later correspondence reveals that there were apparently no hard feelings in the matter. The Syndicate has a long history of "family" disputes. These include a lawsuit by the widow of one of the original Syndicate, Amos Babcock, that stretched over three decades. Legal proceedings became a fact of life for the company, none of which seems to have been much more than burdensome and time-consuming. Its last major legal challenge came in 1923, when Texas courts ruled that the state inadvertently handed the capitol builders an excess of 50,000 acres of Panhandle land. In 1889, Capitol Freehold stockholders voted to accept the board's calculations of just over 2.9 million acres as sufficient exchange from Texas. Over time, the Syndicate relinquished claim to nearly 150,000 acres back to Texas.[39]

Before Matlock arrived to clean house, Boyce did his best to salvage the parched herds. He knew he had to move thousands of cattle farther north quickly. Despite Haley's narrative suggesting the ease by which purged employees were replaced, Boyce lacked horses and manpower for the job. Boyce asked Ab Blocker, who was delivering a herd to a neighboring rancher, if he and his men could help. Blocker eagerly pitched in. By August 3, Boyce and his punchers had moved what he was told was 19,000 head, but which Boyce estimated to be closer to 16,000, north onto the Spring Lake and Escarbada pastures, the latter about at the midpoint of the ranch's north-south reach. While this was being done, Boyce was informed of many cattle in various locations dying of thirst, and of a well that had been plugged with mud by untended thirsty cattle. There were more cattle bound for the ranch, too. He soon discovered even more unfinished wells in the area. As he turned his attention to the project, the man responsible for wells in that area, B. F. Williams, left the ranch during the crisis, claiming his sick wife needed a doctor's attention. Boyce got what information he could from Williams and put men to work moving well equipment to those sites where water could most quickly be captured. By the time that Boyce, joined by Matlock, gained a measure of control, they counted 746 dead cattle. Boyce later wrote Findlay, who had returned to Chicago earlier, "[I] am rather surprised that I succeeded in saving the cattle with so small a loss."[40]

By that fall, mostly with Boyce's firm guidance, work on the XIT was progressing nicely. Windmills and wells came in time to quench thirsty cattle and spare losses. Fencing and building operations at the various ranch outposts progressed efficiently. Another 32,000 head had streamed onto the XIT in 1887, bringing it to about 110,500 head of cattle, including 10,000 calves born that spring. Still, the ranch was not producing the expected profit. Taylor or John V. Farwell occasionally accompanied the agents of their British investors on inspections of the ranch. Concerned about their interests, the British sometimes chose to send their own observer independent of the Farwells or Taylor.[41]

Matlock proved no better at soothing relationships with XIT neighbors than had Campbell, and he quite probably had reason to fear for his life, too, after the uproar his activities created. Despite his diminished role, he continued his involvement with the ranch operation. He soon became one of the group's most ardent land promoters and its town builder. Taylor, watching the capitol construction project wind down, sought to cement a role for himself in the ranch operation. A plan by Taylor to ship the first XIT cattle to Chicago markets to impress a British visitor backfired when cattle prices dropped beneath already low prices. Boyce, who had taken a herd of the ranch's choicest young steers east to a railhead in Oklahoma Territory, sold 714 of the beeves at $16 a head before Taylor, in Chicago to oversee the ranch's first shipments, could stop him. Taylor, changing his mind after seeing the unexpectedly low prices, ordered Boyce to return the remaining three hundred beeves to the ranch.[42]

The British agent, investor Henry Seton-Karr, arrived in October 1887. He and Boyce got along fabulously. Won over, the Englishman reported glowingly to his colleagues in London. John V. Farwell asked Boyce to assume the ranch manager job with the assistance of Findlay, who was sent back to Texas as the ranch business manager. Boyce agreed. He would hold the position for the next eighteen years. As Campbell had discovered, it was sometimes difficult to tell who was making the decisions for the ranch. Taylor was the central figure regarding XIT operations at the time. John V. Farwell asserted his authority regarding Boyce. Once the capitol building was completed, Taylor faced a similar fate when Farwell exercised his position as managing trustee to take over as ranch general manager, with both Boyce and Findlay reporting directly to him. Taylor did not leave the company and retained an active role in ranch business, but his role in the cattle business declined over the next several years.[43]

Boyce and Findlay made a good team. Despite his bookish appearance and city ways, Findlay had experience in the cattle business that went beyond what most knew. In partnership with James Anderson, another Scottish immigrant, in 1878 he imported and developed the first Aberdeen-Angus cattle herd in America. By the end of 1887, both he and Boyce had made a good impression on the employees, suppliers, and neighbors of the XIT. Most freight for the ranch still came by wagons powered by oxen or mules. Findlay bristled at the high prices he felt transporters were charging for the shipments. Boyce reorganized the well- and dam-building operation. Better prices and better workers showed immediate results. The new manager more clearly delineated ranch duties. Findlay and Boyce both supplied monthly reports to Chicago whence, in turn, more reports were sent to London. The Capitol Freehold Land and Investment Company produced many records and documents. Under Findlay and Boyce, that practice increased. As it had with Campbell, meticulous record keeping and continuous questioning from business partners wore on Boyce's patience. He took a strong leading role in the ranch operation. For most of his considerable reign he complied with all that was asked of him.[44]

As the originally mandated capitol completion date of January 1, 1888, neared, the extension to 1891 supplied in the contract for granite appeared less and less necessary. A few last controversies arose around the project. On May 1, 1888, the capitol was dedicated in a solemn occasion marked by a long speech from Temple Houston. As the grandson of Texas hero Sam Houston droned on, a thunder-storm passed overhead. The roof leaked. Other niggling issues prevented the state's full acceptance of the building and thus the thirty-fifth and final transfer of the Capitol Reservation lands. Benevolent during the project's final stages, Taylor offered to warrant the construction for a fixed period following final acceptance of the building. That date finally came on December 8, 1888.[45]

John V. Farwell continued to expand his control of the XIT Ranch. He stayed in England for many months shoring up the support he received from Seton-Karr and another shareholder, J. Garnett, who visited the ranch in the early summer of 1888. By the time of Capitol Freehold's annual meeting in March 1889, Farwell had put his plan for the ranch and the company in place. The chairman of Capitol Freehold, the Marquess of Tweeddale, announced that the Farwells and Taylor agreed to lease the land and cattle for a term of five years. The arrangement had the Americans paying Capitol Freehold $0.15 per acre on the land and 5 percent annually on an estimated 96,000 head of cattle valued at $19.50 each. They further agreed to pay all expenses in the United States. The payments would be applied "first to the payment of Debenture Interest and London expenses, and second to the improvement of the Company's property, including the construction of a line of railway from north to south of the Company's lands," Tweeddale told the gathering. The agreement also included a commitment to leave 150,000 head of cattle on the ranch should the lease be terminated. This last point would later lead to years of litigation.[46]

By 1889, with a herd that had grown beyond 100,000 head, the company had not realized a profitable cattle sale. Two years of significant calf crops contributed to the large size of the herd, but most of the XIT's livestock were common cattle purchased from southern Texas. Range fires, drought, hard winters, and poor planning had cost the upstart ranch thousands of dollars in cattle losses and demonstrated the limits of even three million acres in Texas. Farwell, his name and money on the line, took firm control of the ranching operations. Something had to be done to create a profit.[47]

Now recognizing the limitations to profitable stock raising, the Syndicate sought a plan to overcome the obstacles. "Breeding up" had begun at the ranch earlier but now became a preoccupation of the operation. They began buying higher-grade bulls, initially shorthorns and Herefords—some from Goodnight. At Findlay's suggestion, the ranch even purchased some of the diminutive, sheep-dog-looking Highlander bulls in their attempts to breed the best kind of beef, both for the market and for the harsh conditions present on the XIT. Until about 1892, the increasingly popular Aberdeen-Angus accounted for only about 15 percent of their bull stock. Boyce, always rubbed wrong when new ideas were presented, sounded a bit disappointed in the ranch's success when he wrote John V. Farwell that the "more I see of the black cattle the more I like them." The ranch operators increasingly depended primarily on Angus bulls for their commercial production while maintaining a purebred Hereford herd to provide brood cows and for show. Still, by 1889 high-grade beeves were a few years in the future for the XIT. The ranch's rangy coasters, the only saleable cattle they then held, could not compete with cattle from a growing number of Midwest farmer-feeders or with competitors stocking the northern ranges.[48]

Although Haley wrote that no "large movements of cattle" onto the ranch occurred after 1887, his own research disputes that. According to company reports, 3,000 cattle were purchased the next year. J. E. "Ealy" Moore, a longtime cowhand, wagon boss, and division foreman at the XIT, wrote Haley that the Syndicate purchased another 10,000 head from the King Ranch in 1889, shipping them to Rivers. Only 3,341 head came from the King Ranch, however, but another 6,564 shipped from Dennis O'Connor's South Texas ranch. The ranch purchased another 625 head in North Texas from W. N. Staples of Cleburne.[49]

Higher demand for livestock on the northern ranges in the late 1880s found plenty of southwest cattlemen eager to sell. But the cheapest to be found were on the wrong side of the quarantine line. If you had room in the Texas Panhandle or just across the boundary in the western Indian Territory or eastern New Mexico Territory and could get South Texas cattle past inspectors (and Panhandle ranchers), there was a good chance you could sell them to northern operations. Some Panhandle and West Texas operations purchased cattle in quarantined areas to supply stockers and feeders up north. Through cattle spent little time in Panhandle pastures. Those operations' locations in Texas added strength to claims that their northbound cattle met certification conditions for the various states and territories imposing quarantines. Texas had faced quarantines for a very long time, Louis Atherton wrote, "and had learned much concerning the problems and difficulties involved."[50]

To some extent, it was a question of to whom the cattle belonged rather than from where they came. Senator T. C. Power from Montana, powerful in his home state's cattle business among his numerous interests, corresponded with an associate regarding cattle purchases planned for the senator the spring of 1890. His buyer sought beef in New Mexico and Texas and was well aware of quarantine restrictions. The buyer, confided Power's agent, would "get enough Coloradoes to mix in & avoid the [quarantine laws]." The correspondent wrote, further, that the buyer would "fix his bill of sale papers so there can be no trouble about it." George Findlay, on the threshold of a shipment north, once wrote Boyce asking him to write an affidavit declaring "that all of the cattle are from north of the 36 parallel," perhaps acknowledging that many of them were not, although they had wintered above the line.[51]

Experimenting with plans for finishing their cattle, the company began corresponding frequently with farmer-feeders in Kansas, Nebraska, and Iowa. They inquired about possible opportunities in Indian Territory. They contacted people around the country with ranching interests, investigating potential deals to supply XIT cattle to stock growers in the Dakotas, Wyoming, and Montana. In 1889, Abner Taylor made a deal with J. W. Driskill, the son of legendary Texas cattle drover J. L. Driskill and then-owner of the Austin hotel named for him. The younger stockman took 15,000 head of XIT steers to graze along the borders of the soon-to-be-established states of South Dakota, Wyoming, and Montana that spring. Not waiting for results from that experiment, the company vigorously pursued other alternatives. The government again prohibited non-Indian ranchers from grazing cattle on Indian lands. The Cherokee Strip of Indian Territory soon opened to settlement, ending the XIT's hunt for pasture there. The Cherokee Strip, or Cherokee Outlet, ran across much of the northern tier of Indian Territory adjacent to Kansas. Originally reserved during the Cherokee removal of the 1830s as a hunting and grazing area, after the Civil War portions of the territory were offered to other Indian tribes, possibly as a response to the Cherokee Nation's brief alliance with the Confederacy.[52]

President Grover Cleveland, during his first administration, had barred white cattlemen from grazing arrangements with Indian reservations. The ban never really worked, but the policy continued into Benjamin Harrison's term. Harrison's priority seemed to be opening the land to white settlers rather than protecting Indians from exploitive ranchers. His proclamation in February 1890 ordering stock growers out of the Cherokee Strip helped push the Syndicate to invest in a satellite operation on the northern Great Plains. Taylor, in Congress at the time, had the previous year supported a plan to open various portions of Indian Territory and the unorganized Neutral Strip of today's western Oklahoma to settlers:[53]

We had an amendment put into the Indian Appropriation Bill opening Oklahoma and the Neutral Strip north of us for settlement in the Proclamation of the President. The President has issued the Proclamation opening this land April 22nd so that brings this into market and it will be settled very rapidly. This I consider of great advantage for our property as it will bring settlement right up to us. Land offices are being established by the government for the sale of this land. A United States Court has been established with T. B. Needles an Ill. Man for United States Marshall— which will bring law & order to that country.[54]

The Syndicate's interest in grazing undoubtedly focused on opportunities offered by Harrison's order, rather than on any impediments. They saw two possible benefits in the president's action. First, the order clearing the Cherokee Strip anticipated the government opening the region to settlement; any plan that brought potential buyers closer to their land in Texas suited XIT ownership. Second, the closing of Indian Territory grazing—long used by South Texas cattle raisers as an intermediary stop to condition quarantined cattle before shipping them north—meant that those stock raisers would have to look elsewhere to pasture their stock.[55]

The XIT—north and west of the "tick line," as the quarantine line became known—began leasing portions of its huge reserve to other ranchers. This, in turn, required them to reduce the projected number of cattle they could maintain in Texas, which did little to increase the ranch's profitability. The Syndicate began transforming Texas acreage into a breeding ranch focused on developing high-grade young cattle intended to supply outside finishing operations. They decided, too, that real estate was becoming a viable option. Prospects for land sales increased in 1889 when C. F. Meek, president of the FW&DC, agreed to buy 6,400 acres in Dallam County. The company refused a speculator's offer of $5.00 per acre, stipulating that "our sales should be to bona fide settlers." The Syndicate began laying the groundwork for further settlement by establishing experimental farms growing a variety of crops and surveying town sites along potential rail routes. They began "sectionizing" portions of the property in the reserve's more commercially fertile areas and began enticing farmers and investors. In the meantime, they sought a solution that provided a finishing factory for the high-quality beeves they hoped the XIT could soon begin providing. The company's plans, along with many others in the range cattle business, evolved in reaction to word of the president's intentions. Taylor rejected a Kansas City commission house that offered the company pasturage in the future Oklahoma beyond the reach of the president's order. "I do not think we will put any cattle in Indian Territory this spring," Taylor wrote. And to another offer, of Wyoming grazing range this time, Taylor replied, "We arranged last week with Driskill to take 15,000 head of cattle to his ranch in Wyoming & and I do not think we will put any more up there this year." For months, Taylor and others queried operators around the nation about grazing and feeding options. The company's solution to the limitations faced on their Texas property soon made the Syndicate the biggest player on a field spanning the west from Texas to Montana.[56]

~

CHAPTER 6

The Big Open

"Teddy Blue" Abbott, claimed by Larry McMurtry to have authored "the best" of the cowboy memoirs, said in his classic *We Pointed Them North* that "the Yellowstone River in Montana . . . was the goal of every cowpuncher's ambition." Reaching there July 30, 1890, whooping Texas cowboys aboard determined horses urged 3,500 Texas cattle into the river just north of Fort Keogh, Montana. They represented the last of nearly 10,000 XIT steers driven "over the trail" from the Union Pacific railhead at Wendover, Wyoming. The XIT cattle were headed to range on the "Big Open" north and east of the river crossing. The XIT Ranch, its three million acres in Texas not big enough, was expanding into eastern Montana. George Findlay and Osceola C. Cato sat aboard a wagon on the north side of the river watching the action unfold before them. An experienced Texas cowhand and trail boss, Cato, at thirty-two years old, hired on to manage the ranch's operation in Montana. Cato (O.C. to friends and among his men, but to outsiders and when addressing their boss he was "Mr. Cato") soon became a leading figure in eastern Montana's economic and political development.[1]

Naturally at home in a boardroom, Findlay, the Chicago-based accountant charged by the XIT's owners with making the Texas land and cattle company profitable, had become nearly as familiar with beeves as with balance sheets. His professional experience included a partnership in an Aberdeen-Angus breeding operation in Illinois and two years as business manager at the XIT's Texas operation. Findlay's presence at the herd's fording of the Yellowstone reveals an important aspect of the circumstances that created the iconic western scene. By 1890, large cattle operations like the XIT Ranch depended heavily on their professional

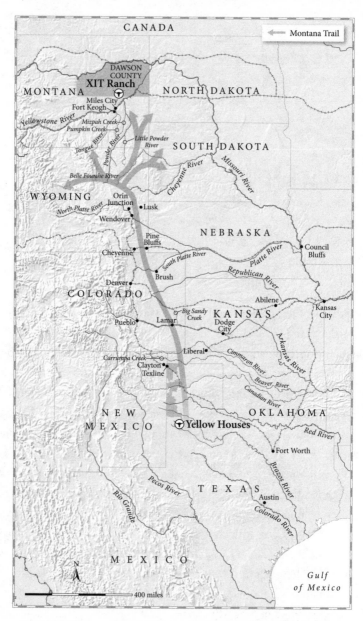

There is no official Montana trail. There is no official Texas or West Texas trail. There never really was an "official" trail. By the late 1880s, the big cattle outfits were just trying to outmaneuver the railroads, but that meant outmaneuvering settlement, too, and, as always, that defined the route. The trail went where the drovers could get from Texas, usually, to the northern range of the Dakotas, Wyoming, and Montana. The cowboys or the merchants and townspeople gave a trail its name, probably based on the most common response to "where you headed?" or, possibly, "which way to Montana?" The places listed here document XIT drovers' cattle drives through their correspondence and financial transactions between 1889 and 1897, when the last XIT beef went "up the trail."

accountants and the analysts who tracked the flows of capital in a rapidly evolving industrial market economy. In this, they differed little from other Gilded Age businesses. Skillful men like Cato in Montana and A. G. Boyce in Texas managed the livestock and the on-the-ground operations, but it was the interests of capital, managed by men like Findlay, that drove cattle and cowboys alike into eastern Montana.[2]

Traveling from Texas on FW&DC rail cars, the beeves represented a fresh wave of cattle ranching on the eastern Montana prairies and other parts of the northern ranges. Just three years before, the region had suffered the disastrous Big Die-Up of 1886–87. Plenty of cattle outfits and other entrepreneurial capitalists found opportunity in the misfortune brought to many by the bad winter. A network of financial and political forces dominated this new era of the imperial ranch and came to wield near hegemonic power within these regions, where inexperienced new state governments, stretched federal resources, and financially burdened railroads were unable or unwilling to regulate land use. The operators of the XIT joined that group the summer of 1890.[3]

The Syndicate's lease on the entire Texas property from Capitol Freehold the previous year included the cattle on the XIT Ranch at the time. The Syndicate's ranch operation essentially became a division of the John V. Farwell Company. The group agreed to pay Capitol Freehold about $400,000 per year over the next five years, along with debenture interest. Elected to represent Illinois in the House of Representatives, Abner Taylor joined Sen. Charles B. Farwell in Washington in 1889. This, no doubt, pleased the Farwell brothers. Taylor's growing tendency to get distracted by side projects troubled his partners. Taking a firm grip on the XIT enterprise, John V. Farwell quickly had ordered his protégé, Findlay, back to Chicago to coordinate ranch operations. Taylor wrote Findlay informing him of the change in November 1889:

> We are expecting to ask you sometime soon to commence spending a part of your time in Chicago instead of all of it in the Ranch. I shall be compelled to go to Washington in a few days to be there the most of the winter and we think from your familiarity with the Ranch you are better informed to advise what course to pursue in certain matters than any new man would be and having great confidence in your judgement, we think

you could be of more assistance to spend part of your time here than all of it on the Ranch.[4]

Although he was never without advice and direction from Taylor, the Farwells, or heirs to the company, Findlay filled the role, if not in title, of the XIT's chief operating officer throughout the remainder of its operation. He later became a trustee of Capitol Freehold. After the British company's dissolution in 1915, Findlay served as an influential leader for its successor, Capitol Freehold Land Trust.[5]

Findlay assumed Taylor's furious correspondence with agencies of the meat industry. His contacts included feeders and stockers, bankers, buyers, railroad men, commission men, and icons of the cattle business such as Charles Goodnight, Ike T. Pryor, and E. S. "Zeke" Newman. Uncommitted to a specific plan for their finishing operations, the Syndicate seemed at first to prefer an option that sent XIT cattle to others for the task. Despite President Benjamin H. Harrison's proclamation banning ranchers from the Cherokee Strip, and probably with ulterior motives, Findlay wrote Pryor, "What would be the chances of procuring a good beef pasture in the Indian Territories next season?" Findlay told the old trail boss he wanted pasture that could "turn the beeves off rolling fat." Less interested in Indian Territory grazing than he was in gaining the attention of the influential cattleman, Findlay knew no XIT cattle would go to the Territory. "The Proclamation of the President," he wrote to a suitor for Syndicate business, "renders it impossible for us to bring cattle into that country." Instead, Findlay wanted it known around the industry that the XIT was ready to expand its role in the beef business. Throughout the winter of 1889–90, he stirred the pot looking for interest and parried offers of a variety of schemes from an array of sources. Taylor could be decisive, but he was mercurial. Logical and determined, yet personable and warm, Findlay was single-minded when set to a task.[6]

In the spring of 1890, Findlay, along with Boyce and Matlock, attended the Interstate Cattle Convention held in Fort Worth beginning on March 11. Heavily attended by Big Four representatives, the commission houses, and the railroads, the nationwide gathering met to address the cattle industry national issues, particularly disease and quarantines, transportation and shipping, grazing laws, and cattle prices. No Montana representatives are represented in the convention's official program.[7] At least two men attending with substantial interests in the cattle business in Montana were there, however. John Clay Jr. was the legendary

Wyoming cattleman and head of the livestock commission house Clay, Robinson & Company, which was headquartered at "The Rookery" building in Chicago— what some saw as the main palace of the beef empire. Clay was the de facto leader of Wyoming's big cattle business, and his operations there cast a wide shadow around him. Seth Mabry, a Kansas City livestock and land broker was there, too. Mabry, a well-known and pioneering trail contractor, among his many endeavors, represented one-half of Mabry and Carter, the operators of the legendary Circle Ranch "on the Redwater" in what was then northwest Dawson County, Montana. Mabry arrived late in Fort Worth, but Findlay was able to meet with him prior to departing, and he wrote to Taylor regarding their discussions. Circumstantial evidence suggests that Findlay met with Clay there as well. Both men contacted Findlay again in the coming days, he having returned by then to Chicago.[8]

Findlay wrote Taylor in some detail regarding his inquiries. He told Taylor he had met with several parties offering grazing range in Indian Territory, "but there is so much uncertainty about what the Government will permit that it was impossible to do anything definite." On the continuing uncertainty about Indian reservation grazing leases outside those covered in Harrison's order, Findlay told Taylor that "some of the Indian Agents outside the Cherokee Strip have been instructed to keep cattle out of their districts." Regarding moving XIT cattle to northern ranges, Findlay wrote, "Seth Mabry [made] a proposition . . . which I look upon as a very fair proposition." The multiyear proposal offered to host 15,000 XIT cattle the first year, with Mabry guaranteeing the Syndicate an average of $17 per head. Mabry would pay 8 percent interest on the cattle until sold, at which time Mabry and the Syndicate would split profits equally. The Syndicate was to pay the costs of transporting the cattle to Mabry, but Mabry would be responsible for market shipments. After two years, the Syndicate could exercise an option to take over Mabry's entire range for themselves. "I firmly believe it is the best ranch in the country," Mabry told Findlay. To Taylor, Findlay wrote that Mabry carried a reputation for being "sharp," but that he heard often that his ranch was "a very fine one." Continuing, the one-time bookkeeper informed the congressman, "The prices he names strikes me as being very good considering the quality of our cattle [as a] large number of the cattle . . . would be the Coasters brought up last year."[9]

Asking Taylor to telegraph his thoughts as soon as possible, Findlay continued that, should Taylor not approve, he had other offers that he would personally attend to. "One party from Miles City offers to run our Cattle at 80¢ p head per annum We paying taxes & shipping expenses & we to pay him 25¢ p head to receive the cattle at Wendover & drive them thru to his range," Findlay penned. "No one I meet favors driving up, as they say if a bad winter follows the loss will be much heavier than if the cattle are shipped in. If we take up a range of our own we would require to send about 100 head of horse up there to be wintered in order that they might get acclimated & fit for the work next summer."[10]

Taylor rejected Mabry's proposal, to which Findlay diplomatically responded, "You do not put the construction on Mabry's letter that he intended." The accountant reminded Taylor that Mabry got nothing until he paid for the cattle allowance and interest. The agreement split sales evenly subsequently. It also gave the Syndicate an option on "the best range in the country," as Mabry had called it. Notified by Findlay, Mabry withdrew his original offer but then proposed another. Findlay was less impressed with the second proposal, but he outlined it to Taylor and asked if he might continue negotiating. He told the congressman that he also was to meet with John Clay Jr. the following day. Mabry, Findlay told Taylor, volunteered to meet the congressman in Washington should that be necessary to close a deal. Taylor's reply indicated that he felt a better deal could be made with J. W. Driskill, who was managing the XIT cattle in Wyoming. He had not given figures to Findlay, however, prompting the Scotsman to ask, "Will you let me know what he offered as it would be a great benefit to me when figuring with others?"[11]

Fielding offers from across the country for northern ranges, Findlay decided that only his personal attention could secure a decision. His attention focused on Montana. The new state stood second only to Alaska with its millions of unsurveyed public acres. Montana and its neighbors offered the XIT a second chance at "open range" ranching, a term relaying some irony considering the effort put out for the undertaking.[12] He immediately began arranging a trip to Montana. He boarded a westbound train in Chicago on the evening of April 3, 1890. Earlier in the day, he added to the Syndicate's frenetic business correspondence. He forwarded general instructions to Boyce in Texas concerning several ranch projects then under way. Additionally, Findlay told the manager he wanted cattle prepared for delivery by rail or trail somewhere in Montana, Wyoming, or the Dakotas. Exactly where and when to deliver them and how they were to get there remained a mystery for the moment—even to Findlay.[13]

He fired off a briefer post to fellow Chicagoan Henry A. Blair—a Wyoming stock grower, Chicago banker, and future executive for Chicago's elevated railroad. Blair shared business interests with John Clay Jr. and often represented Clay in business negotiations. Clay and Findlay communicated several times after the Fort Worth convention. Clay insistently wrote Findlay to "call upon me . . . without fail." It is unknown whether Blair was then acting for Clay. Findlay's letter, however, offered a sharp rejection of Blair's earlier offer of a northern ranch—a Montana ranch. Findlay seemed offended that Blair had questioned the Syndicate's motives for seeking northern cattle range. In the earlier letter, Blair called the company's inquiries part of a "scheme." His true goal was "fatter cattle," Findlay shot back. Nothing else "compelled" his company's interest, but, in any case, he found Blair's asking price much too high. "I go north tonight," Findlay concluded to Blair, dismissively.[14]

The Scottish-born accountant did not much fit the image of the viceroy of a cattle empire when he stepped off a Great Northern Pullman in the northeastern Montana town of Glasgow a few days later. He traveled in the company of Anne Anderson, the younger daughter of his partner in the Angus breeding operation. She was also Findlay's future second wife, following Findlay's brief marriage to her older sister Mary, who died during or shortly after the birth of their son James. Met at Glasgow by Charles Hawley, a local businessman, and accompanied by a well-known "wolfer" named Joe Butch, Findlay took a long look at the Milk River country in the north as well as south toward the Missouri River valley. Taken by the whole country, Findlay seemed sold when he wrote Boyce after his return to Chicago, "I think I found a place between the Milk and Missouri Rivers that will suit us. It is in Montana, on the Great Northern Railway & until recently has been an Indian Reservation, & is consequently a virgin range." Findlay stayed at the Park Hotel in Great Falls on April 8. It is quite likely that he met with representatives of John T. Murphy and T. C. Power in either Great Falls or Helena. Both men were extensively involved in the cattle rush in the state and would have been critical to Capitol Freehold's recognition and entry into the six-month-old forty-first state's livestock oligarchy.[15]

A decade earlier, Findlay and John V. Farwell had consulted with Power regarding the first stock with which the Montana merchant pioneer began to build his prize-winning herd of Angus cattle outside Helena. Later in 1890, one of his agents wrote Power, then a Montana senator, in Washington suggesting that he should speak with fellow senator Charles Farwell about acquiring some cattle. Power corresponded with Findlay numerous times through the 1890s to inquire about further cattle buys and wintering Power's more valuable purebred stock. Murphy, a powerful banker in Helena, held interests in numerous ranch operations, and his influence was expanding. Although Power and Murphy had long been competitors and rivals, they also knew best how to exploit opportunity and how to cooperate at it. It is hard to imagine that any large enterprise in the eastern part of the state would find success without some contact with these men.[16]

Findlay showed interest in the ranges of both the Bay State Cattle Company and the Fort Shaw Live Stock Cattle Company, both in north-central Montana. Findlay also contacted Alfred Myers of Myers Brothers near Livingston. Myers was another early pioneer and among the first to raise cattle in the eastern part of the territory. He operated three ranches in the Yellowstone and Shield river valleys at the time, but he claimed to know of good range for Findlay north of Great Falls. Findlay also corresponded with Capt. William Harmon of Miles City. Harmon, another early resident, had a ranch near Ekalaka, farther east near the Little Missouri River. Myers and Harmon were charter members of the Montana Stockgrowers Association. Harmon had earlier told Findlay that he had no interest in selling his range but thought he could take some of the Syndicate cattle on contract. He urged Findlay to speak with John Clay Jr. about other opportunities. Findlay's original plan was to make a side trip to see Driskill on his return to Chicago, but he later apologized for being unable to make it. Undoubtedly, Findlay would have taken advantage of the early arriving attendees of the stock growers' annual meeting opening April 15 in Miles City. Introduced by Harmon or Myers, or others, he likely met with local and out-of-town attendees there. Many of the state's most influential members would have been in town that weekend in anticipation of the meeting. Nothing has been found to confirm Findlay's whereabouts after visiting Great Falls. Whatever he did, he did it fast and was back in Chicago by April 16, 1890.[17]

Findlay returned to Texas by mid-May but still had not settled on a range. He was weighing options in Wyoming on the Powder River offered by Zeke Newman and for range just east of Yellowstone Park in the Shoshone Mountains offered by the Hardin, Campbell Company out of Chicago. He strongly contemplated the Musselshell and Milk river valleys—considering Cowering Squaw, Lodge Pole, Sage Hen, and Booth creeks for potential locations. The Milk

River country impressed him, but he lamented both the additional distance and hazards represented in going that far north. He hoped for something nearer to Driskill but learned that much of the region south of the Yellowstone was being taken up quickly by settlers and was already overstocked with cattle.[18]

Findlay, as well as Boyce, juggled several issues that had developed. They were selling cattle to a Kansas feeder named James Lee and trading cattle with the neighboring Snyder brothers. Findlay still was dealing with legal issues regarding the southern cattle they bought the year before, most of which would soon board north-bound trains on a long trip to Montana. The complaints about this livestock began just as Findlay was assuming his new duties in Chicago in December 1889.[19]

Findlay had written to Abner Taylor about the fever crisis. Apparently, Texas fever had infected several neighboring herds in the Panhandle and fingers pointed at the Syndicate, which of course had been buying thousands of mostly steers out of southern Texas. Rumors, even lawsuits, charging the XIT with infecting neighboring cattle with splenic fever raged. In the fall of 1889, seventeen cattle operations represented by Wallace and Crutchfield, a Tascosa law firm, made claim against the XIT for bringing infected cattle to the Panhandle. Findlay was skeptical of such claims and recommended that the company not pay them. The Scotsman reasoned that cattle not exposed to the southern cattle the Syndicate had brought in died as well. He pointed out that the XIT's three hundred "black northern bulls . . . more so than any cattle in that country to take the Splenic fever," suffered no ill effects despite occupying the same pasture as many of those they purchased from southern Texas. Findlay told Taylor that he was not too worried, but he fretted that "if suit was brought in Tascosa Court the jury there might give verdict against us," once again highlighting some of the animosity faced by the Syndicate's operation. He closed, however, by assuring the congressman that "the LS does not make a claim with the others for their loss." This was important to Taylor because he and the Farwell brothers were just then involved with W. M. D. Lee, one third of the LS ownership, in a deepwater port project on the Texas coast (see chapter 7).[20]

No record of the outcome of these claims has turned up. Account books for the year 1890 do not show any kind of damages payment. A letter from Findlay to Matlock, who represented them in the suit, seems to be its last mention. Findlay was returning interrogations he had completed in the matter. He explained his reasoning and suggested the position the lawyer should consider in further proceedings. He told Matlock that "there were some considerable fatalities among the Southwest Texas Cattle themselves," explaining that the disease "does not kill the cattle with whom it originates." It would be nearly two years before government scientists identified the coastal cattle tick as the source of splenic fever. Findlay's defense of the XIT cattle reflected the arguments Texas cattle raisers had voiced for years.[21] Whatever the outcome of the claims, they did not seem to impede Findlay's present plans. He had already reminded Boyce that men sent north with the cattle should be equipped with papers affirming their latest origin above the quarantine line.[22]

Sometime during the month, Findlay and Boyce hired Cato. Boyce probably approached Cato in April when Findlay first inquired after a "good man." Ike Pryor may have recommended Cato, since he "knew him well." Cato carried a reputation as a superior trail boss and cowman. Leaving shipping to Boyce, Findlay and Cato left Texas and made their way to Wendover, Wyoming, by May 31, 1890. Presumably there to meet the cattle and arrange supplying the trail crews, they become difficult to track for the next few weeks. Once unloaded at Wendover, the cattle and cowboys still faced a nearly two-month journey ahead if their destination was the Yellowstone River. Again, even at this stage, it is not clear that Findlay had selected a destination.[23]

His increasing workload, particularly those tasks associated with the Montana project, prompted "old man Boyce" to fire off an angry letter to John V. Farwell, who was then in London, demanding to know if it was he, Boyce, who was in charge and hinting at an annual raise to $3,600. He complained that, since Findlay had chosen the northern range, he should also have been the one who arranged to get cattle there. The company dithered too long on the plan, he felt, and shipping the cattle had been an "unsatisfactory" expense. At the time, both Boyce and Findlay were under stress as they tried to get 10,000 head of cattle shipped north. Boyce's letter prompted a nervous exchange of correspondence between the Farwell brothers and Taylor. Boyce's complaining letter likely reflected frustration with the current circumstances rather than any dispute or animosity he held with or toward Findlay. A month later, with the ranch's many ongoing projects seemingly running smoothly, Boyce wrote to Farwell again: "If there was ever any friction growing [between he and Findlay] I know nothing of it."[24]

F. A. Lisk, a well-known Miles City resident, reported to the town's *Daily Yellowstone Journal* on April 10, 1890, having just returned from a hunting excursion with "Mr. and Mrs. Cameron." This was Ewan and Evelyn Cameron, touring British aristocrats at the time who soon became permanent residents in the area. Ewan gained modest popularity in British ornithological journals. Evelyn learned photography and frequently contributed photographs for her husband's articles. The pair lived far from a pampered life in Montana and, although both received a remittance from family in England, the allowances hardly supported them. Evelyn took photographs of friends and neighbors, sheepherders, homesteaders, cattle, and cowboys. She did not get paid much for each photo, but they spread far and wide. Little known until late in the twentieth century, she belatedly emerged as one of the premier photographers documenting the end of the great ranch empires and the beginning of the nation's last great homestead boom.[25]

Lisk and the Camerons had bagged a bear. Display of its head and hide and tales of the pursuit stirred much excitement over the hunters among the townspeople. Lisk's report on range and cattle conditions that he observed on the expedition also excited the paper's editor. Lisk told the newspaper he had looked over many fine specimens of N Bar N, LU Bar, and Bow & Arrow cattle, and the grass was in good shape. He was just the sort of person Findlay would have wanted to talk to, and they were very likely in town at the same time.[26]

By early July, Findlay was back in Montana and had enlisted Lisk to assist in locating a range. On July 11 a notice appeared in the *Daily Yellowstone Journal* that "the IXT [*sic*] brand of about 10,000 head of cattle will locate on the northside." The *Stock Growers' Journal* reported the next day that "F. A. Lisk piloted messers. Cate and Finley, foremans for the IXT brand [*sic*], to the Porcupine [a creek drainage] country." Lisk recommended Findlay and Capitol Freehold's application to the Montana Stockgrowers Association. Official approval awaited the next annual meeting, but the group's secretary, R. B. Harrison, the son of President Harrison, accepted their ten-dollar membership fee, and the Association registered the iconic XIT brand that summer. On July 14, William Courtenay, a local land and cattle broker, wrote to Findlay at the MacQueen Hotel in Miles City: "Mr. Tusler has wired to his partner at Terry . . . if we can make a trade." Findlay sent a telegram to Colin Hunter in Wyoming the next day informing the cattleman that he had secured the Tusler range so would not be taking Hunter's offer for his

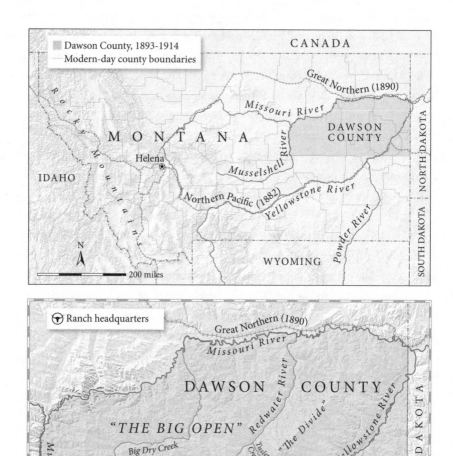

Dawson County was unorganized when Montana Territory was originally created but was one of fifteen counties by statehood in 1889. The Syndicate purchased about 400 acres of riparian land there between 1890 and 1895. There are claims, but no evidence, that the XIT operators leased two million acres in the "Big Open," the broken, high prairie east of the Musselshell River lying mostly between the Missouri and Yellowstone rivers. Big cattle operations, many of them owning no land at all, shipped thousands of beeves from there between 1890 and 1910. It was, perhaps, the United States' last "free" livestock range.

Sand Creek range, even though "the grass was very fine." On July 16 the newspaper reported, "The XIT outfit yesterday purchased Tusler and Kempton's range on Cedar Creek, near Terry. The consideration paid we did not learn." According to company books, for "Ranch & Range, Tusler Kempton Cattle Co., for Ranch buildings, fences & Corrals in Dawson County," the Syndicate paid $1,500.[27]

The *Daily Yellowstone Journal* informed its readers on July 22 that "O. C. Cato and J. D. Corlis of Minneapolis were visitors in the city yesterday." John D. Corlis was a top hand on the XIT in Texas. Nothing explains the newspaper's claim of Minnesota origins for the pair or why they were just then arriving by train. Cato had made his debut in the area days earlier. The cattle remained a week away. Seth Mabry was likely about the country in early July observing his own arriving beeves. The Circle Ranch manager, John Carter, told a Glendive reporter he would be bringing 6,000 southern steers to their Redwater range beginning in early July. Mabry probably met with Findlay and Cato. The Circle's range intersected what would become the XIT's on the "divide," a rise of high ground splitting the water runoff of the country into that flowing to the Missouri and that which flowed to the Yellowstone. Other new neighbors of the XIT, the Niedringhaus brothers of St. Louis, owners of the region's largest operation, the Home Land and Cattle Company—the N Bar N—were also there to oversee their arriving trail herds.[28]

Handpicked Texas cowboys trailed the Texas steers from Wendover that year. A spur line of the Union Pacific railroad edged near the North Platte River there. Taylor had been vague about his wishes regarding shipping rather than driving the cattle all the way from Texas, as Driskill had the previous year. As late as April 21, 1890, Findlay corresponded with Boyce about the obstacles to trailing the cattle north. Despite those, the option was under serious consideration. Concerned with their tardiness, a relentless Findlay pounded railroad officials and convinced the FW&DC to carry the cattle and most of the men from the Texas Panhandle for $55 a car, nearly half the rate the company initially quoted. Typical cattle cars at 30-, 33-, and 36-foot lengths carried from twenty-three to thirty-three steers. They loaded at Cheyenne Pens, a rail siding just northwest of Tascosa, and Rivers, Texas, and probably in Clayton, New Mexico Territory. Shipping delays soured Findlay on the FW&DC, increasing the mounting tension between the two companies.[29]

Findlay and Boyce enlisted sixteen hands and four trail bosses, along with two cooks on well-equipped chuck wagons. Each of the four trail crews managed 2,000–2,500 head. The ranch sent 185 horses. A nine-horse "string" seemed a bit of a luxury for any cowpuncher, but the Syndicate intended most of them for the future use of the northern outfit. The country around Wendover was rather barren, but moving into northern Wyoming and southern Montana, even in a dry year, the rolling foothills there grow tall with grass. Undoubtedly, the cowboys on the trail allowed the cattle to graze leisurely on the rich grass there, easing the rigors of the journey on cow and cowboy alike. When they arrived at the Yellowstone, a river like none other in Texas or in between, a ferry was available to move the crews' wagons across. Horses not then serving as mounts went first and, usually accompanied by a rowboat, punchers drove lead steers into the water. Other cowboys, whistling and shouting, encouraged the rest of the herd to follow.[30]

Attracted by newspaper announcements, people often gathered early on the riverbank to watch the cattle herds crossing. It had become a tradition by the time that Texas outfits—as nearly every nonlocal trail cattle crew was called, no matter their origin—began to arrive. Frequently, several herds arrived at once, but these new Texans with the big brand were arriving late. Other outfits by this time were driving cattle in the opposite direction, crossing the river from the north to begin loading the year's beef roundup at rail yards in Miles City or down the river at Fallon. No matter the direction, it was no small task, and the process could be quite entertaining.[31]

Crossing the Yellowstone often provided high drama and entertainment, and that day produced an event few would forget. As the cowboys prepared to swim their mounts across the river, a call came up from the water that one of the punchers had lost his leg. The report stirred the bystanders, but the crowd's fears melted away when, with another rider's help, the stricken waddy hopped up on the riverbank. The one-legged cowboy joined in a laugh with his mates as the crowd discovered their mistake. With the cattle safely on the north side of the river, his pals took him to Miles City, where a "skillful carpenter" was able to "splice the broken member" recovered somehow from its journey downstream. The cowboy's feelings were no doubt soothed in one of the town's many watering holes.[32]

With the cattle spreading across the new range, Findlay departed for Chicago on August 7, 1890. Driskill had arrived in Miles City just a few days before that, and the two men likely discussed the important upcoming sale of fat cattle. The XIT's Texas ranch manager, Boyce, started shipping on the Atchison, Topeka & Santa Fe at Panhandle August 21. Driskill began loading cattle onto cars from the Fremont, Elkhorn & Missouri Valley Railroad in Spearfish, South Dakota, a few days later. By September 3, Boyce had shipped nearly 3,000 head, all but sixty-three of them steers. Driskill shipped just over 1,400 steers during the period. The Texas cattle averaged 1,057 pounds and brought an average $2.68 per hundredweight. Driskill's "finished" steers averaged 1,090 pounds and returned an average $3.48 per hundredweight. The news delighted the Syndicate and the British bondholders. Lower prices for the Texas cattle likely left Boyce feeling less than enthusiastic about the result.[33]

Findlay, who spent much of the month overseeing cattle sales at the Chicago stockyard, had little time to enjoy the small victory. Much of his attention was on the Montana operation as he focused on the winter ahead. The memory of the Big Die-Up remained fresh and vivid among livestock producers. Findlay spoke of it with his new Montana friends, and he wrote Abner Taylor to ease the congressman's fears. "Everyone tells me," Findlay wrote, "the less the cattle are handled in that country in the winter time the better they will be." Still, the XIT herds had arrived late, and there was much cause for concern. Cato, however, marveled at the favorable conditions well into autumn. "I think this is as fine of a watered country as I ever saw it has springs all over it," he wrote on September 1. Later that fall he told Findlay, "We have had as good wither as I ever saw in any country this far." Cato no doubt had more to learn about the country, but he was a quick study. In subsequent years, he lamented the cost to keep extra men on in the winter. While he continued to cut hay, Cato maintained the mindset of the Texas free-range ideal that less was best and that cattle should be left on their own as much as possible.[34]

Findlay seemed surprised when notified of a tax bill from Custer County, Montana, that arrived at the Chicago office. "I will not pay taxes twice on cattle," Findlay wrote the county's treasurer, T. J. Thompson. Indeed, the Syndicate had already paid over $12,000 to Texas tax collectors at the end of 1889. Findlay engaged the legal services of Strevell & Porter in Miles City to dispute the assessment. Judge Jason Strevell, a pioneering member of the local and state stock growers' associations, a former judge, and a prominent lawyer in eastern Montana, led the firm. Whether these particular cattle were assessed in Texas for 1890 is not clear. One entry in company account books in November 1890 says, "Cattle driven north, taxes for the year, 1890 0.00." Did that mean in Montana, Texas, or both? Regardless, the company's lawyers prevailed before Custer County's board of equalization. This would not be the last of the company's appearances before a tax board. The Syndicate, like many of the larger livestock companies, went to great lengths to limit their local tax liabilities.[35]

Until joined by his family a year later, Cato identified Miles City, in Custer County, and the MacQueen Hotel as his residence. The family continued to live primarily in town rather than on one of the ranches. The Syndicate paid its greatest share of personal and property tax in Dawson rather than Custer County. Both the original XIT tract purchased from Tusler and Kempton and the Hatchet Ranch, purchased finally in 1895 from Cyrus B. Mendenhall, were in Dawson County at the time. Both sites became part of Prairie County in 1915, which adds to the problems of trying to track property ownership and taxes going back over one hundred years.[36]

The land and range practices under way in Montana are highlighted by the Syndicate's acquisition of Mendenhall's Hatchet Ranch. Prized for its reliable water and proximity to the Yellowstone crossing to railroad holding pens across the river in Fallon, the place—a few rough-made buildings, wagons, and some equipment—provided the Syndicate a second claim to the surrounding grazing ranges. Mendenhall first came to Montana in 1866, but he did not stay long. He later got involved in the cattle business in Colorado, then found his way back to Montana in 1882 and established himself in the Big Open in 1884. The Big Die-Up destroyed Mendenhall's herd of, reportedly, 16,000 head. Tax records for Dawson County, however, indicate that Mendenhall paid taxes up to 1896 on as many as 1,600 head of cattle per year. Mendenhall also owned and operated the popular Hunter's Hot Spring Pleasure Resort and Sanitarium near Livingston, Montana. He purchased the resort in 1885 and it apparently covered his Big-Die Up losses, even providing for a modest cattle herd overseen by a reliable foreman.[37]

Mendenhall and Findlay corresponded before the Syndicate expanded to Montana. On March 8, 1890, Findlay wrote Mendenhall of his desire to pasture 15,000 head of two- and three-year old steers in the "Northern Country." He had been talking to John Clay Jr., Findlay wrote, and Clay told him he had been in contact with Mendenhall regarding pasturing some of his cattle. Failing a deal with Clay, "we would be glad to hear from you," Findlay wrote, requesting Mendenhall's figures on "teams, facilities for grazing & watering cattle," and its location. Mendenhall responded in detail a few days later, informing Findlay that his was "most assuredly one of the finest Ranges in Montana."[38]

Mendenhall's response outlined the terms he had offered to graze Clay's cattle, an arrangement that proposed charging $1.00 per head annually for managing the cattle and $0.50 per head for gathering and shipping them. Under the contract, hay, taxes, and cattle losses (by weather or accident) were to be the responsibility of the cattle owner. Mendenhall said the offer was for Clay, but he would extend the same terms to the Syndicate. "I should be pleased to answer any question," Mendenhall closed his letter, "and if my proposition does not meet with your views make me one so I may consider the business."[39]

An agreement did not materialize at the time. The Syndicate seemed satisfied with the Tusler and Kempton operation. Locals soon called it the XIT, and so it has long been remembered. Obviously, an agreement benefitted their Montana operation. William Courtenay stayed close to the business, and thus negotiations seem to have picked up again at the end of the following summer. The broker wrote Findlay in September that he had not yet heard from Mendenhall "with the information you wish about his cattle and range." He went on to summarize what he knew of the Mendenhall "plant"—meaning the cattle and ranch improvements, a few modest shacks and outbuildings. "I think John Clay Jr. holds a mortgage on his plant and Hunter's Hot Springs & should you see Clay," Courtenay continued, "you can probably get further particulars from him."[40]

Negotiations continued into the autumn with Courtenay insisting that Mendenhall's proposal of a single payment of $45,000 "would be cheap at that figure." Findlay, probably at the behest of Taylor or Farwell, wanted the cattle sold by class and distinct from the other ranch property, which Mendenhall refused to do. "I know that I can sell beef enough over the next 3 years to make up that amount and have a good herd left," Mendenhall told Courtenay. "I want to clear up the whole business at once [and] I have asked a very low price," a seemingly frustrated Mendenhall told the broker. "I guess there is no use corresponding further," Courtney wrote Findlay, his tone sounding a bit dejected. Undaunted by this setback, however, the businessman continued to work with Findlay on many projects. Beyond his continued work to expand the Syndicate's presence in Montana, in the next few years Courtenay devoted considerable time to selling XIT stock cattle to ranchers and farmer-feeders throughout the beef empire.[41]

Resurrected again late in 1893, the Mendenhall deal nearly failed for good when the Syndicate hesitated to react when Courtenay brought it up. "I think I have at last got C. B. Mendenhall to offer his cattle for sale, also his ranch, horses, etc.," Findlay read, along with a list classing the cattle by age and sex. Mendenhall had about 1,600 head and contracts for an additional 1,400. The Syndicate would pay Mendenhall $16 per head for cattle rounded up and marketed in 1894 and 1895. If there was a good market in those years, the Syndicate would profit nicely. As was standard practice, the proposal waived charges for each year's calf crop. He would sell his Hatchet brand for 10 percent of the 1895 roundup proceeds and his ranch improvements for $1,500. That included, of course, the land claims Mendenhall made. Courtenay told Findlay that he expected Mendenhall to sell horses, wagons, and his other equipment at very reasonable prices. Still, the Syndicate seemed reticent. Courtenay even threatened, "Kindly advise me promptly, as several other parties north of the Yellowstone are nibbling at it."[42]

The Syndicate remained unmoved, apparently, by Courtenay's pleading, and yet another year passed. Then, in the spring of 1895, Cato wrote Findlay. "I am glad to hear Mendenhall has concluded to accept your offer as I believe his range will be worth that much to us," Cato told his boss and friend, moving quickly to briefly discuss the weather and an increase in wolf bounties for the year. The exact details of the final agreement are somewhat hazy. The Syndicate certainly acquired Mendenhall's ranch, range, and improvements. The cattle seem to have been managed on a shared basis with Clay & Forrest, John Clay Jr.'s livestock commission business. The Hatchet brand remained registered to Mendenhall, according to the Stockgrowers Association brand book for 1899. The name, Hatchet Ranch or Hatchet Creek Ranch, went with the place. The Syndicate now claimed two satellite ranches: the XIT on Cedar Creek and the Hatchet on Bad Route and Hatchet creeks.[43]

The Syndicate, usually as Capitol Freehold Land & Investment Company, paid taxes in Dawson and Custer counties. The *Glendive Independent,* in Dawson County, regularly reported on both the county board of equalization and, usually later in the fall or winter, the county's heaviest taxpayers (see table 1). The XIT did not appear on the list for 1890, of course. Aside from railroads, the Niedringhaus brothers' Home Land and Cattle Co., the N Bar N, had been Dawson County's heaviest tax contributor for a few years. In 1889, Pierre Wibaux purchased the stock and range of the Green Mountain Cattle Company to challenge the Niedringhaus operation as the county's largest livestock grower. The Home operation held on to the top spot during the 1890s until closing out in 1897. The XIT first joined the top owners in 1891, when "O. C. Cato," presumably representing Capitol Freehold, was assessed $2,020 on cattle and improvements in Dawson County. The "XIT Cattle Co." paid about $1,380 in Custer County that year. For most of the 1890s, the Syndicate was among both counties' top five taxpayers. The tax rolls swelled further when the Syndicate finally concluded drawn-out negotiations for Mendenhall's ranch in 1895. Capitol Freehold paid $3,950 in 1897 in Dawson County. The Syndicate's largest known payment came in 1898, when they deposited $5,553 into Dawson County's coffers. Similar tax bills came from Custer County, although its rates were often lower, perhaps due to the large number of Stockgrowers Association members there. Later that year, in a letter to Findlay, Cato deadpanned, "Think I shall remember this enormous rate of taxes when I give in our assessment for next year."[44]

During the period 1890–1900, excluding railroads, no other entity paid more taxes in a year than the N Bar N did in several. In 1891 they paid Dawson County $10,078. The lowest Home payment was the year they closed out their Montana cattle operation, 1897, when they paid $4,705. Capitol Freehold paid $3,950 that year. Records suggest that Cato did report the company's property strategically. Assessments depended on self-reported figures and other information gathered by the commissioners. Cato's 1891 payment in Dawson County represented a claim of roughly only 4,600 cattle—about half the number that arrived the previous year—at a value of about $84,200. Custer County assessed Cato and the Syndicate for about 4,100 head of stock. The XIT had trailed north just over 10,000 head in that summer, however, and reported shipping about half the cattle brought in the previous year. This would have left about 16,000 XIT cattle in both counties.[45]

A tax listing for Capitol Freehold in 1892 has not been located. Nevertheless, the company brought over 11,000 steers in 1892 and shipped nearly 7,000 that year. Company records for 1894 indicate that there were approximately 29,000 head of XIT cattle on the Montana range before the fall beef shipment. Dawson County assessed the company for 150 horses and 5,000 cattle that year. In the highest of the two years Capitol Freehold led the "heavy taxpayer" list, 1898, the company claimed to own 12,850 cattle in Dawson County. The operation sold about three-fourths of the cattle it was sending north by that time. When the company closed out for a four-year span in 1898, it was clearly benefitting from the county equalization board's charitable tax assessments.[46]

TABLE 1

HEAVY TAXPAYERS, DAWSON COUNTY, 1889–1899

1889	Tax ($)
Home L & C, Co.	9,186
Moran, E.	1,175
Mendenhall, C. B.	933
Phillips L & C Co.	754
Day, J. S. & Co.	681
1890	
Home L & C, Co.	8,890
Hubbard & Sampson	1,517
Sampson & Fahnstock	1,085
Wibaux, Pierre	974
Day, J. S. & Co.	719
Phillips Cattle & Land Co.	574
Phillips & Slaughter	506
Butterman, Nick	497
1891	
Home L & C, Co.	10,078
Cato, O. C. [Capitol F&I]	2,020
Hubbard & Sampson	1,649
Wibaux, Pierre	1,422
Carter, W. M.	1,243
Sampson & Fahnstock	1,063
Phillips & Slaughter	1,045
Day, J. S. & Co.	874
Clay & Forest	800
Phillips C & L, Co.	621
Smith, A. C.	569
Wilson, J. B.	428
Detroit & Montana Cattle Co.	415
1892*	
Home L & C, Co.	10,325
Mabry & Carter	1,950
Pioneer Cattle Co.	1,712
Wibaux, Pierre	1,506
Hubbard & Sampson	1,378
Sampson & Fahnstock	1,352
Day, J. S. & Co.	1,087

TABLE 1 *(continued)*

1892*	Tax ($)
Phillips & Slaughter	975
Milner Cattle Co.	700
Phillips C & L, Co.	645
Mendenhall, C. B.	635
Hedrick, Geo.	527
Detroit & Montana Cattle Co.	400
1893	
Home L & C, Co.	7,672
Wibaux, Pierre	2175
XIT Cattle Co. [Capitol F&I]	1,998
Hubbard & Sampson	1,279
Sampson & Fahnstock	1,147
Mabrey & Carter	990
Phillips & Slaughter	779
Day, J. S. & Co.	584
Phillips C & L, Co.	540
Mendenhall, C. B.	473
Douglas & Mead	428
Kellogg, McCoy, & Rumsey	400
1894*	
Home L & C, Co.	11,450
Sampson & Fahnstock	2,317
Wibaux, Pierre	2,075
XIT Ranch [Capitol F&I]	1,950
Hubbard & Sampson	1,645
Sawyer, McCoy, & Rumery	825
Day, J. S. & Co.	757
Phillips & Slaughter	412
Kellogg, McCoy, & Rumery	412
Mendenhall, C. B.	400
1895	
Home L & C, Co.	7,368
XIT Ranch* [Capitol F&I]	5,401
Wibaux, Pierre	1,986
Sampson & Fahnstock	1,691
Hubbard & Sampson	1,541

(continued)

TABLE 1 (*continued*)

HEAVY TAXPAYERS, DAWSON COUNTY, 1889–1899

1895	Tax ($)
Phillips L & C Co.	1,468
Sawyer, McCoy, & Runnery	750
Day, J. S. & Co.	733
Kramer Bros.	696
Douglas & Mead	601
Coleman, A. M.	530
1896	
Home L & C, Co.	3,081
XIT Ranch [Capitol F&I]	2,735
Wibaux, Pierre	2,000
Towers & Gudgell	884
Phillips, H. R.	715
1897	**Tax ($)**
Home L & C, Co.	4,705
The Capitol F. & I. Co.	3,950
Wibaux, Pierre	2,438
Cruse, Thomas	1,678
The Montana Cattle Co.	1,479
Phillips L & C Co.	1,369
Hubbard & Sampson	1,023
Douglas & Mead	821
Hodgson, H	563
Krug, Charles	457
1898	
The Capitol F. & I. Co.	5,553
Wibaux, Pierre	3,590
The Montana Cattle Co.	2,301
Phillips L & C Co.	2,237
Cruse, Thomas	1,487
Douglas & Mead	1,017
Hubbard & Sampson	956
Ryan Bros.	941
Hodgson, H	646
Gilmore, J. W.	632
1899	
The Montana Cattle Co.	3,052
Cruse, Thomas	2,034

TABLE 1 (*continued*)

1899	Tax ($)
Phillips L & C Co.	1,900
Wibaux, Pierre	1,887
Hubbard & Sampson	1,396
Douglas & Mead	1,296
Cotter, Thomas	1,167
Gilmore, J. W.	832
Cato & Johnson	689
Maine & Montana Ranch Co.	655
The Capitol F. & I. Co.	438

Note: The yearly Dawson County, Montana, tax information consists primarily of figures published in the *Glendive* (Montana) *Independent* newspaper as "Heavy Taxpayers" for those years. Where exact figures were unavailable, company information or archival documentation from the WPA Montana Writers Project available on microfilm from the Montana Historical Society was used. The Northern Pacific and Great Northern railroads at the time were always the leading taxpayers and are excluded. With a few exceptions, these figures generally exclude taxes below $400. Taxes are on *all* personal property, although nearly all of the operations listed here are cattle concerns. Names and spelling are reflective of the source document. Beginning in 1897, large sheep operations begin to make the list, e.g., Charles Krug.

*For 1892 and 1894 estimates, horses are valued at $20, cattle at $15, and use a mill value of 25. For 1896 and the XIT Ranch in 1895, horses are valued at $25, cattle at $17, and a mill value of 26 is used.

The state established the recommended valuations for property in each county, and each county board of equalization confirmed the assessment with property owners before levying a mill value to calculate tax payments. Livestock values varied over the years, but for most of the 1890s horses were assessed at around $25–$30, stock cattle at about $14–$18 (Texas steers), and beef cattle (graded) at $20–$24. For example, in 1891 Cato paid Dawson County $2,020 and the N Bar N paid $10,078. Assume all cattle valued at $18 for both, even though the distinction between "beef" and stock cattle is not always clear. According to Cato's records, Custer County assessed "beef" at $25 per head and "three year old steers" at $16 per head. In Dawson, the assessment was $22 and $15, respectively, with horses at a surprisingly low $15. A typical "mill rate" for both Custer and Dawson could be anywhere between 14 and 24. A mill is one-thousandth of the assessed property value. In 1891, Dawson County's mill rate was 24. Property tax was calculated as tax = (assessed valuation × mill rate)/1,000.[47]

Using this formula and assessing cattle only—most cattle raisers' assessments were primarily for cattle, anyway—Cato's payment in Dawson County that year tallied about 4,600 stock cattle—about half what they brought the previous year. Those cattle, at $18 per head, represented about $84,200. For the Home outfit, tax that year included about 23,300 cattle valued at nearly $420,000. That is a lot of beef, but in both cases the figures seem not to completely reflect the reality of Dawson County ranching at the time. Still, if you use the same formula for Custer County, but use a lower mill rate, which was often the case for Custer County, Capitol Freehold paid taxes there on 4,100 cattle. The combined 8,700 total is a much closer reflection of the XIT herd size there.[48]

During the 1890s, Home, Capitol Freehold, and Wibaux headed the "Heavy Taxpayer" list each year except 1899, when John T. Murphy's Montana Cattle Company—the 79 Ranch—topped the list. Capitol Freehold topped the list two years during the decade. In the highest of those, 1898, they probably claimed about 12,850 cattle in Dawson County. According to Capitol Freehold's annual report for 1894, the Montana range hosted an estimated 26,919 steers prior to that year's shipping season. Peaking in 1898, the Syndicate eliminated the Montana operation until 1902, after which XIT herds grew even larger. According to shipping records provided to investors, Cato had sent 20,131 beeves east by the same point. The operation was selling only about three-fourths of the cattle it was sending north by that time. When the company closed out for a four-year span in 1898, it was clearly receiving generous assessments from that county's equalization board.[49]

Texas counties appear generally to have assessed cattle at lower rates than those in Montana, as table 2 illustrates. But the Syndicate owned three million acres there and far less in Montana. County tax records from the ten Texas counties where the XIT Ranch owned property reveal that in 1897 Capitol Freehold paid over $17,000 in school, county, and state taxes. Oldham County far outpaced neighboring Dallam and Hartley counties, collecting $7,088 for its coffers from the company. Cochran County, which contained less than a league of Syndicate property, apparently received nothing from the company, while its neighbor, Hockley, collected the lowest among the other nine—$226.80. The records indicate payment on at least 1.8 million acres of property but are more precise on the numbers of cattle. The operation reported 93,000 cattle and over 1,000 head of horses. Capitol Freehold paid the two counties in Montana in which it operated about $8,000 in 1897, about 46 percent of their Texas taxes—32 percent of their total tax bill. Still, perhaps Cato was right about the high tax rate in Montana. Or

TABLE 2

CAPITOL FREEHOLD LAND AND
INVESTMENT TAXES, TEXAS, 1889

County	Tax ($)
Castro	187.92
Dallam	1,070.20
Deaf Smith	1,131.58
Hartley	873.10
Oldham	6,444.57
Parmer	856.05
Farwells & Taylor	1,153.12
Misc. Tax	383.73
Total	12,100.27

Note: In Oldham County, Texas, in 1889, the company reported 406,810 acres valued at $1.25 per acre. Figuring additionally in the county total are 164 horses and mules valued at about $32 each, 12,000 cattle valued at $7.50 per head, and miscellaneous other charges. "Texas, County Tax Rolls, 1837–1910," *FamilySearch* (https://familysearch.org).

perhaps Texas just showed its reputation as a small-government, low-tax location ideal for big business true.[50]

After 1889, Texas pastures supported the XIT Ranch's breeding program and cow/calf operation. Two-year-old steers were sent to the northern ranges, other young steers and spayed heifers went to midwestern farmer-feeders. Old cows, old bulls, and other surplus cattle sold from Texas. Cattle pastured up north, and those being fed in the Midwest enjoyed better proximity to railroad shipping points as well as higher selling prices than beeves sent directly from Texas. Maybe the agents of the meat industry just did not like Texas. The packers may not have liked buying their beeves there, but they did not mind buying Texas-born cattle fattened on well-watered grasses in Montana, the Dakotas, and Wyoming, or on surplus corn, sorghum, and sugar beets at Kansas, Iowa, or Nebraska feeding farms. The XIT sent thousands of beeves north for double-wintering. Thousands more went to farm-ranch feeding operations on the central plains. In the years that followed the XIT's invasion of Montana, a good many of the beeves taken there walked all the way from Texas. Bitter arguments with the railroads and pure stubbornness on the part of the Syndicate kept the cattle trail well traveled, despite the barriers posed by exploding western settlement. The last XIT trail herds went north in 1897, the same year the company decided to replace the legendary XIT brand with a more conservative "long X."[51]

The last decade of the nineteenth century took the XIT Ranch to new heights in the cattle business. It is unlikely that any single entity up to that time had ever controlled so many cattle spread across so much territory. The XIT Ranch employed about 150 men to manage the cattle and horses as well as maintain the fences, windmills, and crops with which the ranch was experimenting. Other employees, from Channing to London, sat at desks, compiled ledgers, reports, and financial statements, addressed the company's correspondence, and tried to ensure that the cogs of the cattle business turned smoothly. The principals hired good men to oversee the ranch operations. They, in turn, ensured themselves with good hands. To promote the ranch's interests, the company encouraged XIT employees to participate in local government. The foundation essentially laid by John V. Farwell allowed the Syndicate a network of similarly engaged operators to grow beyond the horizontal model of production practiced by the XIT and other ranches, into a vertical model in which the cattlemen hoped to play a larger role in the "beef trust."

This building in Channing (formerly Rivers) became the XIT Ranch's central office in 1892. It continues to stand today. Panhandle-Plains Historical Museum (catalog #832-580).

Escarbada gained a reputation as the toughest of the XIT divisions after former Texas Ranger Ira Aten took over in 1895. The range had been plagued with cattle rustlers coming across the line from bordering New Mexico Territory. Aten discouraged them "through fear" for the next ten years. The division headquarters building was dismantled and reassembled at the National Ranching Heritage Center in Lubbock, Texas. Panhandle-Plains Historical Museum (catalog #832-563_001).

Charles B. Farwell's Chicago home. Ryerson and Burnham Libraries, The Art Institute of Chicago (digital ID #16405).

Farwell Block, 1886. Chicago headquarters of John V. Farwell and Company. Ryerson and Burnham Libraries, The Art Institute of Chicago (digital ID #000000_120210_081).

XIT punchers in Texas gather a Montana-bound herd in 1891. Nita Stewart Haley Memorial Library (catalog #J. Evetts Haley Collection I-30-11).

George Findlay, the Scottish bookkeeper who became the key manager of the XIT's business operations. Nita Stewart Haley Library (catalog #J. Evetts Haley Collection I-H-48).

A. G. Boyce saved the ranch from catastrophe when he took charge of the ranch range operations after Barbecue Campbell's departure in 1887. He retired from the ranch in 1905. Panhandle-Plains Historical Museum (catalog #799-1_001).

O. C. Cato (left), the manager of the XIT's Montana operation, holds his favorite cutting horse, Old Cabe, alongside Nicholas Buttelman, a local horse rancher. Photo Archives, Montana Historical Society (catalog #PAc 90-87 G078-004).

Going to work. A cowboy's life could be hard, and you were not going to get rich doing it. Most did it because they liked it. Photo Archives, Montana Historical Society (catalog #946-482).

Cutting out a big steer. A careful look at the big steer's hip reveals the "Long X" brand the ranch began using in 1897. Photo Archives, Montana Historical Society (catalog #981-1110).

A horse might step in a badger hole chasing down a renegade steer. It could go badly for both the horse and rider. The caption handwritten on this photo reads "A Cowboys Funeral." The other inscription appears to be "Bar 7L" and may be the brand of the outfit the deceased puncher rode for. Photo Archives, Montana Historical Society (catalog #946-495).

Technology brought sweeping changes to a cowpuncher's role in the West. Ranching changed, too. A windmill crew works on a well in the Escarbada division. Nita Stewart Haley Library (catalog #J. Evetts Haley Collection I-30-09).

A field of wheat on the Texas ranch. Panhandle-Plains Historical Museum (catalog #832-577_001).

A threshing crew harvesting wheat in eastern Montana. Photo Archives, Montana Historical Society (catalog #PAc 90-87 G059-004).

Cutting prairie hay in eastern Montana. Photo Archives, Montana Historical Society (catalog #PAc 90-87 G003-008).

A cow looks back through a barbed wire fence on the Escarbada range. Nita Stewart Haley Library (catalog #J. Evetts Haley Collection I-35-30).

Looking southeast from the Big Open across the Yellowstone River. Terry, Montana, can be seen on the river's south side. Photo Archives, Montana Historical Society (catalog #PAc 90-87 G074-004).

Photographer G. V. Barker wrote, "This is the finest picture I have in 40 years at the business." He called it "the last trip of the XIT," but it is dated 1908. The company did not completely close out the Montana operation until 1909. In another photo taken at the time, Barker documents a "cavy of 165 head of saddle horse." He also put the photo's location "at the forks of Burns Creek, 20 miles north of Glendive." Photo Archives, Montana Historical Society (catalog #946-379).

COPYRIGHT BY C. V. BARKER OF
LEWISTON IDAHO

CHAPTER 7

Empire

The Capitol Syndicate's ranch operations peaked during the 1890s, as an empire that operated in both Texas and Montana, but that decade also proved to be one of challenges and changes. Modernization began overtaking the business of raising cattle. The change shows in the company correspondence as the younger members of the beef empire began typing their work and correspondence. Market reports from the numerous commission houses around the country appeared at the Chicago office regularly, neatly prepared by clerks and secretaries delegated to such tasks. Although in many ways the business of cattle remained quite personal, it became far more professionalized as the century closed. On the XIT Ranch in Texas, telephones connected the widely separated division headquarters, greatly improving the operation's efficiency. That ranch's numerous artificial water projects continued to expand to meet demands for production. Transportation needs also brought new challenges. Political allies helped with legal problems but entangled the Syndicate in Texas politics. Nearly everyone on the XIT Ranch in Texas directed some effort toward land sales. Farm operations became more intense as the Syndicate sought to identify the best crops for each area to entice land buyers. Cattle remained the primary focus in both Texas and Montana, which prompted efforts to introduce new stock varieties and improve the herds. All of this, of course, transformed not only ranch operations but cowboys themselves, as the stereotypical western cowpuncher gave way to the modern herd manager.[1]

Lewis Nordyke wrote that the XIT Ranch was "organized on a grand scale," with grand problems to match. It was the "Goliath of the Cow Country" and swarmed by little Davids. By the time Ab Blocker drove the first stock onto the

Buffalo Springs range, fencing pliers were a necessity in every cowboy's saddle-bags. Fence riders maintained a never-ending patrol around ranch boundaries, keeping up the thousands of miles of barbed wire surrounding ranches like the XIT. The classic era of free-range grazing and contract trail cattle was essentially over in Texas by 1885. Quarantines, railroads, herd improvements, surplus beef, and civilization slackened the market demand for Texas cattle. Yet an investment boom begun earlier reached a stage at which operations stubbornly crashed forward in hopes of reaching profitability. The corporatization of the western ranch, the privatization of great stretches of range land, and the commoditization of its product changed the nature of a ranch hand's work. Organizational charts and balance sheets took control of the cattle ranges.[2]

Cowboys found themselves doing their jobs from somewhere other than the back of a horse. On the XIT in Texas, several men spent much of the year plowing firebreaks around the ranch's contiguous acreage. Others worked the experimental farms the Chicago men felt were key to future development on the lands. To rid the ranch's growing herds of the threat from wolves that lingered in the Panhandle, some older cowboys became "wolfers." Other men who worked these tasks were not ever cowboys. In XIT records, many employees are recorded as "not a cowboy." A significant number of current and former cowboys, however, carried out the auxiliary roles of the operation. Employees came and went, but many stayed for years at a time. The days when it was special enough to just be a good man with a horse were ending. As ranching became a more diversified and structured operation, many cowboys settled down, too, often to become farmers or homesteaders on the very ranges on which they once gathered beeves. The cowboy who knew something about all the operations was the one who kept working.[3]

In a place that did not like to give up its water easily, well-drillers required specialized equipment and expertise. Drought in the 1890s required an unending effort to keep XIT herds watered. Contractors generally provided drilling service, but permanent crews needed to service those wells. A fellow named John Wingo apparently earned a promotion when he moved from "artificial water laborer" to "artificial water teamster." Another XIT employee, Thad Whitley, variously appears in XIT records as an artificial water carpenter, hand, and mill tender. Water on the Texas ranch was the priority. Drilling and windmill construction crews were kept busy across Capitol Reservation lands throughout the ranch's operation. Cowboys exchanged their catch ropes for wrenches and hammers to keep water flowing. Insufficient water resources remained the XIT operators' primary concern throughout the ranch's existence.[4]

Although the Syndicate continued to pursue Amos Babcock's and Abner Taylor's dreams of striking a fast-flowing artesian source, they misunderstood the geology beneath the Texas ranch. The shallow, spongelike Ogallala Aquifer, its presence beneath much of the Great Plains unknown until the end of the century, provided the subterranean water on the ranch. Even the ranch's best wells failed to provide anything one could describe as fast-flowing. Wind, steam, and horses powered pumps to bring water to the surface. The few areas of surface water depended on small springs and precipitation runoff. By the late 1880s, the Syndicate was investigating the possibility of irrigating up to a thousand acres on its Buffalo Springs division. Taylor enlisted J. S. Greene of Denver to examine and propose a plan for the project. He grew frustrated over the summer when Greene failed to show up for the examination. "If you could not make it as you promised," Taylor wrote in his typical direct manner, "it would seem to me that you should have notified me." When it became too late in the year to accomplish much on the project, over the winter George Findlay took charge in Chicago and the Syndicate's primary attention shifted to herd improvements rather than irrigation. But the Syndicate never stopped working to secure the ranch's most precious resource—water.[5]

In the XIT's earliest days, workers on the ranch came up with ingenious contraptions to collect and capture water from hand-dug wells. To quench thirsty cattle, older "condemned" horses turned machines hauling a series of linked half-gallon buckets that continually pumped water into a trough. Dams were excavated, and when technology failed to make them hold water the cattle themselves provided the best solution. After attempts with cement and tar returned poor results, someone decided to place a salt feeder in the middle of an excavation. The visiting cattle, concentrated within the dam basin, packed the ground solid and provided a partial solution to the need to store water. Charles Goodnight had brought the first windmills to the Panhandle in 1883. These went up across the XIT Ranch as fast as wells could be drilled and fences could protect them. By the beginning of the twentieth century there were more than five hundred reservoirs on the Texas ranch and some three hundred windmills mining the subterranean treasure.[6]

A sustained drought throughout much of the first half of the 1890s drove ranch operators to consider questionable methods for bringing rain to their parched pastures and fields. In 1891, Gen. Robert G. Dyrenforth received a commission from the U.S. Department of Agriculture to lead an expedition to undertake experiments with rainmaking theories on the southern plains. Someone observed that, after battles during the Mexican War and the American Civil War, heavy rains often fell over the battlefields within days. The expedition used balloons filled with a mixture of hydrogen and oxygen. Scientists launched the balloons attached to lengthy wires to an altitude of about 1,800 feet, then exploded them with electrical charges. Apparently, demonstrations of the techniques in Washington produced "great alarm throughout the adjacent suburbs." Reportedly, however, a heavy rain fell in the area the next morning. The expedition had been promoted by Sen. Charles B. Farwell, the Syndicate member, who also introduced and succeeded in passage of a $9,000 federal appropriation for the project. Quite a large expedition departed for Kansas and Texas to face the "severest conditions of climate and season," equipped with "eight tons sulphuric acid, ten tons iron borings, two tons chlorate of potash, quantities of manganese, carbonates, and other chemicals." There is no record that this worked, but another rainmaker, Prof. Richard Meagher, gained attention that fall by suggesting that a network of towers be erected high in the sky that could generate and inject electricity into the sky.[7]

Water witching is a time-honored talent among a rare few, but during dry times the ranks of these gifted individuals swell with the usual assortment of zealots, charlatans, frauds, and thieves. People become foolish when facing financial ruin. Newspapers in the 1890s bombarded readers with "scientifically proven" cures of everything from dyspepsia to piles. Watching hungry, thirsty cattle die and being presented with a "scientific" plan to bring water to parched pastures could be tempting to anyone. Even Findlay, the wary Scottish accountant, approached by a man promising to "make rain" during the middle of one of the Syndicate's worst years, considered a proposal.

C. B. Jewell worked in Goodland, Kansas, as a dispatcher for the Chicago, Rock Island & Pacific Railway. As Jewell put it, "The road has helped me . . . by furnishing me all material called for, expenses, etc." The dispatcher and amateur scientist tried hard to get Findlay to listen to his promises to make rain. Their correspondence continued throughout the autumn of 1893, then seemingly lost

Findlay's ear that December. Findlay, staving off financial problems, hotly pursued cattle sales to other ranchers well into the next year. He likely was ignoring the inventive entrepreneur, heeding the advice of a railroad lawyer who knew of Jewell's trials. "I confess, I have very little faith in the success of Mr. Jewell's method of producing rain," M. A. Low told Findlay.[8]

Even in the Big Open, up in Montana, surrounded by two of the country's greatest rivers, drought and limited surface water represented a real challenge to ranchers and farmers during the 1890s. A 1901 survey of the township on which the Montana XIT Ranch buildings sat shows fences surrounding the upper reaches of Cedar Creek and its tributaries. Securing reliable water sources explains the four hundred acres the company purchased in Montana. The company held deeds for contiguous and noncontiguous parcels along Cedar Creek and tributaries on both sides of it, along Upper Bad Route and Hatchet creeks, and on Tusler Creek across the divide. In a place where the range was vast and water sometimes scarce, it did not matter how much land one owned. The value came from its location. Scarce and highly valued, available property adjacent to rivers and streams provided operations control over much more of the range.[9]

Transport was also a tremendous challenge for the XIT Ranch in the 1890s. For several years after the XIT's expansion into Montana, a seemingly unending dispute with the railroads serving Texas meant that a good many of the cattle sent north walked all the way from Texas. Arguments with the railroads and pure stubbornness on the part of the Syndicate kept the cattle trail well traveled, despite the barriers posed by exploding western settlement.[10]

Plenty of other outfits kept the trail north busy, and many enterprising individuals found methods to exploit cattle drovers everywhere along the route. Some fenced water holes or river crossings and demanded tolls from the trail bosses. XIT cowboys first drove cattle up the long trails from Texas to Montana in 1891. In what was then known as "No Man's Land," today's Oklahoma panhandle, "inspectors" jailed trail bosses and impounded cattle herds. Company ledgers for that summer report the company paying $51.15 to the "Sheriff of Beaver Co. O. T. for court exps," for their arrested trail bosses. They also paid a $150 inspection fee on "5,000 head leaving O. T.," and, later, $25 in Guthrie, Oklahoma Territory, for a legal "opinion for cattle detained in No Man's Land." Trail boss Ab Owings revealed his frustration in a scrawled note to George Findlay in May 1891: "I have paid them off until I am broke. . . . everybody I meet has to have a few dollars for something." Truly reflecting the mythical cowboy image, Owings expressed his determination to his Chicago boss. "I will get throw [through] as cheap as I can," he concluded his report. The sincerity and determination reflected in the trail boss's report likely endeared him to spendthrift owners. Owings bossed many herds north to Montana for the company.[11]

J. E. (Ealy) Moore, who worked many years on the XIT Ranch in Texas, served as the wagon boss on drives from the Texas ranch to Montana in 1892, 1893, and 1894. Moore kept a log of his journey and expenses on the 1892 drive. "Payed Eight Dollars to Powers Co Land Irrigation Co. for crossing 3 ditches" and "Payed to J. W. Galladge $5 Five Dollars for crossing canal," Moore recorded. He continued with the sundry charges: "Payed to Frank Stephens per M. S. $10 for crossing herd across South Platte" and "Payed to A. J. Elliott $15 for watering herd and driving through pasture."[12]

The last XIT herds trailed north in 1897. More than 12,000 XIT-branded cattle managed to make the journey during 1896, but it took determined puncher "Scandlous John" McCanless, a well-known cowhand in Texas, Montana, and in between, to get his charges through that last trip. When XIT cattle from Texas began arriving again in 1902, they came on rail cars and unloaded at Glendive and Fallon.[13]

Enormous amounts of preparation went into the transportation, whether by rail or trail, of Syndicate cattle from Texas to their northern range and to markets. Spring shipments of feeder and stock cattle added another shipping season to the traditional fall beef shipments to market. Correspondence with railroad representatives by Findlay or his protégé, Francis W. (F.W.) Farwell, a secretary and bookkeeper in the Chicago office, intensified during the shipping seasons. Findlay drove a hardnosed bargain with the FW&DC people for the XIT's initial move to Montana. Although the company at times shipped some cattle to Wyoming and Montana until 1898, in most years the company stubbornly insisted the XIT's Montana-bound two-year-olds follow an increasing difficult-to-transit trail north.[14]

Besides the railroads, the Syndicate dealt with railcar manufacturers, which led to much arm twisting at times. Cattle injured during shipment received lower prices, so shippers began to look for safer livestock cars. A stiff competition ensued between several manufacturers, chiefly the Hick's Stock Car Company and the Street's Western Stable Car Line, both in Chicago. The Rock Island line offered its own version of these "palace cars," known as the Montgomery. Findlay favored Hick's cars. Street's heavily lobbied the company for shipments of XIT cattle in 1893 from both Texas and Montana. A Street's representative stopped by the Chicago office while Findlay was in Montana. F. W. Farwell wrote that the man, C. J. Miles, had asked about rumors that Findlay would use only Hick's cars that year. He expressed to Farwell his company's hope that the Syndicate would use Street's for "northern" business and consider them elsewhere as well. He cautioned the Syndicate that they "ought to consider the subject very carefully" before selecting Hick's. Miles told Farwell his competitor overpromised the cars they could deliver. The Hick's company was in a financial squeeze, he told Farwell. This proved somewhat prescient; the Street's company later absorbed Hick's.[15]

Rock Island people reminded F. W. Farwell when he visited their offices that the cattle shippers did not pay the railcar suppliers. Nevertheless, they informed him that Hick's cars would be delivered to Liberal, Kansas, for XIT cattle. Findlay had also been negotiating with the Santa Fe officials about supplying Hick's cars to the FW&DC for shipping cattle for Montana. When the Rock Island refused to deliver cars to Liberal, cattle had already been put on the trail there by Boyce. The railroad had even located watering stations for the company. Young Farwell, upon discovering the news, authorized the Santa Fe palace cars, and understanding that Findlay would not be happy counseled his mentor: "I do not see how we can make them furnish Hicks' cars under the circumstances." It is not clear that Findlay's pursuit of an exclusive arrangement with the Hick's company ever worked out. In Montana, he was told that the Great Northern could supply all the Hick's cars the ranch could use. The Northern Pacific did not use them, and no documents of shipments of XIT cattle over the Great Northern have been uncovered.[16]

Perhaps a bigger problem than the kind of car supplied was the number of cars supplied. The FW&DC seemed to suffer a constant shortage; hence Findlay dealt directly with the Hick's and Santa Fe people. But rail service for the XIT in Texas never satisfied the Syndicate, which got along better with northern railroads. The Interstate Commerce Commission held hearings on the matter in St. Louis in December 1906. H. S. Boice replaced A. G. Boyce after the XIT legend's eighteen-year reign as general manager ended in 1905. Testifying before Congress on the matter, Boice said: "For the last few years we have had great inconvenience in making our shipments in the fall of the year . . . on account of not being able to get the cars. We placed [an] order [for 125 cars] on the 20th of September to ship on the 13th of October. We were able to ship at that date, but were not able to get anything off until the 20th of October." Boice told the federal commissioners that it was December 11 of that year before he completed the work. It took five separate trains to complete the fall shipping, during which time the cattle were held in closed pastures. Managing and feeding them while waiting to load kept ranch hands from other tasks. Boice said that he had the same problems whether he used the Santa Fe, Rock Island, or FW&DC. He told the commission that there was no shortage of cars for the operation in Montana and expressed his greatest concern regarding the many delays their shipments met after they were loaded—on all the lines.[17]

The Syndicate, as did most large shippers, employed stock inspectors at the various railheads and stockyard destinations. This meant finding reliable and reputable cattlemen to look not just for the XIT brand in other shipments but for stray brands among the Syndicate cattle. F. W. Farwell wrote to Fred De Boice, a ranch bookkeeper in Tascosa, that "some time ago" Findlay had told him "that Mr. Boyce had appointed an inspector at the Kansas City yard." The Syndicate employed inspectors in Chicago, St. Louis, and Omaha as well as Kansas City. Later they would have a man in South St. Paul, Minnesota, too. "If you have not sent him the brands of the O'Conner cattle," Farwell reminded De Boice, "please do so." He urged immediate action if no inspector had yet been appointed. "Strays are likely to be landed there any day and we are losing money by delay." Remarkably, livestock operators took great care in reimbursements to the owners of strays. Inspectors looked for their employer's cattle among other incoming shipments and for other people's cattle among those shipped by their employer. In some cases, a region's livestock association also hired inspectors who kept a lookout for members' cattle. In Montana, proceeds from stray sales were turned over to the state's Board of Stock Commissioners for distribution to owners. There are many instances of correspondence among even the chief men in the largest of operations enclosing a check for $20 or whatever the misguided beef may have brought minus shipping, feed, and commission. Some inspectors also served as range detectives hired by stock associations to investigate rustling and other livestock-related crimes.[18]

William McDole (or W.M.D.) Lee—"Mac," friends called him—earned the respect of most. He was occasionally feared by some. With the last buffalo gone there, Lee saw opportunity in the Panhandle, and he took it. Lee may have been the most powerful man in the Panhandle, and his influence spread widely. He resented the agreements the government made with railroads regarding land and subsidies. Lee reportedly called railroads a "public nuisance." He resented the advantage that Texas and federal laws gave to railroads. Mostly, Lee wanted what was best for Lee. He wanted the railroads to come and take away his cattle, but he was not eager to see his LS Ranch prematurely restricted by the farmers he knew the trains were bringing. Lee, like many of the large cattle operators, was nevertheless pragmatic about these things. As Charles Goodnight told a Texas newspaper, "No one is foolish enough to fight the inevitable." Lee joined with the XIT legal counsel A. L. Matlock to influence the course of the FW&DC as it pushed northward in 1887 and 1888. Lee and Matlock sparked a decade-long feud with Tascosa, leading to the cow town's demise after they convinced the builders of that railroad to bypass Tascosa and establish freight warehouses, depots, and loading pens adjacent to or on LS and XIT land. This location became known as Cheyenne Pens.[19]

Lee, convinced of the soundness of a plan to dredge the Brazos River mouth and establish a deepwater port there, lured Sen. Charles B. Farwell, Abner Taylor, and even both Matlock and Findlay into his scheme. Incorporated as the Brazos River Channel and Dock Company in 1888 with Lee as the company's president, the North Texas firm shared officers with two other companies created at the same time: the Texas Land and Immigration Company and the Velasco Terminal Railway Company. These companies together owned substantial land in the area and built a railroad spur from the International & Great Northern rail line. The Brazos project had also named Gus Wilke, the chief builder on the capitol project, as the contractor for the harbor work.[20]

Other plans like it soon were being promoted. It seems deepwater ports on the Texas Gulf Coast were in high demand. A law enacted by the Texas legislature in 1887 to encourage development of waterways, harbors, and coastal facilities prompted the creation of several companies, apparently to the chagrin of government agencies that had already looked at many of the proposals being offered. Mentioned repeatedly by supporters of the harbor schemes were the prohibitive rates charged by railroads shipping Texas goods out of the state. One advertisement for investors in the Aransas Harbor City and Improvement Company claimed the company had in-hand capital reserves of $6,000,000 and, within

a year, could provide deepwater port services that would save shippers of "surplus products of the West . . . $120,000,000 PER ANNUM." A list of the company's
stockholders included some well-known names from around the country and the
conspicuous presence of some of the Texas cattle business's foremost men. Besides
Findlay and Matlock, the list included Henry B. Stoddard, Charles Goodnight,
R. E. Maddox, Ike T. Pryor, J. G. Wheeler, and W. A. H. Miller, all of whom
were Texans engaged in developing refrigeration, slaughter, and canning facilities
in Fort Worth and on the coast. This company, associated with the Aransas Pass
Harbor Company, paralleled the Brazos harbor project supported by Lee, Taylor,
and Senator Farwell.[21]

Congress ordered an investigation and report on the Brazos company's progress in 1896 to "ascertain the character and improvements" that it had put into
the projects. The appointed board delivered their report to Congress in 1897. By
that time, Lee no longer served as an officer for the company, but Taylor served as
president and Senator Farwell continued to be an officer of the corporation. The
effort to untangle the vast network of business and finance schemes promoted by
the cattle and land interests of Texas remains a work in progress or, perhaps, the
work of another historian.[22]

The federal engineers' report offered a scathing assessment of the company's
efforts in the project. The authors of the report found little to distinguish the
different companies involved in the undertaking as independent firms and essentially dealt with them as if they were the same company. Offering little confidence
in the scheme, they questioned the wisdom of further development activity. The
authors did admit that the plan's only hope rested in the government adopting
the operation. Correspondence in the report from Taylor and other company
representatives remained optimistic, outlining the great benefits that would come
to Texas and the rest of the country if the venture were to be continued. Taylor,
ever the eager optimist, argued that, although he understood the undertaking was
too big for private enterprise, it remained the right thing for the nation. Taylor
and the company presented their costs to the review board should the government
want to take the job out of their hands. Taylor's figure of the company's costs on
the project, including the railroad, was listed at about $1.4 million. The reviewers
dismissed outright several of Taylor's figures and ridiculed the management of the
entire operation. "That this amount [$768,830] was actually spent the Board has
no reason to doubt," the report declared. "That much of it was unwisely spent is

also beyond question." In truth, none of these private ventures seemed to work effectively, and eventually the creation of Texas's deepwater ports became dependent upon the efforts of the federal government and the Army Corps of Engineers. In the meantime, XIT cowboys continued to drive cattle north on the trails or load them on railroad cars, if and when they became available.[23]

The federal review of the river and harbor improvement scheme was, of course, not the first time that Syndicate members dealt with government investigations and criticism. Political power and networks of influence played a central role in the operation of the XIT Ranch. Beginning with the Syndicate's acquisition of the capitol contract, intrigue permeated the operation. Taylor spent considerable time lobbying Texas legislators and governors. Men like Matlock, as a state representative and senator in both the 1881 and 1883 Texas legislatures, were recruited by the Syndicate in part to influence Texas politics. Both Farwells and Taylor influenced politics in Chicago and at a national level. Upon Amos Babcock's death, a newspaper headlined him the "Dictator of the fortunes of the Republican Party in [Illinois]." Neither recently appointed Sen. Charles B. Farwell nor newly elected Rep. Abner Taylor were new to Washington politics. Farwell had served earlier terms in the House of Representatives, and Taylor long sought more political influence in Illinois.[24]

Taylor saw himself as an exceptional negotiator, hard bargainer, and prescient businessman. His partners, the Farwell brothers, were less impressed with Taylor's decisions as time passed. The impulsive Taylor undoubtedly stretched an already failing business association when he eloped with Amos Babcock's daughter late in 1889. The relationship long had troubled the elder gentlemen, who had tried to discourage it. The news of the union, spread by some of the country's largest newspapers, probably did little to comfort Babcock at a time when he was just discovering that his interests in the XIT operation were quickly diminishing while John V. Farwell dealt with British investors.

John V. Farwell himself played no small role in politics. He had grown his mercantile house in Chicago from essentially nothing into one of the largest wholesale businesses in the world, with offices in France and Britain. He had served as one of President Ulysses S. Grant's Indian commissioners while the former general sought to make a final peace with the indigenes of the West who were trying in vain to slow the flood of Americans anxious to fulfill the destiny that the nation's leaders had long promised them. John V., or "Dutch," as he was known to close friends, certainly held the highest hand in ranch operations in 1885, but he strengthened his hold after the completion of the capitol contract in 1888. Taylor's departure for Congress in 1889 worked perfectly toward his intention to secure the ranch's direction under his control.[25]

Farwell spent considerable time in England and, although he attended to his European wholesale interests while there, he focused primarily on ensuring that skittish British investors maintained their interest in the endeavor. Extremely persuasive and not easily rebuffed, Farwell was direct in his manner and speech. Confident in his decision making, he put more than his money on the line for the operation. In March 1886 he, his wife, company lawyer Thomas A. Drummond, and William Sturgis, who had been crucial in gaining British investors for the ranch operation, were returning from London aboard the S.S. *Oregon*. A schooner struck the steamer amidships not far outside New York's harbor, necessitating the rescue of the passengers and crew. Although the schooner was lost with all hands, there were no fatalities aboard the *Oregon*. The ship, however, could not be saved. Drummond received a slight head injury, but the others in his party were unhurt. Farwell gave his account of the sinking to a newspaper and reported the inadequacy of lifeboats. He noted the fine behavior of the ship's crew and captain but commented that "some of the steerage passengers . . . jumped into the loaded boats upon the heads of women and children." One of the crew threatened to kill one unruly passenger, and when some boats tried to depart without being full "Mr. Wm. Sturgis, putting his hand into his hip pocket, called . . . 'come back and take a full load or I will shoot you.'" The boats returned, according to Farwell. Sturgis and his wife later filed suit against Farwell, challenging his compensation in the Capitol Freehold deal. It was another in a lengthy line of legal disputes brought by associates, former and current.[26]

At odds with the State of Texas almost continually from the relationship's inception, the Syndicate strongly promoted their interests there. During Texas governor James Stephen Hogg's two terms from 1891 to 1895, the legislature, at Hogg's urging, sought to reverse some earlier Texas land transactions. Calls to deny out-of-state and foreign corporate control of Texas land and businesses were commonplace. Lawmakers sought to place the same restrictions on non-Texas corporations as the 1876 Texas constitution had placed on railroads. Their land allotments were granted, but if the companies were unable to dispose of them to "actual settlers" the grants reverted to state control after twelve years. Hogg, elected attorney general in 1886, admired the efforts "Oxcart John" Ireland had taken to protect the state's public land. As governor, he continued that fight. The Syndicate took offense at Hogg and legislative actions that seemed to single out Capitol Freehold. The company battled accusations that the ranch fronted for a foreign-owned corporation, stripping Texas of its greatest legacy.[27]

Having both completed their service in Washington, D.C., Abner Taylor and Charles B. Farwell visited Texas in the spring of 1893. Farwell, still involved in the deepwater shipping scheme in Velasco and beef packing in Fort Worth, spoke out about the criticism of the Syndicate. In a memorial to both houses of the legislature in April, the senator, who reportedly never visited the ranch and seemed a somewhat reluctant partner in the cattle business, suggested his willingness to return the reservation for the price then being asked for the state's school lands— $2.00–$3.00 per acre. Moreover, if the state accepted the offer, the company, he proposed, would lease what land the state wished of it back at rates equal to what the state was then offering leases in the region.[28] As in the past, A. L. Matlock served as the spokesperson and proxy of the Chicago men in this contest with the state government. A few days later, after Farwell's proposal circulated, Matlock told newspapers that the company did not expect the legislature to act immediately on the offer, but to put "the entire matter before the people [so they have] a clearer and better understanding of the position we occupy." He implied that there were other options but insisted "the offer is made in good faith, and we are willing to carry it out."[29]

The Syndicate's history with Hogg reverberated into his governorship. As the attorney general, Hogg sat on the Capitol Commission as the Syndicate completed Texas's new statehouse in May 1888. Hogg, only months before that, praised the building to the state's sheriff's association. "When they [the sheriff's association] are through in San Antonio," he bubbled in his apology for missing their convention there, "call and see the grandest capitol building on earth." Hogg, according to the Syndicate's building contractor, Gustav Wilke, called him into his office in early 1888. Hogg said he had timbered farmland to sell in eastern Texas. The property reportedly belonged to Hogg's father-in-law. He offered it to the builder for $25,000. Wilke declined the offer. The contractor suggested that a man sent down from Chicago by the Syndicate to investigate delays in acceptance of the completed capitol might be interested. That man reported that Hogg solicited him to pay $30,000 for the ranch. Abner Taylor himself stated that he had been offered the property for $40,000 and declined. Each man believed that Hogg approached them with the offer as an exchange for relenting on his complaints of defects in the capitol's construction and delaying its acceptance. This led to bad feelings. When Hogg initiated his gubernatorial campaign in 1890, the Syndicate, represented by Matlock, with his own ambitions for the governor's office, led the way in opposing Hogg's candidacy. Findlay, in a postscript after inquiring after Matlock's Syndicate duties and briefing him on the move to Montana, joked that "about this time I expect you are throwing your hat up for Hogg."[30]

Hogg supported a constitutional amendment that created a state railroad commission to set rates and oversee the railroad industry in Texas. Matlock's faction of the state's Democrats, with ties to the railroads and Texas cattle interests, opposed Hogg and the commission. Despite their differences with railroad companies, the forces opposed to the creation of a state commission preferred to control their agreements with the carriers. Many of the state's most prominent players in the livestock business supported the refrigeration and harbor schemes. The latter might well come under the jurisdiction of a new commission. By June, it appeared that Hogg was well on his way to the gubernatorial nomination in August. Hoping to sideline the parade to the attorney general's election, Matlock sought out the state's newspapers and reported, without any specific accusation, the attempts by Hogg to entice the Syndicate or its associates into the land deal.[31]

Hogg never denied that he had offered the land. In fact, he had little to say whatsoever on the matter, although nearly every newspaper in the state posted editorial criticisms of Matlock's barely cloaked accusations. The original contract for the capitol building called for its completion on January 1, 1888, but a change in the contract when the company agreed to use granite for the primary building material had extended the deadline to 1891. Dignitaries dedicated the building on May 1, 1888. Although a few issues, including a leaky dome, kept the state from fully accepting the building until December, there is no evidence that the items on the state's punch list were nitpicky. Without a doubt, Hogg offered the land. Taylor wrote to the attorney general in August 1889 to say that a decision "in relation to that land" depended on the return of John V. Farwell from Europe "the last of this month." Taylor's tone was friendly but not very encouraging to the future governor. "My other associates here," he wrote, probably referring only to Senator Farwell and, possibly, the Farwell brothers' sons, "did not think favorably of it as they thought our investments in Texas . . . were large enough."[32]

Hogg had written to Taylor at the end of July 1889, eight months after the closing of the capitol contract. Had Hogg been trying earlier to coerce a land sale, it would seem odd that he continue to offer the sale without the same leverage. He did cultivate a populist, anticorporate image and certainly was looking at the governor's office, so he may have been encouraging the sale to effect some quid pro quo between him and the Syndicate regarding their supporting his candidacy. The price for which Wilke and Taylor were offered the land clearly was greater than the property's assessed value of about $5,700, but Texas real estate was seldom assessed at its full commercial worth. The land appears to have held harvestable timber, one of Texas's most valuable resources at the time. Still, that Wilke and others confirmed their stories, and that Taylor wrote Matlock that he had the letter offering the land and his response and should be happy to show them to the press, seem to represent a serious indictment of Hogg. Taylor suggested to Matlock, "Get him to deny the letter and transaction. . . . if he does not deny it outright he will likely tell some lies about it." He seemed confident that the whole story would scandalize Hogg and ruin his political career: "I do not see how he can make a statement in relation to this matter that will not put him in an embarrassing position." Taylor misjudged.[33]

Matlock continued his attempts to foil Hogg's political plans in 1892. That August, after a parliamentary battle with Hogg forces, Matlock and at least fifty other delegates "bolted" from the Democratic state convention. Matlock supported attorney George Clark, who often represented railroad interests in the state. In the year that the national People's Party made its biggest mark on politics, Hogg positioned himself between the populists, building on his earlier efforts at land reform in the state, and the antiregulation forces arrayed behind Clark. The election outcome was up for grabs in the days before the election, with both the People's Party candidate, Thomas Nugent, and Clark supporters predicting victory.[34]

When the final counts were in, however, Hogg was reelected with a plurality, with Clark second and Nugent a disappointing third. Speaking to a reporter, Matlock, serving as Clark's executive committee chair, blamed misreported estimates from campaign leaders, particularly in the state's southern regions, for his preelection prediction of at least a 30,000-vote majority. He also discussed Hogg and "the negro vote," casting yet another attack on the character of the governor. "That fraud and intimidation were resorted to in many places by the

Hogg managers cannot be questioned," Matlock told the reporter. The defeat did not seem to cause much friction between the party standard bearers. Clark was soon back representing the state in the Greer County case, concerning a dispute between the State of Texas and the federal government over what is today the southwest corner of Oklahoma.[35]

Like most of the large ranch operators, the Syndicate tried to ensure that its men held some influence in local politics. Findlay held a county commissioner seat until he returned to Chicago in 1889. His replacement was another XIT employee. Boyce and Matlock also worked hard to promote Syndicate interests in Texas, particularly in Oldham, Hartley, and Dallam counties.[36]

They helped get veteran Texas Ranger Ira Aten elected as sheriff for Castro County and in 1895 hired Aten as foreman of the extensive Escarbada division of the XIT, which covered much of the western half of Deaf Smith County to the New Mexico border. Its pastures suffered the worst of the ranch's trouble from rustlers because thieves took advantage of the division's remoteness, escaping with their booty across the state line. The previous range boss, James M. Cook, had sought Findlay's help in enlisting Pinkerton agents to run down the thieves. Although rustling was a real problem, the occasional innocent may have suffered at Aten's hand. Small ranchers and settlers moving into the eastern reaches of the county challenged the Syndicate's dominance there, and Aten presented a powerful and intimidating presence on his division. Still, for much of the ranch's existence, the Escarbada division remained among its most important. XIT owners, seeking to soften their image to potential settlers and townspeople, reined in Aten as the century ended, although he remained a valued division foreman until 1905.[37] Rustling continued to be a problem, however. News accounts reported more than a thousand two-year-old steers stolen over a period of months from the XIT during the winter of 1901–2.[38]

Challengers and critics of the XIT made the political influence of the Syndicate critical. The company encouraged ranch employees to purchase school lands adjacent to the ranch. In some cases, these applications were legitimate and the cowboy or other worker acquired it as his own place in cooperation with the big operator. More often, it allowed large landowners in the region to both aggrandize land and maintain a buffer against "undesirable" settlement. This was a civil matter that could be resolved in favor of the XIT with the right person in power, but even criminal cases could benefit from having the right ally. In Hartley

County, political rivals planted marked steers among XIT beeves destined for Montana. After stamping the XIT brand on these cattle, the XIT cowhands could not identify the former owners, which prevented them from following the customary practice of reimbursing former owners for strays that wound up in a trail herd. The steers were later revealed to be someone else's, and Boyce was indicted for cattle theft by a Hartley County grand jury. The charge highlighted the growing resentment toward the ranch, but Boyce's eventual acquittal demonstrated the importance of having political influence. No doubt the populist fervor at the state and national level created animosity against the ranch during this period, and this was enhanced by the heavy hand of political contract by the Syndicate. But perhaps the tight grip of the closely held, out-of-state enterprise was justified at times.[39]

The Syndicate's political connections are nowhere more evident than in the settlement of a boundary dispute between Texas and New Mexico Territory. The latter claimed that surveys incorrectly identified as much as a two-mile-wide swath of land along the Texas line, most of it controlled by the Capitol Syndicate; this land rightly belonged to New Mexico. John V. Farwell Jr., who later succeeded his father as president of the John V. Farwell Company, contacted his old college friend William Howard Taft, then working as the U.S. solicitor general, to plead against the claim. At the same time, Senator Farwell and Representative Taylor introduced bills in the Senate and House of Representatives, respectively, concerning the border. The resulting law confirmed the boundary line between Texas and New Mexico that had been established June 5, 1858. A rider on New Mexico's later petition for statehood included a dismissal of the boundary claim.[40]

Matlock, while involved in politics, remained engaged with the Syndicate's original goal of selling land within the Capitol Reservation. W. S. Mabry, the one-time district surveyor who had guided Amos Babcock on the first inspection of the property, expanded his association with the Syndicate after overseeing a resurvey of much of the reservation during 1886. Mabry managed fence and townsite surveys and was responsible for "sectionizing" the most likely agricultural parcels of the lands. He showed potential buyers around the ranch. He also was part owner (subsidized by the Syndicate) of a hotel in Channing, which stood near what became the local headquarters for the XIT Ranch in 1890. The hotel, and others like it constructed by the Syndicate, served the growing flow of prospective buyers whom they hoped would purchase land. Mabry, visiting in Chicago, explained that he had left "the Hungarian gentlemen" in the hands of A. G. Boyce, who was just then beginning his transition from cowman to real estate agent—and not expressing too much excitement in the duties. Mabry hoped that the old drover could close a deal on "a colony somewhere on the south end." Although stating that he was "satisfied [Boyce] feels that the Panhandle has some redeeming features tho' he's never willing to admit it," Mabry nevertheless mused on Boyce's ability for "talking up the country."[41]

Mabry became one of the Syndicate's most important promotion agents and eagerly anticipated the arrival of more railroads to the Panhandle. Pushing his aspirations, he wrote Findlay to pass on the latest intelligence he had heard. He hoped that Findlay would urge John V. Farwell, as a member of the board of the Santa Fe Railroad, to encourage the company to speed up its plans for a road southwest out of their Panhandle City terminus. He was also anxious to know the plans of the Rock Island line, then terminating in Liberal, Kansas. "I hope you will not think I am a visionary railroad builder and full of schemes," he wrote to Findlay, "but this information might lead to something and can't do us any harm." Findlay was also negotiating with the resurrected Texas Central Railway for a line northwest out of Albany, Texas, but this was not going well. "I have been led to expect more assistance from you than you offer," the company's general manager complained to Findlay, but that is probably only part of the firm's reasons for failure.[42]

Findlay had other ideas to promote land sales as well. Matlock wrote to him in 1893 to introduce Sue Greenleaf, a writer from Fort Worth at the time. She was "writing up the country along the Fort Worth and Denver Ry and the Pan Handle," including the "Capitol lands." Matlock told Findlay of an encouraging plan that Greenleaf had for them and insisted that the Chicago manager would "find her plans worthy of patronage" if he would just meet her in the Chicago office. Greenleaf was an interesting character. She was from Missouri and had apparently lost her father before she was six years of age. Divorced from a husband who had disappeared after a scandal, she lived with her mother in several different locations including El Paso, Santa Fe, and San Francisco, where she authored plays, several works of fiction, and a historical pamphlet for New Mexico. She was active in the women's movement along with her mother and a vocal proponent of women's suffrage; the two of them would later become the first women to register publicly to vote in San Francisco when women gained the vote in California in

1911. More important to Findlay, Greenleaf had written a promotional pamphlet about Fort Worth and was involved with the Women's World's Fair Exhibit Association of Texas, an organization that promoted the construction of a Texas building at the Chicago World's Fair that year. The group also led the effort to collect exhibition material. It is not clear what Greenleaf's role with the group was, but the Texas Building at the fair reportedly featured "special exhibits of great interest, and thousands of curiosities and relics."[43]

As it turns out, Findlay did meet with Greenleaf, who, according to the former, suggested that his company participate in the Texas exhibits while she served as an agent in promoting the Syndicate land. "It would be greatly in your advantage," Greenleaf wrote in October, "to get out a small folder . . . giving some idea of the price & inducements offered to colonize." Extolling the "throng of visitors" the building was receiving each day, she thought a ten- or twelve-page prospectus on the lands, 30,000 copies, would be inexpensive and offered to distribute them for $15.00. In closing, she reminded Findlay that she had "a map up & invariably showed the location of the lands." A few weeks later, complaining of the "beastly cold," she apologized for not visiting the Syndicate office but provided a list of "parties who were very desirous" of having more information about the Capitol lands. Her notes on the people reveal the persistent idea of colonization that from the beginning drove the men of the Syndicate. "A. G. Makenzie . . . [of] Minneapolis . . . has money to invest, thinks of trying to take [?] a colony," she wrote. And there was W. Biens of Mayview, Illinois, who "said several in his neighborhood thought of going down," or H. W. Hines of "Bijou Hills, S. D. [who] is very anxious to work up a large colony in his state & Ill to locate in the Pan Handle." Amos Babcock strongly urged colonization after his visit to the lands in 1882, and the term permeates the XIT correspondence. While Greenleaf solicited land business at the great fair, efforts to sell property at the ranch continued.[44]

Findlay enlisted more than Greenleaf in the Syndicate's marketing campaign. He spoke with an acquaintance, Hugo Dunfalvy, a Chicago attorney. After considering their conversation, the lawyer wrote the accountant: "I would advise your company to commence the Colonization Business on a regular business principal [and] organize a Stock Company for Colonization purposes . . . to interest a foreign syndicate." They needed to make attractive land offers for 10 percent down payments and thereby lure enough early buyers with money to "boom the whole enterprise." Somehow, one must believe that Findlay ignored Dunfalvy's financing advice, because the Chicago operation had more than enough foreign investors. Ultimately, no large "colonies" spawned from the ranch acreage. A sound marketing strategy eventually paid dividends, though. Many people profited from the dispersal of the land, but it took time. Large land sales were still in the future, but an infrastructure was being created that positioned the American investors, essentially the Farwells, for the land's eventual disposal.[45]

The Syndicate endured the rippling effects of the Panic of 1893. F. W. Farwell, Findlay's Chicago stand-in, wrote his boss, tongue-in-cheek, as a conclusion to his summary of recent Chicago cattle prices: "Nothing else new unless it is that money is tight, and you may have heard that."[46] An earlier exchange between the two indicated that the senior Farwells were concerned with finances at the moment but not prepared to give in to quick money options. "You . . . understand the way things are," the younger Farwell wrote of the brothers. "They can use the money . . . but they do not wish to sacrifice the cattle." In the Syndicate's continuing efforts to improve prospects for land sales to settlers, they experimented with a variety of crops. John V. Farwell's annual message to British stockholders always included his vision of an agricultural paradise on the plains. Farwell vigorously pursued the possibility of grape production on their Texas land. The Syndicate renegotiated its lease with Capitol Freehold in January 1893, and no official stockholders' meeting was held during the year.[47] Farwell, nevertheless, completed his usual report for 1892 and outlined the ranch's agricultural outlook. "A good deal is being said of the suitability of the land and climate in the Panhandle for fruit culture," he wrote, detailing a timeline for production. "The planting of vineyards on the high plateau has not been attempted . . . but enough experimenting has been done to prove that grapes can be raised to great perfection." He was not wrong; 80 percent of Texas's wine grape production in the early twenty-first century comes from vineyards operating in a region from just south of Lubbock to Dalhart.[48]

Farwell's ideas and Findlay's determination may have first sparked the industry there. The Syndicate often used mass mailings to advertise their land and cattle. They sometimes solicited expert advice about potential plans by similar tactics. In early 1893, Findlay began to put shape to Farwell's ideas and drafted a letter addressed "to the Postmaster, Anthony, N.M.," in which he inquired if the man might know of someone to assist them "to make some experiments in the production of raisin grapes and wine grapes by irrigation." The postmaster,

Charles E. Miller, promptly replied (in a note on the same letter) by referring Findlay to Hiram Hadley "at the Agricultural College at Las Cruces."⁴⁹

Findlay wrote to Hadley, then president of New Mexico College of Agriculture and Mechanics, on March 3, 1893. Replying on March 9, Hadley told Findlay that what he had to say on the matter was "subject to a great many qualifications." He had carefully examined soil and climate information Findlay had sent him and was optimistic about the possibilities; he noted that some of the XIT Ranch's characteristics matched his location in the Mesilla Valley. "You have a little colder weather in the winter time, but not much," he wrote. Although he found that the XIT generally had more rainfall, he fretted about the lack of alternative water sources and put little faith in windmills. "They are too capricious in their operation," he warned. Hadley felt that perhaps improved pumps would assist with irrigation, but he questioned whether the expenses would be worthwhile "in the commercial sense." Cautioning Findlay to proceed slowly, Hadley proposed several grape varieties he felt might be appropriate and offered suggestions on the year-around care of grape crops in a similar environment (see charts 1 and 2 for comparative climatic data on Montana and the Panhandle).⁵⁰

Findlay also contacted J. P. Onstott, "Grower of Thompson's Seedless Grapes," in Yuba City, California. Onstott replied on April 3, 1893, and indicated his willingness to provide Findlay with arbors from his nursery in Arizona, but he explained that it was too late in the season to plant. Instead, Onstott suggested that Findlay wait for the next year. In a later letter, Onstott said that, although he had not been in the Panhandle, he had toured the Pecos Valley. He fretted some about the cold weather but saw "no reason but you can raise grapes there." He offered to have product samples sent to Findlay and urged Findlay to visit his exhibit at the Chicago World's Fair. Onstott, reflecting on his observations, wrote last, "Apples, I think, would do well there." He did send Findlay raisin samples and again asked to meet him in Chicago. Findlay was in Montana, however, and Senator Farwell apparently met with the grape grower.⁵¹

Perhaps in line with his reputation, Farwell in his 1892 report also suggested the cultivation of prunes. It is not clear if Farwell understood prunes to be dried plums. After describing his hope for grape and prune production, Farwell also discussed attempts at growing wheat by XIT neighbors, which he described as a great success. The ranch's Spring Lake division first succeeded at growing cotton

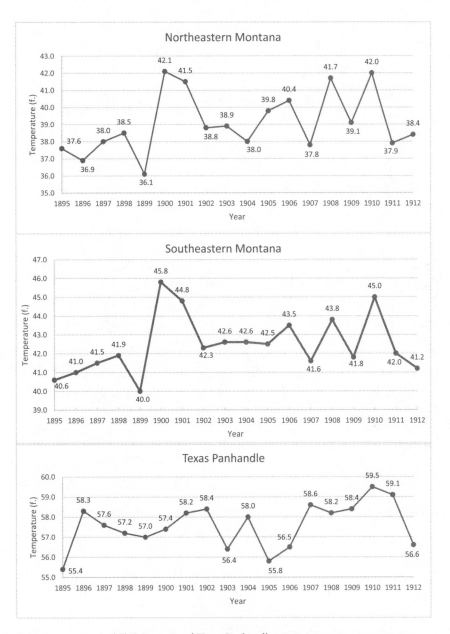

Average temperature (°F), Montana and Texas Panhandle, 1895–1912

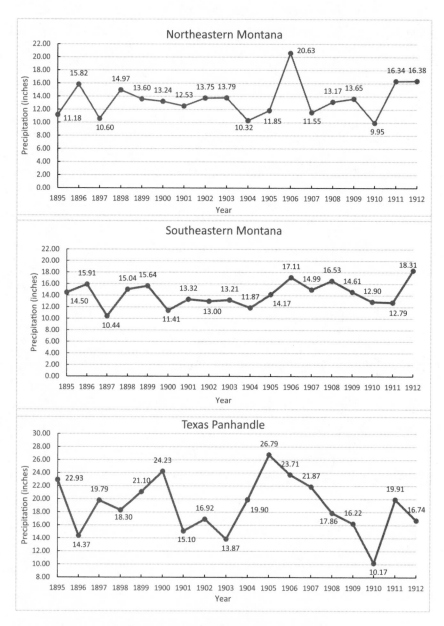

Average precipitation (inches), Montana and Texas Panhandle, 1895–1912

in 1888. In earlier reports, Farwell discussed sugar beet and sorghum production. He once proposed a sugar refinery, but despite his apparent enthusiasm he was not optimistic about the commercial profitability of sugar production just then. He reminded skeptical stockholders that "all of our experiments . . . were undertaken with a view of demonstrating what our lands were capable of producing." The efforts, he wrote, rather than provide profit from the crops, validated the future profitability of the land to potential buyers. "We will have this year most of our cultivated lands in millet, sorghum, or some such forage crop" to feed the only successful cash enterprise the ranch had at the moment—cattle.[52]

With all that occupied the Syndicate through the period, herd improvements continued to be a high priority. Cattle sales, until well into the next century, remained the primary method for keeping British investors at arm's length. These efforts blended the old with the new as the fine cattle they were raising in Texas still found their way "up the trail" to fatten on Montana grass. The Syndicate showed purebred cattle at the Chicago fair. In 1894 the XIT Ranch had about 1,500 purebred Hereford and Angus cattle. More than half were bulls, of which Hereford were the majority. Boyce warmed to the Angus cattle—"the blacks"— which got no argument from Findlay and somewhat bucked the trend of the old Texas outfits. It appears that the XIT managers began scaling back the Montana operation as early as 1893 and selling more young cattle to Corn Belt farmer-feeders. Continuing low prices and the Panic of 1893 had many Kansas farmers, once opposed to a flood of Texas cattle, eagerly seeking them out. F. W. Farwell wrote Findlay late in the summer of 1893 while Findlay was in Montana observing the season's beef roundup. To raise money, the letter instructed Findlay to have O. C. Cato ship everything "marketable, even the three year olds, if they are fat and in condition to bring good prices."[53]

Each ranch division in Texas became more specialized concerning the breed, grade, and character of the cattle it held. The XIT kept thousands of bulls in their own pasture except during the breeding season. Most calves were born in the spring, although a few might come into late summer. In addition to the "XIT" stamped on a calves' right ribs, additional brands on their jaws signified the division from which they came and their birth year. The XIT also used earmarks, particularly after the ranch began producing higher-grade cattle. Yearling steers were sent to Buffalo Springs and conditioned a year before being taken to Montana.

Calf crops on the XIT were massive. Any count under 30,000 represented failure. Montana's DHS ranch, founded by Granville Stuart and one of the best-known western operations, had spring calf numbers of about 5,000. Later, after Conrad Kohrs had bought the DHS, 8,500 was considered a large calf crop. Despite scaling back its Montana operation, in 1894 the ranch began sending a few cows— she-cattle, they were called—to Montana, and bulls in 1895. With breeding cattle to deal with, the Montana ranch work became more extensive and less seasonal in nature. After acquiring the Hatchet Ranch in 1895, Cato delegated responsibility for the two locations, assigning Rufe Morris at the XIT on Cedar Creek and Bob Fudge on the Hatchet as foremen.[54]

The XIT Ranch transformed both the property and those who worked on it in Texas and Montana in ways that belied the stereotypes and legends that arose later about both. Cowpunchers, if no longer the heart of the cattle business, at least still represented its soul. After all, it is their story that proved interesting to most American readers, not the course of capital and the actions of tycoons. These men, the laborers of the classical Old West, spurned the term "cowboy," preferring "cowhand" (or, simply, "hand"), "waddy," "cowpuncher," "vaquero," "buckaroo," or even "hoss stink." Into the 1880s, "cowboy" was mostly a synonym for a drunkard, outlaw, or cattle thief. Murdo Mackenzie, the manager of the famous Matador Ranch, left volumes of letters, memos, and reports, and he never called his employees cowboys. They were his hands, his men, or sometimes his cowhands.[55]

Buffalo Bill Cody first popularized the term "cowboy." Then dime novelists picked it up. Charles Russell painted many cowboys. The Owen Wister novel *The Virginian* further changed the term from one of derision to that of a heroic character, an image that persists. "Horse wrangler, cowhand, bronc breaker and rough string rider," wrote Fay E. Ward, who worked over forty years from Canada to Mexico. As explained in his "cowboy's manual": "The species 'cowhand' is no special breed of human; but he is a special type created by his special way of life. Perhaps, though, it does take a special kind of guy to choose to be a cowhand. The cowhand is possessed by a sort of pioneering spirit; he likes nature—that is, nature in the raw. He doesn't mind taking a chance, win or lose. He can take it on the chin and keep coming back for more."[56]

On the reality of being a cowboy versus the myth, Texas historian Paul H. Carlson writes:

The cowboy changed from rogue to hero. We have . . . sort of corrupted him in reverse. We have made him better than he was. Cowboys were not cattlemen; they were laborers, itinerant workers, seasonal employees. They stole cattle from their employers, and some of them took off at the first sign of trouble. The real cowboy was a common, nineteenth-century working stiff who was often illiterate, often unemployed, and often on the lowest rung of the community's socioeconomic hierarchy.[57]

Some aspects of the myth arguably have an element of truth. Cowpunchers were a distinct sort with a language and tradition all their own. For instance, one never inquired about a man's past unless he brought it up. A person never questioned the name a cowboy gave himself. These were useful practices for ranch managers who needed employees with skills, regardless of their past. But though it was a mark of distinction for a hand to have gone "up the trail," trailing cattle was only one aspect of their work. Of the thousands of cowboys working in the late nineteenth and early twentieth century, only a fraction could claim the honor. The XIT kept about 150 year-around employees, including bookkeepers, cooks, cowboys, wolfers, and windmill men. The numbers swelled in the spring and fall, but the variety remained. This was especially true in Montana, where manager Cato did not like keeping too many men through the winter if he could help it.[58]

It is also true that the cowboy of the American West was generally young, especially trail cowboys. The corporatization of the larger cattle outfits such as the XIT in the 1890s, however, lengthened a cowboy's career with opportunities to learn new skills or to be range and division bosses, or possibly even managers for absentee owners. And they were not all Texans. Texas certainly supplied its share of cowboys, but they came from everywhere. Maybe as many as 20 percent were born outside the United States. Much has been written about black, Hispanic, and even Indian cowboys, all of whom were part of the western cattle business. But fewer black or Hispanic cowboys could be found the farther north you went, such as Montana. Despite the many "buffalo soldiers"—African American soldiers led by white officers—who came west tasked with subduing Plains Indians, little evidence exists to prove that many stayed to become ranch hands there.[59]

Persistence and diversification could bring rewards for those who did stay. Pay for cow work was higher during the early 1870s, but by the mid-1880s, in Texas, cowboys were paid $25 per month. Trail crews received more—$30–$35. Cowboys in Montana generally made $35. Regular cowboys might become "top hands" and earn a bit more based on their skill and reputation. A trail or range boss could earn anywhere from $50 to $75 and a ranch manager at least $100, but some of the latter also became quite wealthy.[60]

The XIT Ranch, and the Syndicate that operated it, faced many challenges and underwent many changes in the 1890s. Having reached its zenith that turbulent decade, the next saw ranching operations steadily slow to a halt. The truth behind this undermines the mythical legacy of what was once the largest ranch in Texas and claimed to be the largest ranch in Montana. Perhaps an analogy can be found in the life of Alden Denby, who worked for the XIT in the 1890s. Born in North Carolina, he got to Texas as fast as he could and was anxious to be a "cowboy" like he read about in the popular dime novels of the period. Barely seventeen years of age, he joined the first XIT drive in 1890, working for trail boss William "Bill" Coats. Throughout Denby's time on the cattle trail, the drovers were mostly young, like him. He did not stick in Montana at first, but like many of the punchers who made their way north he eventually stayed. Denby punched cows for the XIT and others for the next twenty years until marriage bought him a homestead and farm in 1910. By then, the cattle drives had stopped, and the XIT was almost completely out of the livestock business. Sold in parcels to other ranchers, developers, and small farmers such as Denby, the great ranch ceased to exist in 1912.[61]

~~

CHAPTER 8

Closeout

No clear explanation emerges for the Capitol Syndicate's sudden suspension of its Montana operation in 1898. The company had focused on herd improvements throughout the decade. However, whether because of politics among the commission houses, buyers, and owners, or because the XIT cattle were inferior, evidence shows that XIT stock did not always market as well as neighbors' herds. The operation in Montana never enjoyed full support within the company. George Findlay and John V. Farwell certainly were its biggest supporters. Sen. Charles B. Farwell cared little for the range cattle business and favored selling young XIT cattle to feeders in Kansas and Iowa. In his opinion, the sooner he could be done with the whole business, including the land, the better. His offer to return the Capitol Reservation to Texas for a fair price in 1893 came partly in earnest. The senator never visited the XIT Ranch despite occasional visits to Texas. He and his brother, although they shared an office, stopped speaking to one another. No one seems to remember the reason, but for the rest of their lives they communicated only through an assistant who maintained a desk between them. An attempt at mending sibling differences may have been behind the decision to abandon the northern operation. By 1902 the XIT again began raising cattle in Montana. Herd numbers there soon equaled, even surpassed Texas numbers. As large land sales finally began, the herd capacity in Texas fell. Restarting the northern operation proved to be a last hurrah, however, because within a decade the XIT had sold its last cow.[1]

After 1897 stock formerly sent north instead went to farmer-feeders and feedlots in the Corn Belt states. The XIT Ranch established itself as a premier cattle breeder by 1901. The ranch raised Hereford cattle but focused on purebred Angus and high-quality hybrid, Angus-sired, whiteface cattle. Newspapers commonly reported on the ranch's breeding improvements. Market sales to commission houses dropped, presumably offset by sales and leases with the Corn Belt feeders. Compared to range cattle sales, the more complicated structure of the feedlot sales made calculating precise earnings more difficult. As more profitable land sales and demands for payments on overdue debentures increased from London, Capitol Freehold officers there seemed to not always understand how the operation worked. The Capitol Freehold secretary in London, H. Milner Willis, insisted on answers from Findlay regarding certain land transactions and the status of the company-backed hotel in Channing. The cattle were a concern as well: "I am cabling you to-day asking you to send us by first mail full explanations as to the reason for the large decrease in the cattle sales as compared with the previous years."[2]

The letter carried a copy of the company's London auditor's report. Findlay, replying in his typical direct style, allowed a somewhat frustrated tone to seep into his words, as if asking how many more times he must explain this. After reviewing the less concerning issues, Findlay turned to the cattle:

> It is true that the percentage of steers two-years of age and upwards has been diminishing. This is due to the change in our method of operations. We now expect to be able to sell our steers to feeders in the maize growing states every year as two year olds or younger, instead of maturing them ourselves. With this purpose in view we have closed out our Montana business, as you advised your shareholders we were doing in the 13th annual general meeting.[3]

The British investors had become particularly attentive to the herd book, questioning the counts and the Syndicate's lease obligations on the cattle. Stressing cost in responding to the suggestion of an "actual roundup," Findlay highlighted the sales efforts of the previous three years. The "natural result" of the change in method on the XIT required the elimination of the ranch's surplus steers. "Our sales . . . in 1898 and 1899 [included] practically all of our two year old steers as well as some yearling steers and steer calves from our Texas herd in addition to the usual number of matured Montana steers in the former year and a small amount in the latter year." Findlay told Willis how the herd book worked and explained that Willis's Montana herd number of 2,055 did not reflect yearly losses, but he admitted that despite "our cattle [being] all marketed from that country last year," a few others were likely to be gathered in the future by Cato or his neighbors. In any case, Findlay believed that the auditor's number for the XIT cattle-on-hand of 142,868 exceeded the actual count by about 10,000 head. Brushing off any requests for an actual count, Findlay, perhaps remembering his early attempts at a cattle count, told Willis, "We have some experience with such inspections and place very little reliance upon them."

Findlay continued his essay on the Syndicate's ranch business, particularly to emphasize the XIT's efforts at herd improvements. "We have so improved the quality of the cattle since 1892 that the value of the cattle now on the ranch would purchase probably one and one-quarter head of the cattle of the quality they were in 1892." Findlay closed his message to London with a summary of Chicago sales of XIT steers by Midwest feeders so far that year. The two- and three-year-olds averaged nearly 1,250 pounds and brought $5.56 per hundredweight—nearly $70 per head, which was high in a continued weak market.

He added a newspaper clipping, hoping to further soothe the nervous trans-Atlantic investors. He attributed it to the June 20, 1900, edition of the *Texas Stock and Farm Journal*. According to "a recent issue of the Kansas City Journal . . . it will be a surprise to many to know that the top cattle of the day were Panhandle, Tex. raised steers. H. W. Palmer of Spring Hill, Kan. had here sixty three X.I.T. steers . . . that were very smooth and fleshy . . . and would have been a credit to any state [at an] average 1516 pounds and [sold for] $5.50 [per hundred weight], the best price of the day." Indeed, the XIT's cattle had improved tremendously. Those mentioned were Herefords and shorthorns, but Findlay, of course, long advocated the Aberdeen-Angus.

Findlay wrote a detailed account of his experience with the "mulies," as the hornless, mostly black, cattle were often known, for the *Breeder's Gazette* in 1901. Updated and reprinted in the *Aberdeen-Angus Journal* in 1920, Findlay's account is a minutely detailed description of the XIT Ranch's efforts at "breeding up." In it, he showed that his personal interests were not always his greatest concern:

> It is unfortunately too true that there are at the present time too many in
> all the ranks striving to breed exterior color, which has no standing at all
> when the carcass is hanging for sale in that court of last resort, the cooler,

instead of striving to breed quality, which should be the first and last
desideratum with all raising cattle for beef. Breeders who consider color
everything are very much like Mr. Newly Rich, who, wanting to have
as good a library as anyone, ordered so many yards of any kind of books
bound in red and so many in black and so many in white.

Findlay sought to produce the finest, most profitable beef on the XIT. Although
deeply invested in the black cattle, the Scot focused his attention on the
dressed product. The last cattle sold by the XIT consisted solely of purebred
Aberdeen-Angus.[4]

Despite Findlay's strong defense of this change in the XIT's "method of operations," there may have been another reason for the withdrawal from Montana.
Anticipation of a large land sale may have prompted the company's pull-out. A
Miles City real estate firm, Tower and Collins, suggested to Findlay in early 1898
that they had a buyer for the entire Texas property, land, cattle, and improvements. "Last season," the firm wrote, "you did not want to sell the land and
improvements," the mystery partner wrote, reminding Findlay of earlier correspondence. "We have an inquiry for a large tract of land such as yours . . . and
we believe an effective deal can be made. . . . Kindly advise us your pleasure in
this matter." No large-scale sale took place then. It is not clear why the Syndicate
might have shunned a sale. In Texas, workers surveyed town and farm sites anticipating settlers soon arriving. The company anticipated increasing land sales and
was hard at work making that a reality. Texas land sales did accelerate quickly
after the turn of the century and soon overtook cattle ranching as the Syndicate's
prominent business.[5]

The Syndicate tried to favor the interests of settlers in their property. Despite
the tales of animosity between cattlemen and nesters, by the end of the century
most of the large operations had accepted, and even promoted, settlement. The
Panhandle Stock Association participated in promoting the region to the honest,
"law and order" man and encouraged at least some of these newcomers to join,
promising that its members received the organization's full protection whether
the owner of one cow or 10,000. Most of the big operations had incorporated as
cattle *and* land companies, after all. Still, on the XIT, despite their experimental
farms and aggressive promotions, the first major land sale did not come until 1901,
and then to another large cattle operator.[6]

In July 1901, George W. Littlefield, legendary cattle drover and founder of the LIT and LFD operations in Texas and New Mexico, bought nearly 236,000 acres of the Yellow Houses division of the XIT. Days later, J. E. and J. W. Rhea purchased nearly 50,000 acres from the Syndicate near Bovina. Charles E. Harding and William E. Halsell bought parcels of about 18,000 and 184,000 acres, respectively, in the Yellow Houses and Spring Lake divisions and along the north side of the Canadian River in the Rita Blanco and Minneosa pastures. Ewing L. Halsell and Thomas S. Hutton secured another 150,486 XIT acres there as well. Intent on retiring outstanding debentures, the Syndicate offered easy terms to the buyers, who paid an average of $2.50 per acre on about 640,000 acres of the Syndicate's finest land. The following year saw even more large land sales. William J. Tod and F. D. Wight, of the Prairie Cattle Company, an extensive operation in Colorado and New Mexico, purchased 136,560 acres of the Buffalo Springs division. The rejuvenated and expanding Matador gave $2.40 per acre cash for nearly 200,000 acres in the Alamositas division south of the Canadian. By the end of 1902, the Syndicate had sold over 1.1 million acres of its Panhandle holdings. Littlefield used his portions of the former XIT Ranch to subdivide into hundreds of farm plots sold by the Littlefield Lands Company.[7]

Although these earliest large sales, for the most part, were to other large ranching enterprises, the Syndicate remained committed to colonization, and promoters and railroads were anxious to head off a growing movement of farmers into Canada. The company contracted with George H. Heafford, Hardy W. Campbell, and Charles E. Wantland, who later formed the Farm Land Development Company, to sell large sections of the ranch in Parmer and Dallam counties at prices from $2.50 to $6.00 per acre, with generous payment terms. Agents and speculators including the W. P. Soash Land Company and the Western Land and Irrigation Company, purchased large blocks of land. Campbell established an experimental farm in Parmer County. In 1905 the Santa Fe Railroad commenced excursion trains into the area led by a Chicago-organized company, the South and West Land Company.[8]

The Syndicate was unhappy with the results of much of the activities of these agencies and retook control of their sales, focusing on new and eager waves of "actual settlers." In 1905 they appointed F. W. Wilsey as land commissioner to direct their sales efforts. The Montana operation had given the Syndicate many opportunities to become acquainted with Wilsey, a longtime employee of the

Northern Pacific Railway and most recently its assistant land commissioner. Wilsey returned to his railroad work in 1909, replaced by Hoyt King. Garret A. Dobbin followed until Wilsey once again took the position. Fay W. Clark was commissioner in 1916–17. Upon his departure the office remained vacant until Samuel H. Roberts, an attorney for the John V. Farwell Company in Chicago, relocated to Dalhart in 1926. Roberts served in the position for many years. Oversight of land transactions for some time fell to James D. Hamlin and William Boyce when they became the Syndicate's Texas legal counsel in 1900. Boyce's father was ranch manager A. G. Boyce. Hamlin Y. Overstreet, the nephew of James Hamlin, took over as the last resident representative of Capitol Reservation lands after Roberts was killed in an automobile accident in New Mexico in 1940. That company's liquidation in 1950 left only Capitol Freehold Land Trust as the ranch's legacy. Principally the descendants of John V. and Charles B. Farwell, the trust sold the last 20,000 acres of the once great XIT in 1963.[9]

The suspension of Montana operations by the Syndicate left some of its people stranded in the area. By the spring of 1891, Cato had earned the Syndicate's respect, along with a raise. A new agreement allowed him to bring his family north from Texas. The Catos maintained a home in Miles City, although they spent the summers primarily at the Hatchet. They sometimes returned to Texas during the winter. Newspapers recognized his children for academic achievement in Miles City schools. The family quickly became part of the local community. Cato eventually became a bank director in Miles City and then took a seat on the Board of Stock Commissioners. He later owned an ice company. Custer County voters elected him to serve as both a state representative and state senator.[10]

When his commitment to the XIT seemed over in 1898, Cato partnered with another early Miles City stockman, Eugene H. "Skew" Johnson, to run a few cattle on the former XIT range. Johnson was a stock agent for the railroad at the time Cato and the XIT arrived in Montana. He had come to Texas with his family in 1857 at the age of eleven. After mustering out of the Confederate Army in 1865 and not yet twenty years old, Johnson became one of the hundreds of young men joining the great cattle drives north. In the 1870s he was running his own herd in Wyoming. He and another partner, C. D. Graham, established Johnson and Graham Ranch on the Powder River in Montana in 1880. The men sold their operation in 1886, avoiding the effects of the coming winter. In 1889 the Northern Pacific hired Johnson as a stock agent.[11]

Livestock agents, no matter their employer, were always men with long experience in the cattle business. Most started out as regular cowboys. Some had run their own outfits. Most were greatly respected where they worked. Law enforcement was a common trade for unemployed and retired cowboys to try, too. In 1898, Cato, in something of a surprise finish, became the Custer County sheriff on his first attempt at an elected office. The *Weekly Yellowstone Journal* had announced that it was "safe to say Gibbs [was] reelected," referring to Cato's opponent, incumbent John Gibbs. Cato topped Gibbs by eleven votes (178–167). Cato was one of only two Democrats elected in the county that cycle. The position represented a powerful county job. In addition to a regular salary, the county reimbursed the sheriff for his court service, for serving warrants, and for hangings, should the occasion arise. Miles City could still uphold its cow town reputation, but it and Custer County rarely saw anything beyond petty crime and instances of moral turpitude. The sheriff's most important duty to the county included his reports on property tax information to the board of equalization.[12]

Cato's law enforcement career began excitedly before he officially took office. The sheriff's election in Dawson County returned Dominick Cavanaugh to his office. Before the well-liked officer could be sworn to his third term, on the night of December 23, 1898, someone bludgeoned Cavanaugh to death within fifty feet of his own home. While a coroner's jury sat to consider the evidence, county commissioners met to appoint Cavanaugh's replacement. Because Cavanaugh had no deputy at the time of his death, county officials in Glendive asked Cato to come over from Miles City to assist with the investigation. On December 27, county commissioners named Joseph C. Hurst as sheriff for the upcoming term. Hurst had been Cavanaugh's opponent in the late election. Mysteriously, the commissioners voted a second time on December 30, vacating the seat to appoint Alfred E. Aiken as the new sheriff.[13]

The mystery was exposed when, on January 10, 1899, the coroner's panel asked for an indictment of Hurst on murder charges. The inquest report came on January 20. At a preliminary hearing, authorities bound Hurst over to the state district court and scheduled trial on February 27. After picking a jury in the courtroom of Judge Charles H. Loud, the trial began on March 9. The jurors began deliberation

on March 20 and delivered a guilty verdict twenty-two hours later. Loud scheduled sentencing for the following day, March 22. Hurst heard the judge's order
that on May 19, 1899, at a private place established by Dawson County, he "be
executed according to the law, by hanging him . . . by the neck until he is dead."[14]

But Hurst did not hang that day. With affidavits from jurors in hand, his
defense attorneys pleaded to Judge Loud that jury errors warranted a new trial,
which Loud denied on June 12. Hurst waited a few more days for the Montana
supreme court to agree to review his case on June 17. The high court issued its
decision the following January, affirming the district court jury's decision and
upholding Loud's sentence. Appeals to the governor went unanswered, and Hurst
mounted the gallows on March 31, 1900, loudly professing his innocence in word
and letter. Letters left by the condemned man, even the last he wrote his wife,
proclaimed Cavanaugh's death a "mysterious murder" and that "Judge Loud has
done me a great wrong." According to the Catholic priest who attended Hurst on
the gallows, however, the man had confessed to him in his cell. Urged to do so
for authorities, Hurst replied, "damn them. They have thirsted for my blood and
I won't satisfy them to tell them."[15]

Custer County experienced at least two murders under Cato's watch, but the
former cattle boss experienced none with the same lurid details. Cato, while leading the XIT, developed close ties in neighboring Dawson County, where officials
sometimes sought his service. Reporting on stray XIT cattle gathered in the 1899
beef roundup to George Findlay—the two continued to correspond regularly—
Cato detailed the cattle theft charges he had made against a former XIT cowhand. Well known and well liked, Sam Eakers ran a Glendive slaughterhouse.
Along with the stock detective there, William Smith, a former Custer County
deputy sheriff, Cato went to Glendive, where he discovered the hides of several
butchered cattle along with eight that were still alive at the man's shop. Arrested,
Eakers posted a $1,000 bond before promptly skipping town.[16]

Cato oversaw a mostly peaceful administration, but the occasional case arose
to challenge him. The cattle on the Big Open shared the range with pronghorns,
whitetail and mule deer, bighorn sheep, wolves, and a few grizzly bears. Another
commercial animal got there before cattle: some of the biggest cattle ranches
raised sheep to augment their livestock sales. Some of the most respected men of
Custer and Dawson counties based their fortune on the woolies. The annual stock
growers meeting always corresponded with the wool growers meeting. Old-time

cowmen tolerated the beasts, if only out of respect for their owners. But the many Basque herders who solitarily cared for the sheep for months on end received no such respect from drunken or vengeful cowboys, nor did their charges. Cato received a phone call in 1899 from a ranch south of Miles City reporting an attack on a sheep herder and his flock. Attackers clubbed to death nearly two thousand sheep. According to the herder, eleven men with burlap masks attacked his camp and held him at gunpoint while the others took ash clubs to the corralled sheep. Only twelve of his band survived the slaughter. Cato visited the site, interviewed witnesses, and confiscated several bloody clubs. When pressed by the owner, a longtime Wyoming sheep raiser named R. R. Selway, Cato declared that he would arrest the first man to come to his office to claim one of the weapons. The occasional visitor would stop by Cato's office, examine the clubs and announce, "Well, you can't do anything to me. My club's not there." Cato's concern did not impress Selway, who offered a $2,000 reward for information. Many around town undoubtedly knew the perpetrators. Possibly Cato knew as well. In any case, the reward remained unclaimed. Years later, $15,000 was anonymously deposited in a Mile City bank in Selway's name. Selway refused the money. He later unsuccessfully pursued civil action against John B. Kendrick, the owner of the OW Ranch on the Tongue River. The only beneficiaries of the massacre seem to have been the nearby Cheyenne Indians, who scavenged the mutton for days in the aftermath.[17]

Cato completed his term as sheriff in December 1900. He wrote to Findlay in the spring of 1901 to say that he was a bit bored and that it was about time the XIT in Texas sent some cattle to Montana. Prices were low again, and a locoweed outbreak in the Texas Panhandle at the time also concerned Findlay and Boyce. Any grazing animal is susceptible to the neurotoxins in the plant found throughout the West. Not ever their first dining choice, the plant is most palatable to animals in the spring. If other feed is limited, by drought or overstocking, they will turn to it at other times of the year. Ingestion first causes depression and lethargy in the animals, and they stop eating. Sometimes, if removed from the locoweed's location, animals fully recover from the neurological damage, although they become more susceptible to the plant's effects. Pregnant cattle can abort their calves or produce calves with birth defects. If left too long, animals are unable to comprehend feeding, become emaciated, and, finally, starve themselves to death.[18]

Cato suggested that sending excessive or surplus stock north rather than selling at discounts to the corn feeders made more sense and could help their locoweed problem. He wrote that he could easily run two or three times more cattle than the "small bunch" he now managed. Findlay put the question to the Farwells. The brothers, still not speaking, disagreed about the matter. The "Senator is quite averse to moving anything north," Findlay wrote Boyce. John V. Farwell, along with his sons, who had by then assumed their own powerful positions in the organization, "appear to be strongly in favor of going north." Findlay found it a puzzling situation.[19]

The senator so opposed the plan that he lobbied Boyce in opposition to the matter. "As you know," C. B. Farwell wrote, "I have always been opposed to sending cattle to Montana, and am still opposed to it." Farwell argued that ranch confidant Henry Stevens, referring to the two million acres still held by Capitol Freehold, told him a place that could not support a cow on ten acres was not worth having. Offering his apologies for any trouble he may have caused between Boyce and Stevens, Farwell closed, writing, "If you have already decided to send [the cattle to Montana] I wish you could make up your mind [it] is not necessary." A written response from Boyce has not turned up, but within three months the Texas ranch manager had shipped 24,000 head of cattle to the Montana range.[20]

While Syndicate leaders pondered another change in their "method of operation," Cato set out on an adventure. The *Billings Gazette* reported in April that the former XIT range boss "was on his way to Alaska, where he will try his luck in the placer mines." The course of settlement had advanced in the decade since the XIT invaded Montana. This local notice mentioned that several Miles City residents had moved to the "northern country." Findlay called Montana the northern country. To some it was the West. To most, places like Montana and Alaska represented the American frontier. They challenged Frederick Jackson Turner's notions about the end of the westward movement.[21]

John V. Farwell prevailed in the Montana debate, but large land sales pushed the decision as much as the locoweed. Cattle in those parcels would have to be sold or placed elsewhere. Some of those cattle belonged to other owners leasing grazing land from the Syndicate. With cattle prices low at the time, it made good business sense to send them north for range seasoning while owners waited for improved prices. The Syndicate convinced lessees to send their cattle to Montana, too. By April 1902, Findlay had negotiated pacts with other lessees and with three different railroad companies to carry cattle to Montana. He informed one rail executive that they would commence shipping from Texas on May 20, 1902, and load fifty cars per day until completing the chore. Findlay estimated the job would require 450–500 cars in total.[22]

It is not at all clear why Findlay chose the circuitous route by which Texas cattle returned to the XIT's Montana range. The Syndicate stubbornly resisted using the FW&DC after their experiences in 1890. Most XIT cattle went north on the trail in the 1890s. By 1894, cattle could be shipped directly to Montana over Fort Worth & Denver City, Union Pacific, Northern Pacific, and Chicago, Burlington & Quincy tracks. The XIT used the route for smaller shipments of bulls and she-cattle during the period. This time, however, cattle of all different ages and varieties were loaded on Chicago, Rock Island & Pacific Railroad cars at the ranch's Middle-Water pasture and at Dalhart, the Texas Panhandle town incorporated only weeks earlier at the point where the Rock Island crosses the FW&DC road. The Rock Island carried the cattle to Council Bluffs, Iowa, where they transferred to the custody of the Chicago & North Western Railway. Routed from there to Oakes, North Dakota, the cattle then moved to the Northern Pacific for the final leg of the trip into Glendive and Fallon.[23]

Findlay joined Cato in Montana in May 1902 as Boyce commenced shipping cattle from Texas. Nearly 11,000 cattle unloaded from fifteen trains in Glendive and Fallon by the end of the month. Findlay acknowledged that four cars of "XIT cattle" arrived. Boyce continued to load cattle nearly to the end of June. Another 13,000 head went north—a total of about 24,000. The project nearly met doom when Montana's state veterinarian, Morton E. Knowles, threatened to bring charges against the Syndicate for bringing cattle into the state without federal health certificates. The whole dustup may have been a series of miscommunications and some underhandedness by a Montana competitor, Conrad Kohrs. Cato managed to get the first shipments across the river to the range before the Northern Pacific received orders to stop all XIT shipments until the certificates were produced.[24]

Capitol Freehold put more effort and cattle than ever into the Montana operation. Limited cow/calf operations undertaken in 1895 also recommenced. Local celebrity and photographer Evelyn Cameron recorded in one of her many diary entries on September 22, 1903, that during an outing she had passed many "fine shaped XIT cattle [of the] Angus blood." By 1908, two-thirds of all XIT cattle

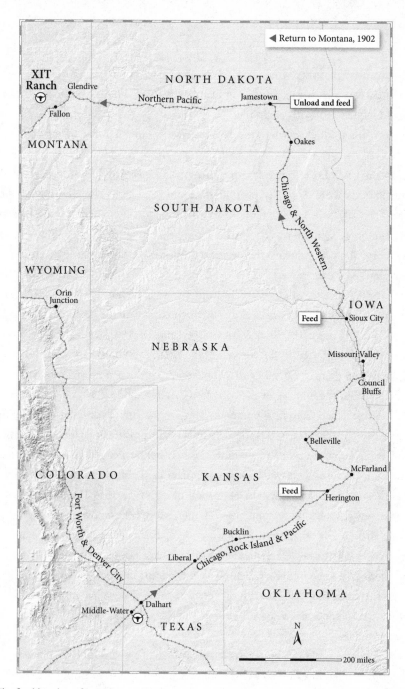

The final big drive from Texas to Montana, 1902. Overall, a total of 24,000 cattle loaded onto Chicago, Rock Island & Pacific Railroad cars at Middle-Water and Dalhart and traveled to Council Bluffs, Iowa. Then a stretch on the Chicago & North Western Railway took them to Oakes, North Dakota, and from there the Northern Pacific delivered them to Glendive and Fallon.

sales came from the Montana operation. The other third divided nearly equally to market sales and sales to feeders and other ranches.[25]

Despite the land sales and herd improvements, British creditors remained mostly disappointed in their investments. Many of those holding the long-matured debentures sold by Capitol Freehold from 1885 to 1889 chose to return them at discounts, some accepting as little as one-quarter the bond's par value. A buyback campaign launched in 1903 failed to convince all their investors to sell. The terms for many of the land deals did not provide large upfront payments. Regarding the buyback plan, a John V. Farwell Company employee in Liverpool, Jonathon Donnelly, wrote to John V. Farwell Jr. that "in no single instance have I received an offer that would warrant cabling you." Donnelly offered Farwell little confidence that the program would be a success. Many of the holders were "moneyed people, & are not inclined to part with their holdings unless at a figure that would pay them for their waiting." Thus, the cattle operation remained necessary for providing ready capital that would appease the thinning group of foreign investors.[26]

The XIT's return to Montana in 1902 became even more critical and central to the cattle operation as the Texas ranch began to look increasingly like a real estate conglomerate. Although Boyce had become an excellent "land man" and undoubtedly was making a lot of money, he decided to part ways with the company as the Texas cattle operation wound down. The company had sent a few cows to Montana in 1895 to establish a breeding program. The breeding operation there resumed after the return in 1902. Disenchanted with real estate and with little ranching left to do in Texas, Boyce retired in 1905. The company brought on F. W. Wilsey, the former assistant land commissioner for the Northern Pacific Railway, to serve as Capitol Freehold's land commissioner in Texas. H. S. Boice and R. L. "Bob" Duke at the same time assumed Boyce's ranch duties. The great XIT manager died in the lobby of a Fort Worth hotel, gunned down by the cuckolded husband of his son's paramour. The killer then assassinated the home-breaking son on an Amarillo street. Three Texas juries refused murder charges against the Boyces' confessed killer. The decision acknowledged, for Texans, the role a man's honor played in his actions.[27]

Amos Babcock became the first of the original primary Syndicate members to die, in 1899. His widow, Margaret, fought a protracted ownership battle against the Farwell's and other members of Capitol Freehold. The lawsuit, initially commenced by Babcock against the Farwells in 1892, asked originally for $750,000. The suit raged in courts in Texas and Illinois for two decades. At one point, representatives of the former partner's estate obtained a court order to take ownership of the Texas ranch property. Boyce met them with a loaded rifle at the door of the company's Channing headquarters. His threat to kill the first person there who tried to seize any ranch property or papers forced a pause in their actions. A countersuit by the Syndicate quickly brought a court order rescinding the seizure. Although the case was resolved in Babcock's favor a decade later, a Farwell appeal had it set aside in 1914. A related suit, called a "friendly," in 1916 awarded Capitol Freehold $1,788,550. This officially concluded the Syndicate's (Farwell heirs') relationship to their British investors.[28]

Charles Farwell and Abner Taylor both died in 1903. Taylor by then had been all but eliminated from Syndicate affairs. The end for the company's operation in Montana came in the same way the cattle business there failed in the 1880s—fickle weather. The winter of 1906–7 in Montana left similar results to the Big Die-Up two decades earlier—some say worse. It was the third killer winter of the new century. Bad winters in 1902–3 and 1904–5 had caused many deaths among the cattle there. The company settled dozens of losses claimed by lessees of cattle Cato grazed on the northern ranch. After the bad winter of 1906–7 and John V. Farwell's death in 1908, the XIT again began closing out its Montana operation. Company heirs by that time showed little interest in the cattle business.[29]

Another legendary Montana ranch, the LU Bar, by then a Swift Packing Company partnership with L. W. Stacy managing, joined the XIT in closing out for good there the same year. The LU Bar, for many years led by H. R. Phillips, always had worked closely with the XIT men. In 1892, Phillips had partnered with Cato and Seth Mabry to contract the exclusive use of the Fallon ferry on the Yellowstone for the three outfits' use during shipping season in the fall. The Big Open hosted extensive homesteading in the first decade of the new century. An old fence law banning public land enclosures began receiving renewed enforcement. The big cattle operations also faced problems other than homesteaders. Sheep became part of the formula for many of the dwindling big outfits. Fences and fields broke up the landscape into a too-crowded range. In 1909, Cato sold off the last large number of XIT cattle in Montana—about 9,500 steers and 6,000 spayed heifers, cows, and bulls. The XIT sold what little land it owned in Montana, mostly to the men and their families who had worked and run the operation for so many years. The Texas Panhandle was settling up, too, and the Syndicate finally found more profit in land than cattle. Few found great wealth in cattle ranching, but most of the XIT's most enduring associates left the ranch better off financially than when they came.[30]

The company redeemed all its debentures by the end of 1909. The Syndicate—mostly the sons and other relatives of John V. Farwell by this time—reclaimed the company's shares from remaining British stockholders in 1915. The company, rebranded as Capitol Reservation Lands, continued actively leasing and selling land into the early 1940s. Farwell family heirs sold the last of their Capitol Reservation property in 1963. Many people claiming to have heard of the ranch seem surprised to learn that it has not existed for more than one hundred years. The once great enterprise left a lasting mark on historical memory, although time burnished those memories.[31]

The imperial ranch closed out the golden age of cattle ranching. Some of the big outfits hung on, diversified into farming and sheep raising; most of those today specialize in game ranching of one sort or another—upland birds, deer, antelope. The laws of the United States contributed the primary blow to the reign of ranches like the XIT. The Homestead Act of 1862 and its successors initially enacted land distribution measures based on the habits of the early settlers of the eastern woodlands west to the Mississippi River. Those laws did not fit the ecology of the Great Plains. Amended several times to address the features of an arid country, the plan for peopling Jefferson's empire of liberty never fit the needs of range cattle operators or, for that matter, farmers on the Great Plains.[32]

The Syndicate sold the last of their Texas cattle and leased the last of their pasturage to Shelton & Trigg in 1912. Reporting the company's final cattle sales in 1912, the ranch's last manager, Bob Duke, included nearly five hundred steers, spayed heifers, and cows sold from the Montana ranges. It seems more than likely that in such a vast country an X-branded steer, cow, or wily bull may have eluded roundups for years, surviving into old age on rich grass and good water.[33]

So, what does all this say of a deal that stirred—continues to stir—controversy in Texas? Delegates at the Texas constitutional convention of 1875 endorsed an idea they hoped would provide the state a suitable house of government. At the same time, they hoped to provide a means by which the state lands could be further developed without the extensive involvement of the state government itself. Not really knowing what they promised, delegates viewed Texas as land rich. Optimistic Texans, glad to have Reconstruction behind them, were anxious to catch up with the rest of the country. By the time delegates allocated three million Texas acres in exchange for the construction of the new capitol in Austin, Ben Munson had already laid his eyes on the Panhandle and developed a plan for its occupation—by cattlemen. He and his partner, Jot Gunter, worked that plan for five years prior to the definition of the boundaries of what became the XIT Ranch.

Although speaking specifically of the western mining industry, William G. Robbins described all the exploitive efforts of the West when he wrote,

> To a significant degree, then, the emerging western industrial program was an extension of capitalist relations in eastern North America and in Europe where surpluses had accumulated. [This] did not come about as a natural consequence of evolutionary processes; rather, human agency effected the historical transformation of the West through conscious and deliberate decisions made in the capitalist marketplace. Clearly the agents of eastern U.S. and European capital . . . provided the vital ingredients driving . . . exploitation in the region.[34]

By 1884 the leaders of the country's beef business gathered in national congress to demand recognition by the government of their role in the industrial dynamism of the country. They compared themselves to the powerhouses of the Gilded Age. The cattlemen, part of a network of finance and commerce permeating a global economy, resisted inclusion in a beef trust controlled by a combine of the railroads and meat packers.[35]

The XIT Ranch, a tool of capitalism, fit the patterns of Gilded Age industry. The Capitol Syndicate extended its financial resources over long distances to exert control of its territorial holdings and to influence the control and exploitation of resources there. The ranch practiced exclusionary tactics to impose company sovereignty on the places its cattle roamed. The Syndicate determined who and for what purpose their land reserves served. The XIT Ranch, for a moment of history, stood among the greatest ranches of America's beef empire.

In 1882, when the Syndicate undertook the Texas capitol project, none of the men had ever looked upon the land that became the XIT Ranch. They made their decision based on Nimrod Norton's report and, no doubt, the general hype surrounding the prospect of owning land out west. The capitol project was cost-ing real money—mostly the Farwells'. The Syndicate hoped to turn a profit from the land quickly. For the Farwells, Taylor, and Babcock, as wealthy, politically connected individuals with other interests, the capitol contract was just another opportunity for them to make money.

The Syndicate's actions often seem indicative of the recklessness of wealth characterizing the Gilded Age. These men failed to turn the quick profit hoped for. John V. Farwell managed to sell gleaming-eyed investors, mostly in England, on the idea of operating a cattle ranch until land sale prospects improved. Under Farwell's leadership the XIT became part of an enterprise of finance and com-merce, a leading and formidable competitor in the global beef marketplace. It returned little to British investors. The XIT ultimately represented the vision of John V. Farwell. His death really ended the dream—or the mirage. No one stepped forward to take his place. As a cattle ranch, its legend outlasted the XIT's twenty-eight years of operation.

The ranching businesses ended for the XIT in 1912. Its role in the Texas Pan-handle did not. By 1920, hundreds of small farms dotted the former XIT pastures. Wheat, in heavy demand during World War I, began to lose its value after the war. Dry weather in 1917–20 resulted in low production but stabler grain prices. Rain returned to the Great Plains for the first few years of the twenties, but grain prices did not recover. Donald Worster's groundbreaking *Dust Bowl* and journal-ist Tim Egan's terrifying *Worst Hard Times* illustrate the depth of what came next. Both works deliver an indictment of the land management practices in Texas and throughout the Great Plains at the time as well as the environmental, social, and practical effects brought about by those actions. Egan is not troubled by casting considerable blame on Texas and the operators of the XIT Ranch for their role in establishing a human environment unprepared for the long-term natural condi-tions the Great Plains had to offer.[36]

The huge tract was perfect for the nutritious native bunch grasses that had supported eons of migrating bison. Its aridness and weather patterns initially kept permanent settlement from the Panhandle. Within ten years of the introduction of domestic cattle, overgrazing and persistent drought had induced irreparable damage to the landscape. The windmill offered large-scale livestock operations their only hope of success. Indian lands in present-day Oklahoma provided some relief, but calls for the elimination of grazing leases for non-Indian stock growers began to draw political support, particularly from the cattle feeders on the central plains. Both presidents Grover Cleveland and Benjamin Harrison ordered white cattlemen out of Indian Territory and off other reservations in the West—not that it worked.[37]

The XIT Ranch and the capitol project impacted Texas and its people. A project intended to provide the Lone Star State with a big new capitol building became much larger than that, affecting lives across the United States and even across the Atlantic Ocean. New sources of revenue were uncovered, railroads expanded, new towns grew, employment opportunities expanded. The complex transaction undertaken by Texas leaders and the Illinois capitalists provided a legacy of history. The memory of the XIT continues to echo today. Businesses named for the ranch dot the roadside heading northwest out of Lubbock toward the old Yellow Houses division. An August weekend in Dalhart features XIT Days, the region's biggest celebration of the year. In Wyoming and Montana, reminders of the XIT appear at roadside attractions, in area museums, and on rural road signs. The brief ranch operation influenced settlement and land use where it operated. The XIT left a mark on local law enforcement, politics, ranching and farming, and, of course, the landscape that supported its thousands of cattle. A dozen or more communities in Texas and Montana pay homage to the role the XIT played in their past. No less significant are the individuals involved with the XIT—the cowboys, cooks, wranglers, windmill men, and wolfers who became inextricable from the social, cultural, and political fabric formed around the ranch in Texas and Montana.

Focusing solely on the XIT's on-the-ground operations across the western plains obscures a larger story. Along with cowboys, cooks, and trail bosses, the XIT Ranch employed clerks, accountants, lawyers, and managers—men such as George Findlay—overseen by officers and a board of accomplished international capitalists. The ranch's associates, owners, and employees engaged in nearly every level of government service. This Gilded Age model profoundly shaped cattle ranching and agriculture in the twentieth-century American West.

Notes

ABBREVIATIONS

CFLIC Proceedings	Capitol Freehold Land and Investment Company Limited Proceedings
DBCAH	Dolph Briscoe Center for American History
MHS	Montana Historical Society
NSHL	Nita Stewart Haley Memorial Library
PPHM	Panhandle-Plains Historical Museum
TBC	Taylor, Babcock & Company
TSLA	Texas State Library and Archives
TXGLO	Texas General Land Office

CHAPTER 1. COWBOYS AND CAPITALISTS

1. Sandoz, *Cattlemen*, 300; Graham, "Investment Boom," 442; Marx and Hobsbawm, *Precapitalist Economic Formations*, 119; Bobrow-Strain, "Logics of Cattle–Capital," 778.

2. Brands, *American Colossus*, 201.

3. Cronon, *Nature's Metropolis*, 252; Garland, *Jason Edwards*, 61, 142; Robbins, *Colony and Empire*, 21. The concept of an "American Dream" was not formalized until James Thurlow Adams's *The Epic of America* in 1931, but the ingredients of it have long been part of the origins story Americans and others believe, if not in their head at least in their heart. See Clark, "In Search of the American Dream"; Adams, *Epic of America*; Adams and Schneiderman, *Epic of America*, ix–xviii; see also Cullen, *American Dream;* Nevins, *James Truslow Adams*.

4. *Amarillo News-Globe*, August 14, 1938, sect. E, 14; Nordyke, *Cattle Empire*, 74–77, 188–92.

5. Haley, *XIT Ranch*, 5; Woods, *British Gentlemen*, 119; Atherton, *Cattle Kings*, 214–15; Brayer, "Influence of British Capitol." For interpretations of the global aspects of the relationship of capitalism and settler societies, see Belich, *Replenishing the Earth*, 8, 57–59, 337–39; Denoon, *Settler Capitalism*, 211–12.

6. Haley, *XIT Ranch*, 52–55; Nordyke, *Cattle Empire*, 190; State of Texas, *Biennial Report* (1886), 195–205. The figure for the building's comparative cost today lies somewhere

between $91 million and $4 billion; see Samuel H. Williamson, "Seven Ways to Compute the Relative Value of a U.S. Dollar Amount, 1774 to present," *Measuring Worth*, 2017, www .measuringworth.com/uscompare. An online calculator puts the payment and tax values today at approximately $135,000,000 and $560,000, respectively.

7. Skaggs, *Cattle-Trailing Industry*, 100; Atherton, *Cattle Kings*, 230–40; Carter et al., "Table Da968–982."

8. Weston, "Cowboy Western," 54.

9. Robbins, *Colony and Empire*, 182.

10. Kens, "Wide Open Spaces?" 177–79. For more on the role of the U.S. Army in opening the cattle ranges of the West, see Rockwell, *U.S. Army in Frontier Montana*; Smith, *U.S. Army and the Texas Frontier Economy*.

11. White, *"It's Your Misfortune,"* 270–71.

12. Haley, *Charles Goodnight*, 325; Osgood, *Day of the Cattleman*, 182–90.

13. *New York Times*, February 22, 1881. See Haley, *Charles Goodnight*, 383–85, for a sense of the stock raisers' thoughts about small farmers and ranchers.

14. Duke and Frantz, *6,000 Miles*, 151; *Amarillo News-Globe*, August 14, 1938; Howard, *Montana*, 164–65; Wollaston, *Homesteading*, 63; "History of Custer County [Winter of 1906–1907]," U.S. Work Projects Administration, Montana Writers Program Records, 1939–1941, Microfilm 250, Reel 18, Montana Historical Society, Helena, MT [hereafter MHS]; Hartmann, "'Our Snow Covered Trail.'"

15. Clay, *My Life*, 328–29; Cronon, *Nature's Metropolis*, 218–24; Haley, *XIT Ranch*, 84–97; Skaggs, *Prime Cut*, 65. See also Carter, Evans, and Yeo, *Cowboys, Ranchers and the Cattle Business*; Foran, *Trails and Trials*.

16. Brown and Schmitt, *Trail Driving Days*, 183.

17. MacMillan, "Gilded Age"; Ball, "Historical Overview of Beef Production," 3; Brisbin, *Beef Bonanza*.

18. Ball, "Historical Overview of Beef Production," 3.

19. Nordyke, *Cattle Empire*. I have borrowed the term "fabulous" from Lewis Nordyke's subtitle, "The Fabulous Story of the 3,000,000 Acre XIT."

20. Capitalism fed and prospered on the exploitable land and people of the West. Resented at the time for the often heavy-handed tactics of gargantuan operations of any sort in the American West—cattle, mining, agriculture, timber—over time, the memories of participants, passed down, exaggerated, and romanticized became the story of the West. The actions of the exploiters were recast with that of the exploited, iconizing the fearless miner, the brawny lumberjack, and the rugged cowboy and masking the entrenchment of the global marketplace into those places from which it draws its raw materials. Ironically, both exploited and exploiter are enriched by a mythical West—the capitalist, economically; the miner, cowboy, and lumberjack, culturally. An introduction to the idea of "cultural capital" can be found in Pierre Bourdieu, "The Forms of Capital," in Richardson, *Handbook*, 241–58.

21. Haley, *XIT Ranch*, 80, 214–16; Nordyke, *Cattle Empire*, 188–92, 209–24. On the reputation of the XIT today, see, for example, Cates, *XIT Ranch*. Extensive information on the principals of the Capitol Syndicate is hard to come by and generally gleaned from an array of resources. See, for instance, Ferry, *Reminiscences of John V. Farwell*; Farwell, *Some Recollections*

of John V. Farwell; Jessica Raynor, "John V. Farwell," *Amarillo Globe-News*, May 19, 2000; *Chicago Tribune*, September 9, 1894; *New York Daily Tribune*, September 24, 1903; Arthur H. Miller, "Charles B. Farwell," Lake Forest College Library Archives and Special Collections, Lake Forest, IL; "Amos Charles Babcock," *Cook County, Illinois, Death Index, 1878–1922* (Provo, UT: Ancestry.com, 2011); Andreas, *History of Chicago*, 2:497 (see Special Index, vols. 2–3, for extensive listings on Taylor and the Farwell brothers).

22. Rathjen, *Texas Panhandle Frontier*, 241–42.

23. Haley, *XIT Ranch*, 80–81.

24. West, *Contested Plains*, 325.

25. West, *Contested Plains*, 244–49, 325–37. On the region of the "northern" ranges, see Schneiders, *Big Sky Rivers*.

26. Robbins, *Colony and Empire*, xii; Crosby, *Columbian Exchange*, 219, 113, 109; Eliza Barclay, "Americans Should Eat Less Meat, but They're Eating More and More," updated October 1, 2016, www.vox.com/2016/8/18/12248226/eat-less-meat-campaign-fail.

27. Ostler, *Plains Sioux*, 46; White, *"It's Your Misfortune,"* 94–117.

28. Dr. William Green, conversation with author, March 12, 2014; Nordyke, *Cattle Empire*, 220; *Austin Weekly Statesman*, April 23, 1891.

CHAPTER 2.   CROOKED LINES

1. *Joint Resolution for Annexing Texas to the United States,* Statutes at Large of the United States, 5 Stat. 797 (8), 28th Cong., 2nd sess. (March 1, 1845); *Joint Resolution for the Admission of the State of Texas into the Union,* Statutes at Large of the United States, 9 Stat. 108 (1), 29th Cong., 1st sess. (December 29, 1845); Campbell, *Gone to Texas*, 185; Kens, "Wide Open Spaces?," 161–67; McKay, *Debates*, 133, 211, 241–45, 289, 418; Miller, *Public Lands of Texas*, 232–43; Nordyke, *Cattle Empire*, 19–22; Rathjen, "Texas State House," 433–34; Texas, 1876 Constitution, Article XVI (General Provisions), Section 57: "Three millions acres of the public domain are hereby appropriated and set apart for the purpose of erecting a new State Capitol and other necessary public building at the seat of government, said lands to be sold under the direction of the Legislature; and the Legislature shall pass suitable laws to carry this section into effect."

2. McKay, *Debates* 93, 120–33; McKay, "Making the Texas Constitution," 117; Moneyhon, *Texas after the Civil War*, 204–5; Miller, *Public Lands of Texas*, 121, 137–41; Pacific Railway Act of July 1, 1862, Ch. 120, 12 Stat. 489 (sec. 3, p. 492). The Texas General Land Office (hereafter TXGLO) has commissioned several studies of itself. TXGLO is an exceptional resource with exhaustive records, and Miller's studies represent the most thorough and coherent analyses of Texas's land policies to date. According to him, 4,651,076 acres were sold by the state for between $0.50 and $1.00 per acre. See also Hazel, *Public Land Laws of Texas;* Miller, *Bounty and Donation Land Grants.* On Texas's governors, see State of Texas, *Texas State Library and Archives Commission,* "Governors of Texas, 1846–Present," www.tsl.texas.gov/ref/abouttx/governors.html. On "beef bonanza," see Brisbin, *Beef Bonanza.*

3. Miller, *Public Lands of Texas*, 121, 137–41, 98–102; Kens, "Wide Open Spaces?," 167; McKay, "Making the Texas Constitution," 114; TXGLO, "Categories of Land Grants in Texas," www.glo.texas.gov/history/archives/forms/files/categories-of-land-grants.pdf;

TXGLO, "History of Texas Public Lands," rev. January 2015, www.glo.texas.gov/history /archives/forms/files/history-of-texas-public-lands.pdf. In total, forty-three companies got 32,153,878 acres of Texas public land in three decades; see Roger A. Griffin, "Land Grants for Internal Improvements," *Handbook of Texas Online*, June 15, 2010, https:// tshaonline.org/handbook/online/articles/mnl04. See also chapter 7 of this work for a fuller explanation of these events.

4. Miller, *Public Lands of Texas*, 98–102, 121, 137–41; Kens, "Wide Open Spaces?," 167; McKay, "Making the Texas Constitution," 114; TXGLO, "Categories of Land Grants"; TXGLO, "History of Texas Public Lands," rev. March 2018, www.glo.texas.gov/history /archives/forms/files/history-of-texas-public-lands.pdf.

5. Miller, *Public Lands of Texas*, 62; Alice Gray Upchurch, "Fifty Cent Act," *Handbook of Texas Online*, June 12, 2019, www.tshaonline.org/handbook/online/articles/mlf01; Kens, "Wide Open Spaces?," 162.

6. Texas Senate, *Journal of the Senate of Texas*, 32; Miller, *Public Lands of Texas*, 252.

7. Claude Elliott, "Ireland, John," *Handbook of Texas Online*, mod. February 24, 2016, www.tshaonline.org/handbook/online/articles/fir01.

8. Kens, "Wide Open Spaces?," 167; Miller, *Public Lands of Texas*, 51–53.

9. Ely, *Where the West Begins*, 3–34.

10. Ralph A. Smith, "Grange," *Handbook of Texas Online*, mod. September 4, 2013, www .tshaonline.org/handbook/ online/articles/aag0; Campbell, *Grass-Roots Reconstruction*, 26, 223–25; Moneyhon, *Texas after the Civil War*, 199–202. Among the ninety delegates to the 1875 Texas constitutional convention, at least forty were members of the Grange. See Kens, "Wide Open Spaces?," 160.

11. McKay, "Making of the Texas Constitution," 71, 95–101, 111.

12. Haley, *XIT Ranch*, 5–6, 50–51.

13. Haley, *XIT Ranch*, 50. On the capitol itself, see, for example, Texas State Historical Association, *Texas State Capitol*, especiallyWilliam Elton Green, "A Question of Great Delicacy: The Texas Capitol Competition," 33–43; Paul Goeldner, "The Designing Architect: Elijah E. Myers," 47. See also Rathjen, "Texas State House"; Greer, "Building of the Texas State Capitol; Mabry, "Capitol Context"; Miller, "Cattle Capitol"; State of Texas, *Biennial Report* (1883), 4; McKay, "Making the Texas Constitution," 168–84, 170; McKay, *Debates*, 459; Judd and Hall, *Texas Constitution Explained*.

14. Haley, *XIT Ranch*, 38–48; Robertson and Robertson, *Panhandle Pilgrimage*, 149–51. The latter source can be found on the *Portal to Texas History*, https://texashistory.unt.edu/ark: /67531/metapth225495.

15. Haley, *Charles Goodnight*, 280; Hagan, *Charles Goodnight*, 25–26; Rathjen, *Texas Panhandle Frontier*, 101–3, 228–38.

16. Rose Englutt, "From the Denison *Daily News*, May 5, 1875," *Denison* (TX) *Herald*, December 23, 1992; George Flournoy et al., in U.S. Congress. House. Select Committee on the Texas Frontier Troubles, *Depredations on the Texas Frontier*, 1–5.

17. Hunter, "Captain Arrington's Expedition"; H. Allen Anderson, "Arrington, George Washington," *Handbook of Texas Online*, mod. October 8, 2018, www.tshaonline.org /handbook/online/articles/far20.

18. Wayne Gard, "Fence Cutting," *Handbook of Texas Online*, mod. September 27, 2019, www.tshaonline.org/handbook/online/articles/auf01; Joseph and Smith, *Ten Million Acres*, 74; Haley, *XIT Ranch*, 55; Liu, *Barbed Wire*, 55–61.

19. Joseph and Smith, *Ten Million Acres*, 74; Gunter, "Jot Gunter." The exploits of Gunter and Munson in Texas land development are mostly untold. Their many Texas land grants include thousands of Panhandle acres. The two remained powerful and respected in Texas throughout their lives. The Munson family continues as an influential presence in North Texas. The iconic Gunter Hotel in San Antonio is named for the lawyer, land speculator, and businessman. Upon news of Gunter's death in 1907, the Texas governor ordered flags lowered to half-staff.

20. *Sherman* (TX) *Herald Democrat*, October 21, 2001. The land certificates could be for as much as 4,428 acres—a league. More likely these were from 320- to 1,280-acre grants.

21. Joseph and Smith, *Ten Million Acres*, 70–71; Miller, *Public Lands of Texas*, 104; TXGLO, search Grantee or Patentee=Gunter and Munson, for the thousands of land grants linked to the pair, https://s3.glo.texas.gov/glo/history/archives/land-grants/index.cfm (accessed February 8, 2020).

22. Miller, *Public Lands of Texas*, 197; *New York Times*, October 20, 1877; *Princeton*, (MN) *Union*, October 24, 1877.

23. TXGLO, "Categories of Land Grants."

24. Kens, "Wide Open Spaces?," 161–62; Hazel, *Public Land Laws of Texas*, 23–45; Miller, *Public Lands of Texas*, 55; Haley, *Charles Goodnight*, 302–6; TXGLO, "Texas General Land Office Land Grant Search," https://s3.glo.texas.gov/glo/history/archives/land-grants/index.cfm.

25. For an example of Texas land scrip, see TXGLO, "Land Grant Search" (search File Number 27658), www.glo.texas.gov/ncu/SCANDOCS/archives_webfiles/arcmaps/webfiles /landgrants/PDFs/8/4/7/847665.pdf. This railroad land scrip (640 acres) shows that it was purchased by Gunter and Munson for $100; that is $0.16 per acre. This quite likely is within the general bounds of the Capitol Reservation.

26. Kens, "Wide Open Spaces?," 167–73; Rathjen, *Texas Panhandle Frontier*, 234; Haley, *Charles Goodnight*, 282–84; Hagan, *Charles Goodnight*, 27–33; Malin, *Grassland of North America*, 99–101.

27. Joseph and Smith, *Ten Million Acres*, 70; Miller, *Public Lands of Texas*, 62; Graham, "Investment Boom," 442.

28. Rathjen, *Panhandle Frontier*, 167; Sullivan, *LS Brand*, 23–25; Donald F. Schofield, "Lee, William McDole," *Handbook of Texas Online*, mod. November 12, 2019, www.tshaonline.org /handbook/online/articles/fle54.

29. Sullivan, *LS Brand*, 30; Schofield, *Indians, Cattle, Ships, and Oil*, 52–53; Donald F. Schofield, "LS Ranch," *Handbook of Texas Online*, December 5, 2019, www.tshaonline.org /handbook/online/articles/apl02; H. Allen Anderson, "LE Ranch," *Handbook of Texas Online*, June 15, 2010, www.tshaonline.org/handbook/online/articles/apl10.

30. Land Records, Land, Taxes, Record of 1894–1895; Abner Taylor to A[lbert] E. Reynolds, Denver, July 12, 1889, XIT Papers, Panhandle-Plains Historical Museum, Canyon, TX [hereafter PPHM]. C. F. Reynolds wrote Findlay on June 17 to arrange to "remove all stock from the strip along the river and adjust . . . fences." C[harles]. F. Reynolds to Findlay, June 17,

1889, J. Evetts Haley Collection IV-A-1, Nita Stewart Haley Memorial Library, Midland, TX [hereafter NSHL].

31. Rathjen, *Panhandle Frontier*, 240–41; Blodgett, *Land of Bright Promise*, 1, 43; Woods, *British Gentlemen*, 23–25, 117–22; Clay, *My Life on the Range*, 129–39; Haley, *XIT Ranch*, 40–48; Graham, "Investment Boom." For more insights on the British investment phenomenon, see Belich, *Replenishing the Earth*, 119–20, 208. For more on Colorado and the Front Range, see Smith, *Rocky Mountain West*.

32. State of Texas, *Biennial Report* (1883), 60–67; Nordyke, *Cattle Empire*, 256; Haley, *XIT Ranch*, 50–51; J.T. Munson, Tone & Munson Real Estate, to Governor O. M. Roberts, May 8, 1879; Roberts to General Walter P. Lane, July 10, 1879, Records of the Capitol Building Commission, Texas State Library and Archives, Austin, TX [hereafter TSLA]. A nearly identical letter of appointment and instruction is transcribed in the *Biennial Report* (1883), 7, and addressed to Nimrod L. Norton. General Lane, a noted participant in the Texas Revolution, the Mexican War, and for the Confederacy during the Civil War, is not mentioned in any other official documents regarding the capitol, and his role in this matter remains unclear. Advertisements for bids were widely published in April 1879 under the title "Advertisement for Bids to Survey the Land to Build the Capitol of Texas"; see Records of the Commission, TSLA. See also Lucie C. Price, "Norton, Nimrod Lindsay," *Handbook of Texas Online*, June 15, 2010, www.tshaonline.org/handbook/online/articles/fno13.

33. Joseph and Smith, *Ten Million Acres*, 69. For J.T. Munson land patents, see TXGLO, "Land Grant Search," Patentee = Munson, J T or Munson, Joseph, https://s3.glo.texas.gov/glo/history/archives/land-grants/index.cfm.

34. Munson to Roberts, May 8, 1879, Records of the Capitol Building Commission, TSLA.

35. Mabry, "Early Surveying," 245; State of Texas, *Biennial Report* (1883), 48, 50; Moore et al., *Temporary Capitol of Texas*, 14; Mabry, "Capitol Context," 96. See also Nolan, *Tascosa*.

36. Haley, *XIT Ranch*, 50–52; Nordyke, *Cattle Empire*, 22–23; State of Texas, *Biennial Report* (1883), 3–8. Not all the survey bids agreed on the acreage represented in a league. At least one prospective contractor measured one at 5,760 acres. XYZ (c/o Dr. Sam P. Wright) to Capitol Board, May 5, 1879, Records of the Commission, TSLA. Many other markers existed in the vicinity. Just prior to New Mexico's statehood in 1912, Texas acknowledged mistakes in the northwest survey. The boundary was not changed. "Boundaries," *Handbook of Texas Online*, June 12, 2010, www.tshaonline.org/handbook/online/articles/mgb02; *Amarillo News-Globe*, August 14, 1938, sec, D, 22.

37. State of Texas, *Biennial Report* (1883), 8; Norton to Roberts, September 20, 1879, Records of the Commission, TSLA. See also September 10 and December 1, 1879; Oran Roberts to N. L. Norton, September 30, 1879, Records of the Texas Governor: Oran Milo Roberts, TSLA; Haley, *XIT Ranch*, 51; Nordyke, *Cattle Empire*, 23. Haley reported that the survey did not begin until autumn and that the drought quickly drove the men from their task. Nordyke wrote, "The men finally had to resort to seepage from alkali lakes." Continuing, he summarized the results of 1879: "After a lonely Christmas . . . one blizzard after another drove the surveyors and Rangers out of the Panhandle." Both accounts appear misleading or incorrect.

38. *Denison* (TX) *Daily News*, May 26, 1880; Robertson and Robertson, *Panhandle Pilgrimage*, 210.

39. Walsh to Roberts, October 21, 1879, Records of the Commission, TSLA (emphasis original).

40. Norton to Roberts, October 12, 20, 1879; Edward Montgomery to Norton, October 31, 1879, Records of the Commission, TSLA.

41. Munson to Roberts, November 10, 1879, Records of the Commission, TSLA.

42. "Contract . . . Setting Forth that a Resurvey of the Capitol Lands Has Been Made," January 11, 1887; Munson to Roberts, April 30 and July 20, 1880, Records of the Commission, TSLA. In this letter Munson wrote, "I find the cost of doing the work will be about double my estimate."

43. *Brenham* (TX) *Weekly Banner,* October 17, 1879.

44. State of Texas, *Biennial Report* (1883), 60–61; Haley, *XIT Ranch,* 43. See also "Gunter, Jot," *Handbook of Texas Online,* June 15, 2010, www.tshaonline.org/handbook/online/articles/ fgu6.html; David Minor, "Munson, William Benjamin, Sr.," *Handbook of Texas Online,* June 15, 2010, www.tshaonline.org/handbook/online/articles/fmu09.html.

45. Frank Sperling to Norton, February 11, 1880, Records of the Commission, TSLA; Haley, *XIT Ranch,* 48; H. Allen Anderson, "Trujillo, TX," *Handbook of Texas Online,* June 15, 2010, www.tshaonline.org/handbook/online/articles/hvt84; *Galveston Daily News,* December 26, 1879.

46. *Galveston Daily News,* November 25, 1879; *Shamrock* (TX) *Texan,* September 14, 1938.

47. *Galveston Daily News,* December 4, 1879.

48. *Galveston Daily News,* December 4, 1879.

49. *Galveston Daily News,* December 4, 1879; Frank Sperling to Norton, February 11, 1880, Records of the Commission, TSLA; Robertson, *Panhandle Pilgrimage,* 136–37, 190; Haley, *XIT Ranch,* 48.

50. Munson to Roberts, March 5, 1880, Records of the Commission, TSLA.

51. Norton to Roberts, December 1, 1879, Records of the Commission, TSLA; Roberts to Norton, December 4, 1879, Records of the Governor: Roberts, TSLA; Gammel and Raines, *Laws of Texas: 1822–1897,* 3:1455–61.

52. Land Records, Record of Land Taxes, 1894–1895 [*sic*], 159, XIT Papers, PPHM; *The Capitol Freehold Land and Investment Company Limited Proceedings of the Fourth Annual General Meeting of Shareholders,* 1889, 2, XIT Papers, PPHM. The annual published proceedings of the Capitol Freehold Land and Investment Company [hereafter CFLIC Proceedings] housed at PPHM have seen varied collection management schemes over the years. The most recent finding aid lists "XIT Annual Reports" in "Drawer 1" and lists several I could not confirm exist. I found no published reports between 1894 and 1906, although there are other company reports ordinarily compiled and submitted for the London shareholders meetings. The XIT Papers are extensive and remain a challenge to researchers and PPHM staff to access efficiently. Texas, *Biennial Report* (1883), 60–67; Norton to Roberts, May 2, 1880, Records of the Commission, TSLA.

53. Gunter & Munson to Roberts, November 25, 1880, Records of the Governor: Roberts, TSLA; State of Texas, *Biennial Report* (1883), 8–9.

54. The Syndicate first corresponded with W. M. D. Lee in August 1882, discussing land and railroad plans "beneficial to all." See Taylor, Babcock, & Co. to Lee, August 29, 1882, XIT

Papers, PPHM. Letters from Abner Taylor, general manager for Taylor, Babcock & Company (hereafter TBC), in 1883 first highlight the land issues presented in the Panhandle. Taylor to John Farwell, June 16, 1883; Taylor to Charles Farwell, June 22, 1883; Taylor to J. Farwell, June 25, 1883, XIT Papers, PPHM; Daniel M. Braid [?], "Map of the XIT Ranche Situated in the Panhandle of Texas, the Property of the Capitol Freehold Land & Investment Co. Ltd." (Chicago: Rand McNally & Co., 1888), XIT Museum, Dalhart, TX. See also State of Texas, "Sketch of 103rd Meridian, W.L. showing conflict of Capitol Leagues, Surveyed and signed as correct by W. O. [sic] Mabry, Surveyor of Oldham County," 1887, TSLA; F. G Blau, "Oldham County Map, 1887 [digital image]," *Portal to Texas History*, April 2, 2010, http://texashistory.unt.edu/ark:/67531/metapth88877.

55. W. M. D. Lee to Walsh, February 1, 1881, Records of the Commission, TSLA; State of Texas, *Biennial Report* (1883), 9; see also Sullivan, *LS Brand*, 30; Schofield, *Indians, Cattle, Ships, and Oil*, 52–59; Donald F. Schofield, "LS Ranch," *Handbook of Texas Online*, December 5, 2019, www.tshaonline.org/handbook/online/articles/aplo2.

56. George Findlay et al. v. State of Texas, 113 Tex. 30, 250 S.W. 651 (S. C. Tex. 1923).

57. *New York Times*, January 6, 1885; Joseph and Smith, *Ten Million Acres*, 99–100; Gunter, "Jot Gunter," 53–54.

58. Rarick, "Michigan Architect"; Haley, *XIT Ranch*, 49–57; Nordyke, *Cattle Empire*, 19–30; Green, "Question of Great Delicacy," and Goeldner, "Designing Architect," in Texas State Historical Association, *Texas State Capitol*, 21–44, 45–61; Mabry, "Capitol Context," 110.

59. Seale, "Symbol as Architecture"; Mabry, "Capitol Context," 111–18. State of Texas, *Biennial Report* (1883), 28, 53; "Notice," ca. April 1882; J. Harrell to Roberts, April 20, 1882, Records of the Commission, TSLA; Texas Legislative Council and Texas Highway Department, *Texas Capitol*, 63–64.

60. State of Texas, *Biennial Report* (1883) 21, 22, 102–5; Daniell, *Personnel*, 44; Thomas W. Cutrer, "Lee, Joseph," *Handbook of Texas Online*, May 1, 2017, www.tshaonline.org/handbook/online/articles/fle15.

61. Haley, *XIT Ranch*, 49–57; Nordyke, *Cattle Empire*, 19–30; Green, "Question of Great Delicacy," and Goeldner, "Designing Architect," in Texas State Historical Association, *Texas State Capitol*, 21–44, 45–61; Mabry, "Capitol Context," 110; "Capitol Fire," November 9, 1881, Records of the Commission, TSLA (thirty-nine pages of handwritten testimony regarding the fire are in the Commission records).

62. Mabry, "Capitol Context," 109, 119–20; State of Texas, *Biennial Report* (1883), 14–15. Frederick Ruffini bid on the new capitol and the temporary capitol, the design of which he was responsible. See also Brinkman and Utley, "Name on the Cornerstone." J. N. Preston was the first of several construction superintendents for the Capitol Commission; Green, "Question of Great Delicacy," in Texas State Historical Association, *Texas State Capitol*, 40–41.

63. D. J. Duhamel to Roberts, June 14, 1881, and September 8, 1881, Records of the Commission, TSLA; Rathjen, "Texas State House," 439; Mabry, "Capitol Context," 120.

64. Nordyke, *Cattle Empire*, 25–26; Haley, *XIT Ranch*, 57. For an example of titles that popularized western investment, see Brisbin, *Beef Bonanza*, 16. Brisbin wrote that he wished to provide interested parties with information "sufficient . . . to convince anyone that the Great American Desert is not such a bad place to live, and indeed no desert at all."

65. *Waco* (TX) *Examiner*, February 8, 1882; Beardsley to Roberts et al., January 31, 1882, Records of the Commission, TSLA. According to the article in the Waco newspaper, besides Babcock, Taylor, and the two Farwell brothers the Syndicate also included Beardsley, identified as the postmaster at Rock Island, IL; J. S. Drake, formerly one of the proprietors of the Rock Island *Argus*, an ex-member of the Illinois Democratic state central committee, and a "wealthy capitalist and contractor"; and A. M. Burel, mayor of Rockdale, TX, and well known as a Democratic politician.

66. Cullom to Roberts, February 3, 1882, Records of the Commission, TSLA. See also the contract, bond, and specification for Schnell in State of Texas, *Biennial Report* (1883), 97–175; Cullom to Roberts (telegram), February 7, 1882, Records of the Commission, TSLA; State of Texas, *Biennial Report* (1883), 31. A follow-up letter from Beardsley, who had sent the earliest telegram about Taylor and the others, is available and conveys positive opinions on the "Syndicate"; see Beardsley to Roberts, February 1, 1882, Records of the Commission, TSLA. On the capitol, see also Rathjen, "Texas State House," 438; Mabry, "Capitol Context," 121; Miller, "Cattle Capitol," 32–38.

67. Haley, *XIT Ranch*, 5; Taylor to Forster and Wennig, April 26, 1882; Taylor to Schnell, June 19, 1882; Accounts: Ledgers, Taylor-Babcock, XIT Papers, PPHM. An 1893 case before the U.S. Supreme Court sheds some light on this topic. In *Burck v. Taylor*, 152 U.S. 634 (1894), the Court declared Burck the rightful holder of "title to one thirty-second interest" in the profits of the Texas capitol project.

68. *Stock Growers Journal* (Miles City, MT), March 13, 1886.

CHAPTER 3.   CAPITOL CAPITAL

1. Green, "Great Delicacy," in TSHA, *Texas State Capitol*, 42; State of Texas, *Biennial Report* (1883), 22–27; Rathjen, "Texas State House," 437.

2. State of Texas, *Biennial Report* (1883), 83–84, 26–27, 88; Taylor to John T. Dickinson, Secretary of Capitol Board, August 29 (1883), XIT Papers; Greer, "Building of the Texas State Capitol," 148.

3. State of Texas, *Biennial Report* (1883), 31, 187–88; Taylor to Thomas N. Anderson, May 27, 1882, XIT Papers, PPHM. Although the pursuit of investors would later intensify, particularly in England, this letter reveals the tentative approach the four men were taking toward responsibility for the project.

4. DeKoven to Lee & Norton, July 7, 1882, XIT Papers, PPHM; Goeldner, "Designing Architect," in TSHA, *Texas State Capitol*, 52; Greer, "Building of the Texas State Capitol," 89–92; Mabry, "Capitol Context," 121–22; State of Texas, *Biennial Report* (1883), 39.

5. Taylor to Hoxie, August 10, 1882; Taylor to Gault, August 28, 1882; Taylor to Norton, August 31, 1882, XIT Papers, PPHM.

6. Daniell, *Personnel*, 42; State of Texas, *Biennial Report* (1883), 37, 194–96; Babcock to "Ike," April 8, 1884, XIT Papers, PPHM.

7. Taylor to John T. Dickinson, April 15, 1884, XIT Papers, PPHM.

8. Rathjen, "Texas State House," 440–41; R. Platt (Acting Mayor, Austin) to Roberts, September 9, 1882; Roberts to R. Platt, Austin Street Commission, March 26, 1883, Records

of the Commission, TSLA; Taylor to W. A. Saylor, Mayor, Austin, January 19, 1883, XIT Papers, PPHM.

9. Taylor to R. J. Brackenridge, 1st Nat. Bank, Austin, August 15, 1882; Taylor to Dickinson, August 22, 1882; Taylor to Wilke, August 31, 1882; Taylor to Ed Creary, September 4, 1882, XIT Papers, PPHM; Vivian Elizabeth Smyrl, "Wilke, Gustav," *Handbook of Texas Online*, May 12, 2016, www.tshaonline.org/handbook/online/articles/fwiam. Rather than a geologic designation, here "water table" refer to an architectural feature created to deflect water away from a building's foundation while also providing a decorative feature.

10. State of Texas, *Biennial Report* (1883), 33, Appendix O; Taylor to Dickinson, August 15, 1882, XIT Papers, PPHM; Greer, "Building of the Texas State Capitol," 91.

11. State of Texas, *Biennial Report* (1883), 102; Taylor to Lee and Norton, August 15, 1882; Taylor to [First National Bank], August 15, 1882; Taylor to Burck, August 16, 1882, XIT Papers, PPHM; Babcock to Capitol Board, April 6, 1883, Records of the Commission, TSLA; Taylor to Lee and Norton, April 9, 1883; Accounts, Ledger, Taylor-Babcock, 1882–1886, XIT Papers, PPHM. TBC again requests payment of the first land parcel. Several earlier letters in the fall of 1882 also refer to Creary and his inaccurate and inconsistent accounting.

12. State of Texas, *Biennial Report* (1883), 37; Myers to Board, September 21, 1882, Records of the Commission, TSLA; Taylor to Myers, October 3, 1882, XIT Papers, PPHM.

13. Taylor to Abner Morgan, October 20, 1882; Taylor to David Nobles Rowan, October 30, 1882; Taylor to Babcock, November 3, 1882, XIT Papers, PPHM.

14. Taylor to Myers, December 30, 1882, XIT Papers, PPHM; Texas Legislative Council, *Texas Capitol*, 33; Taylor to G. W. Turner, August 27, 1883, XIT Papers, PPHM.

15. Taylor to A. J. Peeler, Austin, TX, September 19, 1883; Taylor to Turner, September 19, 1883, XIT Papers, PPHM.

16. Taylor to William Henry Smith, June 23, 1883, XIT Papers, PPHM. Herbert Melville "Hub" Hoxie, an Iowa lawyer, began his railroad career contracting with the Union Pacific Railroad in the mid-1860s, where he was caught up in the Credit Mobilier affair. He later worked for the International & Great Northern Railway and for the Texas & Pacific Railroad, before becoming a vice-president for the Missouri Pacific Railroad.

17. Taylor to Baldwin Locomotive Works, August 15, 1883; Taylor to Burnham Parry Williams & Co., September 17, 1883; Taylor to Baldwin Locomotive, November 14, 1883; Taylor to Burnham, et al., February 1884, XIT Papers, PPHM.

18. Taylor to J. Waldo, VP, Houston & Texas Central RR, August 16, 1883; Taylor to J. V. Farwell, June 25, 1883; Taylor to Hoxie, November 9, 1883, XIT Papers, PPHM.

19. Greer, "Building of the Texas State Capitol," 93, 148; Taylor to Babcock, March 7, 1883; Taylor to Norton, August 29, 1883, XIT Papers, PPHM.

20. Taylor to Dickinson, December 19, 1883, XIT Papers, PPHM.

21. Taylor to Dickinson, December 31, 1883; Taylor to Myers, December 13, 1883, XIT Papers, PPHM; Goeldner, "Designing Architect," in TSHA, *Texas State Capitol*, 54–55. Myers tried to balance several projects simultaneously during this period, including courthouse buildings in Nebraska and Ohio and application for appointment as the U.S. Treasury Department's supervising architect, which he did not receive.

22. Goeldner, "Designing Architect," in TSHA, *Texas State Capitol*, 54–55; Daniell, *Personnel*, 43; Greer, "Building of the Texas State Capitol," 92; "Application of Capitol Building Contractor for Conveyance of Second Installment," February 1, 1884; Dickinson to Governor John Ireland, April 2, 1884, Records of the Commission, TSLA.

23. Baker, *Building the Lone Star*, 9–11; State of Texas, *Biennial Report* (1886), 4–5; Taylor to Burnham Parry Williams and Co., September 17, 1883, XIT Papers, PPHM; Mabry, "Capitol Context," 125; Taylor to J. V. Farwell, June 25, 1883, XIT papers, PPHM.

24. Greer, "Building of the Texas State Capitol," 105; Mabry, "Capitol Context," 125; U.S. Department of the Interior, "Town Mountain Granite," https://mrdata.usgs.gov/geology/state /sgmc-unit.php?unit=TXpCAt%3B0 (accessed February 7, 2020); State of Texas, *Biennial Report* (1883), 51.

25. Taylor to Walker, April 16, 1884; Taylor to W. E. Cutshaw, Richmond, VA, April 8, 14, 1884; Taylor to Myers, April 14, 1884, XIT Papers, PPHM.

26. Taylor to Robert Greenlee, Denver, CO, and others, May 15, 1884; Taylor to James Applegood, Lansing, MI, May 23, 1881; Taylor to Richard Glaister, Lansing, MI, May 25, 1884; Taylor to Greenlee, May 28, 1884; Taylor to Charles E. Williams, Buffalo, NY, April 25, 1885, XIT Papers, PPHM.

27. Taylor to W. R. Allen, St. Louis, MO, June 7, 1884; Taylor to Dickinson, June 10, 1884, XIT Papers, PPHM; State of Texas, *Biennial Report* (1883), 103; Taylor to Babcock, September 16, 1884; Taylor to Myers, December 2, 24, 1884; Taylor to Dickinson, December 26, 1884, XIT Papers, PPHM.

28. Greer, "Building of the Texas State Capitol," 108–9, 113–24; Taylor to Wilke, December 31, 1884; Babcock to Taylor, January 6, 1885, XIT Papers, PPHM; State of Texas, *Biennial Report* (1886), 12.

29. State of Texas, *Biennial Report* (1886), 15.

30. State of Texas, *Biennial Report* (1886), 16.

31. State of Texas, *Biennial Report* (1886), 32–33; Greer, "Building of the Texas State Capitol," 117.

32. State of Texas, *Biennial Report* (1886), 195–205.

33. Taylor to J. A. Hooper, Chairman, Cornerstone Celebration, March 1, 1885, XIT Papers, PPHM.

34. List of Items Placed inside Capitol Cornerstone, Records of the Commission, TSLA; Legislative Council, *Texas Capitol*, 28–29; Greer, "Building of the Texas State Capitol," 101–2.

35. State of Texas, *Biennial Report* (1886), 8–12; Greer, "Building of the Texas State Capitol," 112; J. V Farwell to Norton, September 18, 1885, XIT Papers, PPHM; Daniell, *Personnel*, 44; Message to the Legislature, January 11, 1887, Records of John Ireland, Texas Office of the Governor, Archives and Information Services Division, *Texas State Library and Archives Commission*, March 30, 2011, www.tsl.state.tx.us/governors/west/ireland-capitol-1.html; Vivian Elizabeth Smyrl, "Granite Mountain, Texas," *Handbook of Texas Online*, June 16, 2010, www.tshaonline.org/handbook/online/articles/hrg71.

36. Abner Taylor to G. W. Turner, October 6, 20, 30, 1883, XIT Papers, PPHM.

37. State of Texas, *Biennial Report* (1886), 42–43; Greer, "Building of the Texas State Capitol," 88; Babcock to Taylor, January 6, 1885, XIT Papers, PPHM. Indications of the Syndicate's interest in Wilke taking over the contract emerge as early as August 30, 1884, in a letter from Taylor to Wilke. Greer indicates that Wilke's "services" were $362,000. One presumes that Wilke agreed to do the project for $2.3 million and realized personal earnings at the former figure. Remember, Wilke takes over in late 1885. It is not clear that any money beyond Wilke's salary ever changed hands or that Wilke controlled spending on the project. The Syndicate took faith in his day-to-day decisions but continued to maintain the purse strings.

38. Babcock to J. V. Farwell, June [day missing], 1883, XIT Papers, PPHM; State of Texas, *Biennial Report* (1886), 203–5; "Fear, Force, and Leather: The Texas Prison System's First Hundred Years, 1848–1948," Texas State Library and Archives Commission, August 22, 2019, www.tsl.state.tx.us/exhibits/prisons/convictlease/page1.html; Marjory Harper, "Emigrant Strikebreakers: Scottish Granite Cutters and the Texas Capitol Boycott," in TSHA; *Texas State Capitol*, 63–84. See also U.S. Congress, "Charles Farwell," *Biographical Directory of the United States Congress* (Washington: Office of History and Preservation, 2010), http://bioguide.congress.gov/biosearch/biosearch.asp. Charles Farwell, formerly an Illinois delegate to the U.S. House of Representatives, had recently been considered for the Senate and became Illinois's senator in 1887, filling the vacancy left by the death of the state's long-term representative in the upper house, John A. Logan. Although the labor dispute in Texas might have proved embarrassing to a U.S. senator, the opposite appears the case, with considerable political force brought to bear in the matter. See Lusk, *History of the Contest*, 47–48.

39. "From the State Capitol," *Dallas Morning News*, October 27, 1885.

40. Taylor to Robert C. Greenlee, Tiffin, Ohio, May 28, 1884; Taylor to Myers, December 13, 1883; Taylor to Myers, July 30, 1883, XIT Papers, PPHM.

41. Taylor to Babcock, February 27, 1885; Myers to John T. Dickinson, Secretary of the Capitol Board, February 28, 1885, XIT Papers, PPHM; State of Texas, *Biennial Report* (1886), 11.

42. Goeldner, "Designing Architect," in TSHA, *Texas State Capitol*, 55–56; Greer, "Building of the Texas State Capitol," 163.

43. Taylor to Myers, August 11, 1885, XIT Papers, PPHM.

44. State of Texas, *Biennial Report* (1986), 49–74; Greer, "Building of the Texas State Capitol," 161–63; Goeldner, "Designing Architect," in TSHA, *Texas State Capitol*, 58–61.

CHAPTER 4. CATTLE CONVENTION

1. Skaggs, *Prime Cut*, 70.

2. Nordyke, *Great Roundup*, 113–27.

3. Taylor to David Nobles Rowan, October 30, 1882; Taylor to Babcock, November 3, 1882; TBC to Rowan, January 19, 1883; "Memorandum," January 24, 1883; Amos Babcock to John V. Farwell, June 26, 1883, XIT Papers, PPHM. Letters signed "Taylor, Babcock, & Co." are usually written by Abner Taylor.

4. TBC to Charles Goodnight, Palo Duro, TX, March 28, 1883, XIT Papers, PPHM; *Chicago Tribune*, April 6, 1884.

5. TBC to E. S. Graham, Graham, Young County, TX, January 18, 1883, XIT Papers, PPHM; Clayton and Salvant, *Historic Ranches*, 25.

6. William R. Hunt, "Graham, Texas," *Handbook of Texas Online*, mod. February 23, 2018, www.tshaonline.org/handbook/online/articles/hfg07; Graham Chamber of Commerce, "Graham, Texas," *VillageProfile.com*, 2015, www.villageprofile.com/texas/graham/03/topic .html; Dr. William Green, conversation with author, March 12, 2014. Exploration companies did approach the Capitol Syndicate. See L. M. Davis, President, Ohio Consolidated Oil Co. to J. B. [*sic*] Farwell, December 15, 1904. The Syndicate also held some coal lands in New Mexico; see B. H. Campbell to J. V. Farwell, October 16, 1885; Campbell to Taylor (telegram), October 21, 1885, J. Evetts Haley Collection II-B, NSHL. As with other aspects of Syndicate operations, the Farwell brothers disagreed regarding its disposal. See Francis W. Farwell to William Boyce, Texas Legal Counsel, August 9, 1900, XIT Papers, PPHM.

7. State of Texas, *Biennial Report* (1886), 12, 15–16, 32–33; Miller, *Public Lands of Texas*, 64–65; *Chicago Tribune*, April 6, 1885; TBC to Col. Pullitz, Frankfort-on-the-Main, Germany, June 9, 1884, XIT Papers, PPHM. See chapter 3 for a fuller discussion of the controversy surrounding the capitol building's construction.

8. Miller, *Public Lands of Texas*, 61–67.

9. Taylor to Walsh, September 17 and 28, 1885; Taylor to A. J. Peeler, Austin, September 22, 1885, XIT Papers, PPHM; Greer, "Building of the Texas State Capitol," 162; Haley, *XIT Ranch*, 53–54; Jordan, "Windmills in Texas," 81. The term "artificial water" referred to the creation of dams to capture runoff and wells powered by wind, steam, or horse power tapping a subterranean source.

10. State of Texas, *Biennial Report* (1886), 195–99; Taylor to John T. Dickinson, Secretary, Capitol Board, September 22, 1885; Taylor to William C. Prescott, London, August 31, 1885, XIT Papers, PPHM; Haley, *XIT Ranch*, 72–73; Advertisements in *Glasgow* (Scotland) *Herald*, October 13, 1885; and *London Daily News*, November 21, 1885; Reginald DeKoven (Syndicate employee) to Charles B. (C. B.) Farwell, September 29, 1885, XIT Papers, PPHM; Daniel M. Braid [?], "Map of the XIT Ranche," Rand, McNally, Chicago, 1888.

11. TBC to E. L. Sheldon, London, February 22 and May 3, 1884; Sheldon (telegram), April 17, 18, 1884, XIT Papers, PPHM.

12. TBC to John Stuart & Co., Manchester, England, December 24, 27, 1883, January 9, February 15, April 16, September 12, 17, 1884; TBC to John W. Maugham, London, June 17, 1884, XIT Papers, PPHM; Graham, "Investment Boom," 421–42.

13. Taylor to Campbell, January 3, 1885; Taylor and C. B. Farwell to Campbell, August 24, 1885, XIT Papers, PPHM; *Prairie Farmer*, August 24, 1878; Haley, *XIT Ranch*, 75, 79; Wheeler, "Blizzard of 1886."

14. Nordyke, *Cattle Empire*, 75; State of Texas, *Biennial Report* (1886), 195–99; Haley, *XIT Ranch*, 71–72; *CFLIC Proceedings (Fourth)*, 1889, 6–7, and (*First*), 1885, 4–6, XIT Papers, PPHM; C. B. Farwell to Editor, *Fort Worth Daily Gazette*, August 20, 1889; Woods, *British Gentlemen*, 119–21; Robbins, "Public Domain," 100–101; Graham, "Investment Boom," 441–42; *Dallas Morning News*, October 21, 1885; "Incorporated," from the *Helena* (MT) *Herald*, in *Stock Growers Journal*, March 13, 1886. In British finance parlance, and here, a debenture is a long-term security yielding a fixed rate of interest, issued by a company and secured against assets.

15. William M. Pearce, "Spur Ranch," *Handbook of Texas Online*, June 15, 2010, www .tshaonline.org/handbook/online/articles/aps05; H. Allen Anderson, "Francklyn Land and

Cattle Company," *Handbook of Texas Online*, mod. June 28, 2016, www.tshaonline.org /handbook/online/articles/dsf02; Blodgett, *Land of Bright Promise*, 1, 43.

16. *London Financial News*, July 29, 30, 1885; *London Daily News*, May 27, 1886; H. Milner Willis, "Notice of Debenture Redemption Drawing," July 26, 1906, XIT Papers, PPHM. See also Clay, *My Life on the Range*, 129–39. In 1890, one British pound equaled about US$4.86.

17. Rathjen, *Texas Panhandle Frontier*, 241; Brands, *American Colossus*, 218–23; *An Act for the Establishment of a Bureau of Animal Industry*, Public Law 23–31–60, 48th Cong., 1st sess. [May 29, 1884], 31–33; National Convention of Cattlemen, *Proceedings*, 1–3.

18. Cattlemen, *Proceedings*, 4; *Las Vegas* (NM) *Gazette*, November 19, 23, 1884; *Ft. Benton* (MT) *River Press*, November 26, 1884. For a short, contemporary biography of Hunter, see *Chillicothe* (MO) *Weekly Crisis*, November 20, 1884.

19. Cattlemen, *Proceedings*, 1, 3, 29; Wyoming State Archives, "Joseph Carey," *WyomingHistory.org*, November 8, 2014, www.wyohistory.org/encyclopedia/joseph-carey.

20. Cattlemen, *Proceedings*, 5–8 (see also 32: Colorado Cattle Growers' Association, "Mrs. J. P. Farmer" appears to be the only woman represented at the gathering); Streeter, "National Cattle Trail," 26–27, 59–74; Lewis, "National Cattle Trail," 205–20; Hutson, "Texas Fever," 74–104.

21. Cattlemen, *Proceedings*, 8.

22. Cattlemen, *Proceedings*, 8–15.

23. Cattlemen, *Proceedings*, 11, 15.

24. Cattlemen, *Proceedings*, 8, 15–16; John W. Noble, N. O. Nelson, and Dwight Tredway, Banquet Committee, National Convention of Cattle Men to General W. T. Sherman, St. Louis, MO, October 22, 1884, William T. Sherman Papers, General Correspondence, Library of Congress, Washington, DC; "William Tecumseh Sherman," *Bio* (A&E Television Networks, 2015), updated June 28, 2019, www.biography.com/people/william-tecumseh -sherman-9482051; *St. Genevieve* (MO) *Fair Play*, December 20, 1890. It was not clear in the article exactly what Sherman said about the former Confederate leader to offend the scribe— nearly twenty years after the Civil War's end.

25. Lohse, *First Governor*; Cattlemen, *Proceedings*, 18–29, 40.

26. *Fort Worth Daily Gazette*, November 20, 1884.

27. Cattlemen, *Proceedings*, 52, 74; Stuart and Phillips, *Forty Years*, 2:211; Milner and O'Connor, *As Big as the West*, 252; Clay, "Call to Order," 51; Andrew and Erwin Davis, Samuel Hauser, and Stuart founded the Pioneer Cattle Company, later owned by Conrad Kohrs. The main cattle brand of the outfit was D Bar S, which, when stamped together on a steer, resembled the surname initials of the partners, thus the DHS Ranch.

28. Cattlemen, *Proceedings*, 41, 45; Streeter, "National Cattle Trail," 26. Carroll was later the mayor of Denton, Texas, and spoke at the opening ceremony of the forerunner to the University of North Texas in 1890.

29. Olmstead and Rhode, *Arresting Contagion*, 95; Skaggs, *Cattle-Trailing Industry*, 105; Skaggs, *Prime Cut*, 53; U.S. Congress. House. Committee on Agriculture, *Memorial in Regard to Texas Fever*, 1–8; U.S. Congress. House Committee on Agriculture, *Report on Texas Fever*, 1–5; U.S. Department of Agriculture. *Annual Report of the Commissioner of Agriculture*, 523–50.

30. *Bureau of Animal Industry*, Public Law 23–31–60, 1884, 31–33; Findlay to Taylor, December 9, 1889, XIT Papers, PPHM; Skaggs, *Cattle-Trailing Industry*, 22, 103–21; Olmstead and Rhode, *Arresting Contagion*, 42–62, 97; Olmstead, "First Line of Defense," 332, 334, 339 map; Tamara Miner Haygood, "Texas Fever," *Handbook of Texas Online*, mod. May 23, 2017, www.tshaonline.org/handbook/online/articles/awt01. The parasitic protozoon *Babesia bigemina* is the root cause of this fever, which is characterized by high fever, emaciation, anemia, bloody urine, other symptoms, and eventually death. More information can be found at Carl N. Tyson, "Texas Fever," *Encyclopedia of Oklahoma History and Culture*, www .okhistory.org/publications/enc/entry.php?entry=TE022 (accessed June 12, 2017).

31. Kingston, "Introduction of Cattle."

32. Skaggs, *Cattle-Trailing Industry*, 107, 118–21; Olmstead and Rhode, *Arresting Contagion*, 42–62, 97.

33. Skaggs, *Cattle-Trailing Industry*, 105–6; U.S. Department of the Treasury, *Report from the Chief*; U.S. Department of Agriculture, *Annual Report of Bureau of Animal Industry*, map between 274–75

34. Skaggs, *Cattle-Trailing Industry*, 103–21; Olmstead and Rhode, *Arresting Contagion*, 98–100, 103, 113; Cattlemen, *Proceedings*, 50, 54. See also A. E. Carruthers, M.D., "The Germ Theory of Splenic, or Texas Fever," in Cattlemen, *Proceedings*, 104–12; George Findlay, Chicago, to Avery L. Matlock, Texas Legal Consultant, Tascosa, TX, XIT Papers, PPHM. On pleuro-pneumonia outbreaks, see, U.S. Department of Agriculture, *Annual Report of the Commissioner*, 432–76.

35. Parker, *Report of the Commissioner*, 8, 34–36, 60–64, 88; Rathjen, *Texas Panhandle Frontier*, 180–227; Hämäläinen, *Comanche Empire*, 330–41; Carlson, *Plains Indians*, 155–60; Barnes, *Historical Atlas*, 291–95, 310–11, 336–37; Graybill, *Policing the Great Plains*, 23–63; Sherow, *Chisholm Trail*, 238–49.

36. Findlay to Taylor, March 15, 1890; W. J. Tod, Litigation, 55, 694, XIT Papers, PPHM; Alvin Howard Sanders, *History of Aberdeen-Angus Cattle*, 149–68; Skaggs, *Prime Cut*, 58–64; Libecap, "Rise of the Chicago Packers," 247–50.

37. Miller, *Public Lands of Texas*, 242–52.

38. Cattlemen, *Proceedings*, 54, 58; *An Act to Provide for the Allotment of Lands in Severalty to Indians on the Various Reservations* [General Allotment Act or Dawes Act], Statutes at Large 24, 388–91, NADP Document A1887, www.ourdocuments.gov; Stuart and Phillips, *Forty Years*, 2:224–26.

39. Parker, *Report of the Commissioner*, 7, 25–27, 116, 289; Carlson, *Plains Indians*, 155–62; Miller et al., *History of the Assiniboine*, 15–154; Barnes, *Historical Atlas*, 291–95, 328–29; Malone, *Montana*, 114–44; Graybill, *Policing the Great Plains*, 23–63.

40. Cattlemen, *Proceedings*, 80.

41. *Fort Worth Daily Gazette*, November 1, 1883; Nordyke, *Cattle Empire*, 111; Graybill, *Policing the Great Plains*, 118–30; Wayne Gard, "Fence Cutting," *Handbook of Texas Online*, mod. September 27, 2019, www.tshaonline.org/handbook/online/articles/auf01. The people of the cattle range found many worse things to call homesteaders as they became more prevalent in the western cattle regions, including "Honyockers" and "Scissorbills." See Toole, *Montana*,

228–42. For a discussion of the influence large livestock operators wielded over legal authority in the western cattle regions, see also Elofson, *Cowboys, Gentlemen, and Cattle Thieves*; Elofson, *Frontier Cattle Ranching*.

42. Stuart and Phillips, *Forty Years*, 2:195–210; Brown, *Plainsmen of the Yellowstone*, 400–403; Milner and O'Conner, *As Big as the West*, 219–48; Clay, "Call to Order," 55–59. The new organization merged the Eastern Montana Live Stock Growers Association with the Montana Stock Growers Association, which represented the territory's westside cattle interests, into a single territorial-wide lobby.

43. *Glendive* (MT) *Independent*, July 27, 1889; *Helena* (MT) *Independent*, March 10, July 27, 1889, April 6, 1892; *Miles City* (MT) *Daily Yellowstone Journal*, April 14, 20, 1892; Brown, *Plainsmen of the Yellowstone*, 408–15; Davis, *Wyoming Range War*, 115. For a nuanced approach to this topic, see Belgrad, "'Power's Larger Meaning.'"

44. H. B. Ijams, Secretary, Wyoming Stock Growers' Association to Findlay, March 30, 1893, XIT Papers, PPHM.

45. Cattlemen, *Proceedings*, 81–82, 84.

46. Cattlemen, *Proceedings*, 87–88. Stone is often referred to as Governor Stone. W. M. Stone was the governor of Iowa for two terms (1863–68). He later served as commissioner of the General Land Office in Washington D.C. Stone was a representative of the Southern Colorado Cattle Growers' Association.

47. Malin, *Grassland*, 202–7; Osgood, *Day of the Cattleman*, 194–204; Cattlemen, *Proceedings*, 83. See also McCoy, *Historic Sketches*.

48. Cattlemen, *Proceedings*, 83, 88.

49. Brisbin, *Beef Bonanza*, 13–14, 49. Brisbin is the author of one of the most influential of the many books, pamphlets, and articles written in the late 1870s and early 1880s encouraging the boom of investments in the western cattle business.

50. Skaggs, *Cattle-Trailing Industry*, 110; Cattlemen, *Proceedings*, 88.

51. Cattlemen, *Proceedings*, 89; *Las Vegas* (NM) *Gazette*, November 23, 1884; Skaggs, *Cattle-Trailing Industry*, 110–14.

52. Cattlemen, *Proceedings*, 45, 49. According to Skaggs, D. W. Smith, the president of the National Cattle Growers' Association, withdrew from the St. Louis convention in opposition to the national trail proposal. He called for another meeting exactly one year later in Chicago. See also Bureau of Land Management, "Livestock Grazing on Public Lands," www.blm.gov /programs/natural-resources/rangelands-and-grazing/livestock-grazing (accessed February 7, 2020); Fleischner, "Ecological Costs."

53. *Fort Worth Daily Gazette*, November 30, 1884; Skaggs, *Cattle-Trailing Industry*, 108; Streeter, "National Cattle Trail," 27; Hutson, "Texas Fever," 87–91.

54. Streeter, "National Cattle Trail," 70; Lewis, "National Cattle Trail," 216.

55. Teigen, "Century of Striving," *Montana Stockgrower*, 11; Milner and O'Connor, *As Big as the West*, 250–55; Hopkins, "Veterinarian's Report," 72–79. Montana's territorial governor at the time was Samuel T. Hauser, one of Stuart's partners in the DHS operation.

56. Streeter, "National Cattle Trail," 70; John H. Reagan, in U.S. House Committee on Commerce, *Report on the National Live-Stock Highway*, 1–5.

57. Cronon, *Nature's Metropolis*, 222–24, 236–51; Skaggs, *Cattle-Trailing Industry*, 1–12, 23–24; Dobie and Lea, *Longhorns*, 340–43; Libecap, "Rise of the Chicago Packers," 247–50; George Graham Vest, in U.S. Senate, Select Committee on Transportation and Sale of Meat Products, *Investigation*, 124, 183–84; "The Drovers Journal," *Stock Growers Journal*, August 6, 1892; Babcock v. Farwell, 190 1d 19580 [Ill. App. Ct. 1913], 704 [abstract]; Findlay to A[lbert] G[allatin] Boyce, August 14, 1890; O. C. Cato, Miles City, MT, to Findlay, August 16, 1892; Taylor to Boyce, August 14, 1890, XIT Papers, PPHM.

58. Oscar Canoy, "Livestock History of Custer County," U.S. Work Projects Administration, Montana Writers Program records, 1939–1941, MF 250, Reel 18, MHS; Hoopes, *This Last West*, 57–61; Stuart and Phillips, *Forty Years*, 2:99; Fletcher, "Day of the Cattlemen"; Niedringhaus, "N Bar N Ranch"; Clay, "Call to Order," 48–63. Generally, on Montana, see Toole, *Montana;* Malone and Roeder, *Montana*.

59. Skaggs, *Cattle-Trailing Industry*, 90, 99–100; Cronon, *Nature's Metropolis*, 222–24; Belich, *Replenishing the Earth*, 336–39; Sabin, "Home and Abroad," 318–19; Libecap, "Rise of the Chicago Packers," 247–50; *Daily Yellowstone Journal*, April 13, July 22, 1886; *Great Falls (MT) Tribune*, Weekly Edition, May 1, 1889. On railroading, see Fink, "Fort Worth and Denver City Railway," 1, 250; Stanley, *Story of the Texas Panhandle Railroads*, iii, 45; Athearn, *Union Pacific Country*, 291, 300, 367; *CFLIC Proceedings (Fourth)*, 1989, 6–7.

CHAPTER 5. CHANGES IN THE WIND

1. Osgood, *Day of the Cattleman*, 112–13; Wayne Gard, "Fence Cutting," *Handbook of Texas Online*, mod. September 27, 2019, www.tshaonline.org/handbook/online/articles/auf01.

2. Osgood, *Day of the Cattleman*, 193; George Findlay to A. L. Matlock, March 27, 1890; "Report of John V. Farwell," in *CFLIC Proceedings (Fifth)*, 1890, 33, XIT Papers, PPHM; *Amarillo News-Globe*, August 14, 1938, sec. E, 14; Haley, *XIT Ranch*, 79; Nordyke, *Cattle Empire*, 105; Clay, *My Life on the Range*, 141; Wheeler, "Blizzard of 1886," 453; Fletcher and Russell, *Free Grass to Fences*, 118; Brown and Schmitt, *Trail Driving Days*, 224; Sandoz, *Cattlemen*, 265, 309; Slatta, *Cowboys*, 187.

3. Skaggs, *Cattle-Trailing Industry*, 100–101; Skaggs, *Prime Cut*, 69–70; Libecap, "Rise of the Chicago Packers," 247–50; Haley, *XIT Ranch*, 147–49; H. Allen Anderson, "Bovina, TX," *Handbook of Texas Online*, June 12, 2010, www.tshaonline.org/handbook/online/articles/hjb13. Skaggs lists the eleven members of the "ranching kingdom" in order of output: Texas, Kansas, Nebraska, Oklahoma, South Dakota, Colorado, New Mexico, Montana, North Dakota, Wyoming, Idaho.

4. "Report of John V. Farwell," in *CFLIC Proceedings (Fourth)*, 1889, 33, XIT Papers, PPHM; Haley, *XIT Ranch*, 96; Nordyke, *Cattle Empire*, 121; Jordan, "Windmills in Texas," 81; Walsh and Little, "Ogallala Aquifer"; John Walsh, "Ogallala Aquifer," in Robbins, *Encyclopedia of Environment and Society*; David J. Wishart, "Ogallala Aquifer," *Encyclopedia of the Great Plains*, http://plainshumanities.unl.edu/encyclopedia/doc/egp.wat.018 (accessed February 10, 2015). For an overview of the federal government's assessment of water conditions on the Great Plains as the twentieth century opened, see U.S. Department of the Interior, *Annual Report of Director of Geological Survey*, 692–719.

5. Milner and O'Connor, *As Big as the West*, 252, 258–67; Rackley, "Hard Winter"; *Fort Benton* (MT) *River Press*, October 20, 1886; Freese et al., *Centennial Roundup*, 79.

6. *New York Times*, February 2, 1881; Rackley, "Hard Winter," 52; Haley, *XIT Ranch*, 126; Fletcher, *Free Grass to Fences*, 52. "Through" cattle were purchased by one buyer and then sold to another, generally on a south-to-north trajectory. These, for the most part, essentially were arrangements to "de-quarantine" otherwise prohibited livestock.

7. Avery L. Matlock, Texas Legal Consultant to George F. Westover, Legal Counsel, Chicago, October 9, 1887, in J. Evetts Haley, "Letters" [typescript, ca. 1936–1937], 5–30, XIT Ranch Records, 1885–1889, Dolph Briscoe Center for American History, University of Texas at Austin [hereafter DBCAH]; Haley, *XIT Ranch*, 98–104; Nordyke, *Cattle Empire*, 121–34, 149. See also Matlock, A. L., J. Evetts Haley Collection II-B, NSHL.

8. Milner and O'Connor, *As Big as the West*, 258–67; Rackley, "Hard Winter," 55–59; Howard, *Montana*, 157–64; Sandoz, *Cattlemen*, 263–71; Fletcher, *Free Grass to Fences*, 113–18; Liu, *Barbed Wire*, 79–83.

9. Rackley, "Hard Winter," 55–59; Abbott and Smith, *We Pointed Them North*, 176.

10. Hughey, "Texas."

11. Stuart and Phillips, *Forty Years*, 2:236; Milner and O'Connor, *As Big as the West*, 258–67; Rackley, "Hard Winter," 52–53; Freese et al., *Centennial Roundup*, 179–80; Kens, "Wide Open Spaces?," 178.

12. Wallis, *Cattle Kings*, 69; Schofield, *Indians, Cattle, Ships, and Oil*, 86, 97; Donald F. Schofield, "Lee, William McDole," *Handbook of Texas Online*, June 15, 2010, www.tshaonline .org/handbook/online/articles/fle54; Donald F. Schofield, "LS Ranch," *Handbook of Texas Online*, December 5, 2019, www.tshaonline.org/handbook/online/articles/aplo2; Sullivan, *LS Brand*, 140; Sandoz, *Cattlemen*, 270.

13. Robbins, *Colony and Empire*, 70–71; Milner and O'Connor, *As Big as the West*, 258–65; Stuart and Phillips, *Forty Years*, 2:236–37; Dobie and Lee, *Longhorns*, 200; Stuart, "Winter of 1886–1887." For references to the quarantine and the demand for stock cattle, see *Helena Independent*, April 20, 1891; *Daily Yellowstone Journal*, March 14, 1893.

14. The original digested in *River Press*, October 20, 1886.

15. *River Press*, October 20, 1886; *Daily Yellowstone Journal*, October 29, 1886; Clay, *My Life*, 49, 176–81.

16. *River Press*, March 16, 1887. The letter is from Dan Tovey to Joseph Conrad, dated February 28, 1887.

17. *River Press*, March 16, 1887.

18. *Daily Yellowstone Journal*, April 21, 1887; *Miles City* (MT) *Weekly Yellowstone Journal*, April 21, 1898; *Bozeman* (MT) *Weekly Chronicle*, March 23, 1887; *River Press*, March 16, 1887; Michael L. Collins, *That Damned Cowboy*, 77. The MacQueen was never rebuilt.

19. *Daily Yellowstone Journal*, April 20, 21, 1887; Teigen, "Century of Striving," 12; Collins, *That Damned Cowboy*, 77. Collins mentions in his popular biography that Roosevelt discussed the Interstate Commerce Commission at the 1886 meeting. His resources seem authoritative, but the *Daily Yellowstone Journal* reports on a similar initiative by Roosevelt at the 1887 meeting. See Stuart and Phillips, *Forty Years*, 2:237; *Daily Yellowstone Journal*, August 17, 1887.

20. Howard, *Montana*, 164–65; Wollaston, *Homesteading*, 63; "History of Custer County [Winter of 1906–1907]," U.S. Work Projects Administration, Montana Writers Program Records, 1939–1941, MF 250, Reel 18, MHS; Stuart and Phillips, *Forty Years*, 2:238–39. Congress investigated illegal grazing on public lands many times; see U.S. Department of the Interior, *Report from the Acting Commissioner.*

21. Vest, in Senate, Select Committee on Transportation and Sale of Meat Products, *Investigation*, 81; "Cattle Trusts," *Stock Growers Journal*, January 28, 1888, June 1, 1889, May 10, 1890; Clay, *My Life*, 340–55; *Glendive Independent*, June 1, 1889; Skaggs, *Prime Cut*, 59; Libecap, "Rise of the Chicago Packers," 247–50; Nordyke, *Great Roundup*, 170–76; Welsh, "Cosmopolitan Cattle King"; Gordon, "Swift & Co."

22. Brown and Schmitt, *Trail Driving Days*,185–88; Collins, *That Damned Cowboy*, 113.

23. *Helena Independent*, June 4, 1891; Pringle, *Theodore Roosevelt*, 72.

24. H. J. Rutter and Georgia Rechert, "Cow Tales," SC 35, 25–26, MHS; *Lewistown* (MT) *News-Argus*, December 17, 1995; Abbott and Smith, *We Pointed Them North*, 84–98; Burns, "Newman Brothers," 35; McCumsey et al., "Cowboy and Cattleman's Edition."

25. Haley, *XIT Ranch*, 217; H. Allen Anderson, "Boyce, Albert Gallatin," *Handbook of Texas Online*, June 12, 2010, www.tshaonline.org/handbook/online/articles/fb097; H. Allen Anderson, "Boice, Henry S." *Handbook of Texas Online*, June 12, 2010, www.tshaonline.org /handbook/online/articles/fb0089; Gavett, *North Dakota*, 283.

26. *Stock Growers Journal*, June 1, 1889; Welsh, "Cosmopolitan Cattle King."

27. Niedringhaus, "N Bar N Ranch"; Paladin, *From Buffalo Bones*, 5. The outfit name often described its brand. The Home Livestock and Cattle Company, or N Bar N, used a pair of capital Ns with a thin line separating them as a primary brand, although most large operators had several registered brands. There was an order to reading brands. In this case, stamped with a hot iron on a cow's rump, it looked like this: N-N.

28. Niedringhaus, "N Bar N Ranch," 15–17; H. Allen Anderson, "Francklyn Land and Cattle Company," *Handbook of Texas Online*, June 28, 2016, www.tshaonline.org/handbook /online/articles/dsf02; Frantz, "Texas's Largest Ranch."

29. *Helena Independent*, April 20, 1891; *Daily Yellowstone Journal*, March 14, 1893.

30. Carter et al., "Table Da968–982"; "History of Custer County [Winter of 1906–1907]," U.S. Work Projects Administration, Montana Writers Program Records, 1939–1941, MF 250, Reel 18, MHS; Paladin, *From Buffalo Bones*, 7.

31. Taylor to Amos Babcock, January 31, 1885, XIT Papers, PPHM; Sandoz, *Cattlemen*, 297; Haley, *XIT Ranch*, 100–104; Nordyke, *Cattle Empire*, 154–66; Duke and Frantz, *6,000 Miles*, 100–102.

32. Matlock to Westover, October 9, 1887, in Haley, "Letters," 7–30, DBCAH. Nordyke did not provide many notes in his book. The letter mentioned is from Campbell to John V. Farwell as transcribed in *Cattle Empire*, 161–66. See also Campbell, B. H., J. Evetts Haley Collection II-B, NSHL.

33. A[lbert] G[allatin] Boyce to Findlay, December 3, 1887, in Haley, "Letters," 20–22, DBCAH; Haley, *XIT Ranch*, 101–2.

34. Boyce to Findlay, December 3, 1887, in Haley, "Letters," 23–32, DBCAH.

35. Nordyke, *Cattle Empire*, 157–58, 165–66; Haley, *XIT Ranch*, 101–3.

36. Nordyke, *Cattle Empire*, 167. Governor Ireland had outlawed the carrying of "six-shooters" in 1885; Archive and History Department of the Texas State Library, *Governors' Messages*, 515.

37. Matlock to Westover, October 9, 1887, in Haley, "Letters," 7–30, DBCAH.

38. Matlock to Westover, March 2, 1888, in Haley, "Letters," 53, 55, 61, DBCAH; Nordyke, *Cattle Empire*, 169–70.

39. Taylor to Campbell, Wichita, KS, September 11, 1889; Land Records, Record of Land Taxes, 1894–1895 [*sic*], 159; Babcock v. Farwell, 190 1d 19580 [Ill. App. Ct. 1913], 1, 1170, 1183 [abstract], XIT Papers, PPHM; Babcock v. Farwell, 146 Ill. App. 307, LEXIS 359 [Ill. App. Ct. 1909]; Babcock v. Farwell, 189 Ill. App. 279, 1914 LEXIS 316 [Ill. App. Ct. 1914].

40. Boyce to Findlay, December 3, 1887; Matlock to Westover, October 9, 1887, in Haley, "Letters," 19, DBCAH.

41. Haley, *XIT Ranch*, 83; Nordyke, *Cattle Empire*, 168.

42. Nordyke, *Cattle Empire*, 169, 172–73.

43. Nordyke, *Cattle Empire*, 173–75, 198; Sandoz, *Cattlemen*, 320; Harvey, "George Findlay." Both C. B. Farwell and Taylor were serving in Congress in March 1889, in the Senate and House, respectively.

44. Harvey, "George Findlay," 10; Nordyke, *Cattle Empire*, 118–20.

45. Texas Legislative Council and Texas Highway Department, *Texas Capitol*, 63–64; Nordyke, *Cattle Empire*, 188–90; Haley, *XIT Ranch*, 53–54.

46. *CFLIC Proceedings (Fourth)*, 1889, 6–7, XIT Papers, PPHM.

47. "Report of John V. Farwell," in *CFLIC Proceedings (Fourth)*, 1889, 17–35, XIT Papers, PPHM; Haley, *XIT Ranch*, 81, 187–93; Nordyke, *Cattle Empire*, 55; Harvey, "George Findlay," 63.

48. "Report of John V. Farwell," in *CFLIC Proceedings (Fourth)*, 1889, 32–33; "Report of John V. Farwell," in *CFLIC Proceedings (Sixth)*, 1891, 25–32; Boyce to John V. Farwell, January 13, 1891, XIT Papers, PPHM; Sanders, *History of Aberdeen-Angus Cattle*, 152–68; Findlay, "Famous XIT Range Classic"; these articles originally appeared in *Breeder's Gazette* 39 (1901). See also Findlay, "Aberdeen-Angus on the Range," 334–45; Haley, *XIT Ranch*, 81, 187–93; Nordyke, *Cattle Empire*, 55; Harvey, "George Findlay," 63.

49. Haley, *XIT Ranch*, 83; Taylor to Boyce, June 14, 1889, "Purchases by A. G. Boyce," 1889, XIT Papers, PPHM; J. E. Moore to Haley, February 26, 1927, J. Evetts Haley Collection V, NSHL; Craig H. Roell, "O'Connor, Dennis Martin," *Handbook of Texas Online*, mod. April 9, 2019, www.tshaonline.org/handbook/online/articles/foc10. For more on the King Ranch and southern Texas ranching, see Baker, *Adventures;* Monday and Vick, *Petra's Legacy*. North of the Canadian River and on Capitol Freehold property, Rivers soon was renamed for a FW&DC railroad executive and became Channing. Channing became the ranch's headquarters in Texas in 1890.

50. Atherton, *Cattle Kings*, 8.

51. A. C. Johnson to Senator T. C. Power, Papers, MC55, B24/F3, MHS; see also Findlay to Boyce, April 21, 1890, XIT Papers, PPHM. For more on the late-century cattle business in New Mexico Territory, see Gilbert, *We Fed Them Cactus*.

52. Taylor to J. W. Driskill, Spearfish, DT, March 26, 1889; Taylor to Findlay, April 6, 1889; Taylor (by F. W. Farwell) to Topeka Sugar Company, August 30, 1889; Taylor to Findlay (in Topeka, KS), August [September] 2, 1889; Taylor to J. M. Shade, Liberal, KS, September 3, 1889; Taylor to Findlay, September 7, 1889 (discussing farmer-feeders in Kansas using sorghum: "It was an experiment I wished to[o]"); Findlay to J. V. Farwell, Findlay to Taylor, both January 11, 1890; Findlay to J. L. Driskill, Austin, TX, February 8, 1890, XIT Papers, PPHM; *Stock Growers Journal*, June 22, 1889; Rhodes, "Alive and Well." Financial distress forced the elder Driskill to sell the Austin hotel named for him at about this same time. S. E. McElhinney, an Iowa cattle breeder and associate of George Findlay, purchased the luxurious hotel.

53. Osgood, *Day of the Cattleman*, 217; Howard, *Montana*, 111; J. V. Farwell (in London) to Findlay, December 27, 1889; Findlay to J. V. Farwell, January 11, 1890; Findlay to Taylor, January 11, 1890 ("discussing the advisability of sending 10,000 or 15,000 steers to Montana next spring"); Findlay to Taylor, February 22, 1890, XIT Papers, PPHM; Richardson, *Compilation*, 9:97–98.

54. Taylor to J. V. Farwell, March 29, 1889, XIT Papers, PPHM.

55. In a series of articles on November 9, 30, and December 28, 1889, *Stock Growers Journal* provided an extensive look at the western cattle business just then, including reference to the intended presidential action November 9, 1889. The Indian territories had been subject to federal action against grazers since the Cleveland administration. See also, for instance, *Helena* (MT) *Weekly Herald*, September 3, 1885.

56. Babcock v. Farwell, 190 1d 19580 [Ill. App. Ct. 1913], 703; Dalrymple et al., *Cattle Tick and Texas Fever*, 252; Lea, "Prodigious Growth," 79; *CFLIC Proceedings (Fourth)*, 1889, 4; Taylor to Drumm & Snider Live Stock Exchange, Kansas City, April 9, 1889; Taylor to Hardin & Campbell, Union Building, Chicago, April 9, 1889, XIT Papers, PPHM.

CHAPTER 6. THE BIG OPEN

1. Grant, "Recollections of a Cowpuncher"; Abbott and Smith, *We Pointed Them North*, 60; *Daily Yellowstone Journal*, July 31, 1890, July 13, 1896; "December 1890," Accounts, Ranch, Journal #1, 1889–1892, 116; George Findlay, Chicago, to A. G. Boyce, Texas Ranch Manager, April 21, 1890; F. W. Farwell, Chicago to Findlay, May 31 (Wendover, WY), July 11, 1890 (Miles City, MT), XIT Papers, PPHM; Haley, *XIT Ranch*, 126–44; Nordyke, *Cattle Empire*, 207; Duke and Frantz, *6,000 Miles*, 139–53; Kennedy, *Cowboys and Cattlemen*, 136; Montana Historical Society Library, "Legislative Biographies," vol. 1 (1897–1915), s.v. "Cato," MHS; *Terry* (MT) *Tribune*, May 7, 1915; XIT Association, "Montana Range Manager an Expert Cowman," in *XIT Brand*, 9. For "Big Open," see Brown and Felton, *Before Barbed Wire*, 15. The story of the iconic brand has taken a couple of paths, but its origin is well documented in several sources, such as J. Marvin Hunter, "The Man Who Had Hell in His Neck, by Ab Blocker," in *Trail Drivers of Texas*, 507 (Cato also gains a brief mention at 396); Karen Griswold Stroh, "O. C. Cato," *Find A Grave*, #86012688, February 29, 2012, https://findagrave.com/cgi-bin/fg .cgi/http%2522//trees.ancestry.com/tree/19807769/fg.cgi?page=gr&GRid=86012688; Haley, *XIT Ranch*, 128; Duke and Frantz, *6,000 Miles*, 144–45; Yellowstone Corral Posse, "XIT." See also Schneiders, *Big Sky Rivers*.

2. Haley, *XIT Ranch*, 224–25; Evans, "Angus Origins"; Harvey, "George Findlay," 7–10; Osgood, *Day of the Cattleman*, 90–113; Skaggs, *Cattle-Trailing Industry*, 1–12, 23–24; Starrs, *Let the Cowboy Ride*, 19–37; Robbins, *Colony and Empire*, 19; Milner and O'Connor, *As Big As the West*, 249–58; Stuart and Phillips, *Forty Years*, 2:175–93, 211.

3. D. C. Leary, Agent, Ft. Worth & Denver City Railroad to Findlay, April 24, 1890; Findlay to Taylor, April 26, 1890, XIT Papers, PPHM; Howard, *Montana*, 157–64; Sandoz, *Cattlemen*, 263–71; Fletcher, *Free Grass to Fences*, 113–18; Liu, *Barbed Wire*, 79–83, 103–4; Wheeler, "Blizzard of 1886," 415–32; Stuart, "Winter of 1886–1887."

4. *CFLIC Proceedings (Fourth)*, 1889, 6, 7, 17–35, XIT Papers, PPHM; Taylor to Findlay, November 5, 1889, XIT Papers, PPHM.

5. Haley, *XIT Ranch*, 81, 187–93, 224–25; Nordyke, *Cattle Empire*, 55, 198; Harvey, "George Findlay," 8–11, 63.

6. Taylor to Findlay, Topeka, KS, August [September] 2, 1889; Taylor to J. M. Shade, Liberal, KS, September 3, 1889; Taylor to Findlay, September 7, 1889; Findlay to Ike T. Prior, Austin, TX, January 16, 1890; Findlay to J. A. McCormick, Arkansas City, KS, February 22, 1890; Findlay to E. S. "Zeke" Newman, El Paso, TX, March 19,1890; Newman to Findlay, March 24, 1890, XIT Papers, PPHM. See also Findlay to C. B. Mendenhall, Hunter Hot Springs, MT, March 8, 1890; Cyrus B. Mendenhall, Springdale, MT, to Findlay, March 11, 1890; J. T. Phillips, Phillips Cattle and Land Company, to Findlay, March 19, 1890; E. Coggshall, Miles City, MT, to Findlay, March 28, 1890, XIT Papers, PPHM. On the president's proclamation, see chapter 5 and Richardson, *Compilation*, 9:97–98.

7. Interstate Convention of Cattlemen, *Proceedings*, 11, 99; "The Biggest Gathering of Cattlemen Ever Known," *Fort Worth Daily Gazette*, March 11, 1890; Findlay to Taylor, March 15, 1890.

8. John Clay Jr. to Findlay, March 20, 25, 1890; Findlay to Taylor, March 21, 1890, XIT Papers, PPHM; Hunter, "Seth Mabry," in *Trail Drivers*, 718. Mabry (sometimes Mabrey or Mayberry) is mentioned no less than eight times in Hunter's classic. The "Major" also partnered with the Texas Snyder brothers; see *Stock Growers Journal*, August 23, 1890. Clay is ubiquitous in the western cattle business. His involvement is well reflected in his autobiography; see Clay, *My Life on the Range*, xi–xv. See also "Western Ranches, Ltd: Three Vs," U.S. Work Projects Administration, Montana Writers Program Records, 1939–1941, MF 250, Reel 1, MHS; Grace Gilmore, "The Original Circle Ranch," Montana Writers Program Records, MF 250, Reel 19, MHS; "Stockmen Are in Good Shape," *Daily Yellowstone Journal*, August 3, 1903.

9. Findlay to Taylor, March 15, 1890, XIT Papers, PPHM. These are the 10,000 head purchased from King and O'Connor in 1889.

10. Findlay to Taylor, March 15, 1890, XIT Papers, PPHM.

11. Findlay to Taylor, March 21, 1890, XIT Papers, PPHM.

12. Cram and Hinrichs, *Cram's Standard American Atlas*, 369.

13. Findlay to Mabry, March 31, 1890; Findlay to Boyce, April 3, 1890; Findlay to Seth Mabry [telegram], April 3, 1890, XIT Papers, PPHM. Findlay's telegram to Mabry before he departed asked whether Mabry would "entertain a proposition" similar to an earlier offer.

14. Findlay to Henry A. Blair, April 3, 1890, XIT Papers, PPHM; Chicago Railways Company, *Chicago Railways Company Report*. Davis, *Wyoming Range War*, outlines or implies Clay

NOTES TO CHAPTER 6

and Blair's role in the so-called Johnson County War (see chapter 4). Clay was conveniently out of the country at the time. Blair was in Chicago, but apparently he remained in close communication with the raiders. In fact, he was among the first to examine the diary of the martyr-like Nate Champion (*Wyoming Range War*, 248, index).

15. F. W. Farwell to Taylor, April 8, 1890; Findlay to Boyce, April 19, 24, 1890, XIT Papers, PPHM; H. J. Rutter and Georgia Rechert, "Cow Tales," SC 35, 23, MHS; "Northwestern Cattle Co./Montana Cattle Com./John T. Murphy," Montana Writers Program Records, MF 250, Reel 1, MHS; Paladin, *From Buffalo Bones*, 3–4, 13. Wolfers, in pursuit of bounties offered by state, local, and private associations and agencies, were employed throughout the cattle West and were regularly represented on the XIT payroll. One is left to wonder if Joe Butch, apparently well known during the period, is the same person mentioned by Teddy Blue Abbott as "Buckskin Joe" in his popular memoir; see Abbott and Smith, *We Pointed Them North*, 94.

16. Anderson & Findlay to T. C. Power, June 25, 1880; George Findlay to Power, May 11, 1882; John V. Farwell to Power, February 22, 1883; Anderson & Findlay to Power, October 12, 26, 1891; Thomas Charles Power papers, MC 55, Box 24 Folder 14, Box 459 Folder 2, MHS; T. C. Power to J. V. Farwell & Co., Chicago, December 22, 1892, XIT Papers, PPHM. Findlay was a partner with his future father-in-law in Anderson & Findlay, the first importers of Aberdeen-Angus cattle into the United States; see Evans, "Angus Origins"; Sanders, *History of Aberdeen-Angus Cattle*, 152–63, 172–74, 626–27.

17. J. J. Kennedy, Great Falls, MT, to Findlay, April 24, 1890; G. W. Simpson, Bay State Live Stock Company, Chicago, April 1, 1890, XIT Papers, PPHM; "Myers Bros.," Montana Writer's Program Records, MF 250, Reel 1, MHS; Bernice Myers Summer, "The First Cattle in the County," Montana Writers Program Records, MF 250, Reel 18, MHS; Findlay to William Harmon, Miles City, MT, March 8, 1890; Harmon To Findlay, March 11, 1890; Findlay to Alfred Myers, Livingston, MT, April 2, 1890; Myers To Findlay [telegram], April 8, 1890, XIT Papers, PPHM; "Spring Immigration [arrivals at hotels]," *Great Falls* (MT) *Tribune*, semiweekly ed., April 9, 1890; Findlay to Thomas Drummond, Corporate Counsel, Wheaton, IL, March 16, 1890, XIT Papers, PPHM.

18. Findlay to Boyce, April 26, 1890; George Findlay, "Notes on Northern Country," [April 26] 1890; Findlay to Taylor, April 26, 1890; Findlay to Taylor, September 6, 1890, XIT Papers, PPHM.

19. Findlay to James E. Lee, April 28, 29, 1890; Taylor to D. H. and J. W. Snyder, Georgetown, TX, May 10, 1890; Taylor to Boyce and Findlay, May 10, 1890; F. W. Farwell to Findlay (in Texas), May 28, 1890, XIT Papers, PPHM.

20. Findlay to Taylor, December 9, 1889, XIT Papers, PPHM.

21. Findlay to Matlock, May 6, 1890, XIT Papers, PPHM. Findlay's letter continued:

There are a great many things that might have caused the death of so many cattle last season. Is it not probable that last season was peculiarly favorable for the growth of some poison weed? Some seasons are. We have from a dozen to two dozen cattle die on the River near Skunk Arroyo almost every spring and we have never been able to account for it on any other ground than that of some poison weed. Murrain & other diseases presents symptoms very similar to Splenic fever & it would require an expert & postmortem examination to decide what the disease was.

22. Findlay to Boyce, April 21, 1890, XIT Papers, PPHM.

23. Yellowstone Corral Posse, "XIT," 18; *Terry* (MT) *Tribune*, May 7, 1915; [F. W. Farwell] to Boyce (telegram), May 28, 1890; Findlay to F. D. Brown, Local Treasurer, Denver, Texas & Ft. Worth Railroad Co., Denver, May 5, 1890; F. W. Farwell to Findlay, Wendover, WY, May 31, 1890, XIT Papers, PPHM.

24. Boyce to J. V. Farwell, June 12, 1890; J. V. Farwell to C. B. Farwell [no date]; Boyce to Taylor, July 20, 1890; Boyce to J. V. Farwell, July 22, 1890; Boyce, A. G., J. Evetts Haley Collection II-B, NSHL.

25. Lucey, *Photographing Montana*, 16; *Daily Yellowstone Journal*, April 10, 12, 1890; see also Evelyn Jephson Cameron Collection, Photographs Collection, and Evelyn Cameron, 1868–1928, Diaries (1893–1928), MHS.

26. *Daily Yellowstone Journal*, April 10, 12, 1890. Most cattle outfits were known by their brand. These three companies, respectively, are Home Land and Cattle Company, Phillips Cattle and Land Company, and Rea Cattle Company (also called the Bow Gun outfit).

27. Brown and Felton, *Before Barbed Wire*, 15; F. W. Farwell to Findlay, Miles City, MT, July 11, 1890, XIT Papers, PPHM; "Local Items," *Daily Yellowstone Journal*, July 11, 16, 1890; *Stockgrowers Journal*, July 12, August 16, 1890; Findlay to R. B. Harrison, Secretary, Montana Stockgrowers Association, July 16, August 27, 1890; Harrison to Findlay, September 3, 1890, XIT Papers, PPHM; "Proceedings of Stockgrowers' Meeting," *Daily Yellowstone Journal*, April 22, 1891; *Daily Yellowstone Journal*, July 12, August 1, 20 1890; *Stock Growers Journal*, August 9, 1890; Ranch Journal #1, 41, XIT Papers, PPHM. The use of "IXT" in this article is clearly a typographical error or the reporters' misunderstanding of the new outfit's name.

28. Description of Property #13, Land Records: Land, Taxes, 1894–1895 [*sic*]; William Courtenay, Real Estate & Mercantile Agency, Miles City, MT, to Findlay, July 14, 1890, XIT Papers, PPHM; *Glendive Independent*, April 5, 1890, July 19, 1890; *Daily Yellowstone Journal*, July 6, 16, 22, 1890; *Stock Growers Journal*, July 19, 1890; John D. Corlis, XIT Employee to Findlay, September 21, 23, 1890, XIT Papers, PPHM.

29. Leary to Findlay, April 24, 1890; Findlay to Taylor, April 26, 1890; Findlay to Fred W. De Boice, XIT Ranch Bookkeeper, Tascosa, TX, August 12, 1890; Findlay to F. D. Brown, Local Treasurer, Ft. Worth & Denver City Railroad, Denver, May 5, 1890; Findlay to J. C. Leary, FW&DC, Denver (telegram), June 9, 1890; Findlay to C. F. Meek, FW&DC, Denver (telegram), June 11, 1890; Meek to Findlay, June 22, 1890, XIT Papers, PPHM; Robertson and Robertson, *Panhandle Pilgrimage*, 149–51, 287; Jennie Rose Powell, "Channing, TX," *Handbook of Texas Online*, June 12, 2010, www.tshaonline.org/handbook/online/articles/HLC20.

30. Findlay to Taylor, April 26, 1890; Ranch Journal #1, 61, 117; O. C. Cato, Tally sheet, September 4, 1892, XIT Papers, PPHM; *Daily Yellowstone Journal*, July 12, 1890; Hunter, "The Cost of Moving a Herd to Montana, by Ike T. Pryor," in *Trail Drivers*, 367–68; Brown and Schmitt, *Trail Driving Days*, 184. Texans called the horse herd the "remuda," but in Montana punchers called it a "cavvy."

31. *Daily Yellowstone Journal*, July 3, 1890, July 13, 14, 1896; Brown and Felton, *Before Barbed Wire*, 165–68.

32. *Daily Yellowstone Journal*, July 31, 1890. Cowboys preferred to call themselves "waddy" or "cowpuncher."

33. *Daily Yellowstone Journal*, August 1, 20 1890; *Stock Growers Journal*, August 9, 1890; Homer Taylor to Findlay, July 28, 1890; Findlay to Boyce, August 4, 11, 14, 1890; Findlay to Driskill, August 9, 1890; Findlay to Taylor, August 22, September 5, 6, 1890; Taylor to C. B. Farwell, September 9, 1890, XIT Papers, PPHM. Boyce also drove cattle to Liberal, KS, and shipped them on the Chicago, Rock Island & Pacific Railroad.

34. Cato to Findlay, September 1, 30, 1890; Findlay to Taylor, September 6, 1890, XIT Papers, PPHM. Cato's correspondence often offers unique spelling and punctuation. All quoted material is original except for factual error.

35. Findlay to T. J. Thompson, Custer County Treasure, Miles City, MT, August 25, 1890; Findlay to R. A. Ford, Collector, Plainview, Hale County, TX, December 14, 1889; Findlay to J. M. Robinson, Tax Collector, Tascosa, TX, December 23, 1889; Findlay to Matlock, January 3, 1890; Findlay to Matlock, March 27, 1890 ("Taxes are much cheaper than those in Oldham [County, TX]"); Strevell & Porter, Attorneys, Miles City, MT to Findlay, September 10, 16,18, October 25, 1890; Ranch Journal #1, 92, XIT Papers, PPHM; *Glendive Independent*, July 20, 1895; *Daily Yellowstone Journal*, August 16, 1895.

36. Cato to Findlay, November 20, 1891, XIT Papers, PPHM; "Proceedings . . . Board of Equalization," *Glendive Independent*, July 20, 1895. The "XIT Ranch" originally purchased from Tusler and Kempton is about twenty miles northwest of Terry, MT. The purchase of the Hatchet seems to have been completed in 1895 after years of negotiation. See Cato to Findlay, October 2, 1891; William Courtenay, Real Estate & Mercantile Agency to Findlay, September 16, 23, 24, October 2, 18, 26, November 13, 19, 1891, December 16, 23, 1893; Findlay to Cato, December 29, 1893; Clay & Forrest, Chicago, IL, to F. W. Farwell, April 25, 1895; Cato to F. W. Farwell, May 1, 1895, XIT Papers, PPHM. As his first Montana winter wound down, Cato negotiated to keep his job and move his family to Miles City; see Cato to Findlay, March 16, 1891, XIT Papers, PPHM.

37. Western Historical, "Cyrus B. Mendenhall," in *Illustrated History of the Yellowstone Valley*, 413–15; A. W. Bowen & Co., "Cyrus B. Mendenhall," in *Progressive Men*, 1152–54; Findlay to Cyrus B. Mendenhall, Springdale, MT, March 8, 1890; Mendenhall to Findlay, March 11, 1890, XIT Papers, PPHM; Dawson County [MT] assessments on horses, cattle, and sheep, 1891–1899, Montana Writers Program Records, MF 250, Reel 1, MHS. Mendenhall was assessed tax on 1,600 cattle and seventy horses in 1892 and on 400 cattle and forty horses in 1896. The ranch was named for Mendenhall's livestock brand, a triangle with a bar through its upper pinnacle to form a symbol resembling a hand-ax or hatchet.

38. Findlay to Mendenhall, March 8, 1890; Mendenhall To Findlay, March 11, 1890, XIT Papers, PPHM.

39. Mendenhall To Findlay, March 11, 1890, XIT Papers, PPHM.

40. Courtenay to Findlay, September 16, 24, 1891, XIT Papers, PPHM. The ranch facilities were often "rustic," and absentee owners did not often go out of their way to add luxury.

41. Courtenay to Findlay, October 2, 18, 21, 26; November 13, 19, 1891, XIT Papers, PPHM. On Courtenay's sales effort for the XIT, there are dozens of letters. Good examples are Courtenay to Findlay, January 12, 19, 27, 28, 1893, XIT Papers, PPHM.

42. Courtenay to Findlay, December 16, 1893, December 23, 1893, XIT Papers, PPHM.

43. Findlay to Cato, December 29, 1893, March 15, April 1, 1895; Cato to Findlay, March 13, April 22, 1895; Findlay to Clay & Forrest, The Rookery, Chicago, IL, April 3, 11, 1895; Clay & Forrest to F. W. Farwell, April 25, 1895; Cato to F. W. Farwell, May 1, 1895, XIT Papers, PPHM; Montana Stock Growers, *Brand Book*, 116.

44. Cato to Findlay, October 2, November 11, 20, 1891, XIT Papers, PPHM; H. J. Rutter and Georgia Rechert, "Cow Tales," SC 35, 26–28, MHS; Niedringhaus, "N Bar N Ranch," 22; *Glendive Independent*, June 1, 1889; "Wibaux Ranch," *Stock Growers Journal*, June 1, 1889; Welsh, "Cosmopolitan Cattle King"; Notice, W. E. Savage, Custer County Treasurer, Miles City, MT, October 6, 1891; Notice, J. C. Auld, Dawson County Treasurer, Glendive, MT, October 12, 1891; Dawson/Custer County Assessment, 1891, [Ledger entry duplicates Cato's report, correcting math], Taxes, Montana Ranch, B1–83/2, XIT Papers, PPHM.

45. "Proceedings of the Board of Equalization," *Glendive Independent*, September 21, 1889; Dawson County [MT] assessments on horses, cattle, and sheep, 1891–1899, Montana Writers Program Records, MF 250, Reel 1, MHS; "Heavy Taxpayers," *Glendive Independent*, December 21, 1889, November 22, 1890, November 21, 1891; "Heavy Taxpayers," *Daily Yellowstone Journal*, October 25, 1893; "Heavy Taxpayers," *Glendive Independent*, October 28, 1893, September 30, 1899; "H. Seton-Karr Report: November 8, 1894," in *CFLIC Proceedings (Eighth)*, 1894, 8–29, XIT Papers, PPHM.

46. "Heavy Taxpayers," *Glendive Independent*, October 28, 1893, October 5, 1895, October 2, 1897, September 28, 1898, September 30, 1899; "H. Seton-Karr Report: November 8, 1894," in *CFLIC Proceedings (Eighth)*, 1894, 29; Cato to Findlay, August 15, 31, September 8, 15 1898; Tally Sheets 41–49, September 17, 22, 24, 25, October 1, 4, 27, November 3, 5, 1898 (3,832 steers), XIT Papers, PPHM.

47. "Heavy Taxpayers," *Daily Yellowstone Journal*, October 25, 1893; "Heavy Taxpayers," *Glendive Independent*, October 28, 1893, September 30, 1899; "Rate of Levy in Counties," *Malta* (MT) *Enterprise*, February 17, 1909; "How to Calculate Property Tax Liability," *Tax Foundation*, February 20, 2009, http://taxfoundation.org/article/how-calculate-property-tax-liability-2.

48. "H. Seton-Karr Report: November 8, 1894," in *CFLIC Proceedings (Eighth)*, 1894, 8–29, XIT Papers, PPHM.

49. "Incorporated" (from *Helena Herald*), *Daily Yellowstone Journal*, March 13, 1886; "Heavy Taxpayers," *Glendive Independent*, December 21, 1889, November 22, 1890, November 21, 1891, October 28, 1893, October 5, 1895, October 2, 1897, September 28, 1898, September 30, 1899; "H. Seton-Karr Report: November 8, 1894," in *CFLIC Proceedings (Eighth)*, 1894, 29; Cato to Findlay, August 15, 31, September 8, 15 1898; Tally Sheets 41–49, September 17, 22, 24, 25, October 1, 4, 27, November 3, 5, 1898 (3,832 steers), XIT Papers, PPHM.

50. "Texas, County Tax Rolls, 1837–1910," *FamilySearch*, www.familysearch.org/en, search Abner Taylor, John V. Farwell, C. B. Farwell, 1891–1910; Accounts, Journal, Ranch, XIT Ranch Journal #1, 1889–1892; "Ranch Statement "1," January 1892; Land Records, Land, Taxes, Record of 1894–1895, XIT Papers, PPHM.

51. Nordyke, *Cattle Empire*, 241; Haley, *XIT Ranch*, 143; XIT Association, "No Such Thing as XIT Brand Recorded in Dallam County," in *XIT Brand*, 50; "Brand Listings," *Stock Growers Journal*, May 4, 1905; *Dawson County* (Glendive, MT) *Review*, June 25, 1903, in Scherger, *Synopsis*, 231.

CHAPTER 7. EMPIRE

1. Haley, *XIT Ranch*, 167; Starrs, *Let the Cowboy Ride*, 2–7, 26–29; Harvey, "George Findlay," 42–44; Jordan, "Windmills in Texas," 81.

2. Starrs, *Let the Cowboy Ride*, 26–27; Nordyke, *Cattle Empire*, 144, 208. For an idea on labor resistance on the imperial ranch, see Anderson and Hill, "Cowboys and Contracts."

3. Osgood, *The Day of the Cattleman*, 229; Nordyke, *Cattle Empire*, 186–87; Freese et al., *Centennial Roundup*, 80.

4. "List of Ranch Employees, 1887," XIT Papers, PPHM; Avery L. Matlock, Texas Legal Consultant, to George F. Westover, Legal Counsel, Chicago, October 9, 1887, March 2, 1888, J. Evetts Haley Collection, "Letters" [Typescript, ca. 1936–1937], 5–30, 53–61, XIT Ranch Records, 1885–1889, DBCAH; Haley, *XIT Ranch*, 98–104; Nordyke, *Cattle Empire*, 121–34, 149.

5. Amos Babcock to W. S. Mabry, District Surveyor, Tascosa, TX, May 12, 1884; Abner Taylor to J. S. Greene, Denver, CO, June 17, August 20, 1889, XIT Papers, PPHM. On the Ogallala Aquifer, see Walsh and Little, "Ogallala Aquifer"; Bjerga, "Great Plains' Looming Water Crisis." For an overview of how government scientists viewed Great Plains water issues, see U.S. Department of the Interior, *Annual Report of Director of Geological Survey*, 692–719.

6. Harvey, "George Findlay," 30, 38; Robertson and Robertson, *Panhandle Pilgrimage*, 186; Haley, *XIT Ranch*, 166, 212; Reeves, "Transformation," 6; Baker, "Inventory of Windmills."

7. *Fort Worth Daily Gazette*, August 6, 20, October 20, 1891; "Professor Dyrenforth successful, Midland, C Ranch, Mr. Rannels," *Fort Worth Daily Gazette*, August 28, 1891; Gwynne, "Rain of Error."

8. C. B. Jewell, Goodland, KS, to Findlay, October 9, 16, 18, December 16, 1893; M. A. Low, Law Department, Chicago, Rock Island & Pacific Railway, Topeka, KS, to Findlay, September 29, 1893, XIT Papers, PPHM.

9. Edward W. Beattie, Surveyor General, Township 15 North, Range 48 East, Montana Meridian, Plat Image, DM ID 136390, March 25, 1901, Bureau of Land Management, General Land Office, https://glorecords.blm.gov/details/survey/default.aspx?dm_id=136390 survey DetailsTabIndex=1 (accessed May 25, 2020); West, *Contested Plains*, 248. See Sherow, *Chisholm Trail*, 90–101, for an engaging analysis of the relationship of water sources and patterns of overgrazing during the cattle trail era. I have never seen an actual "title" for the Montana land. The parcels are identified in the Syndicate land records. The Montana parcels are documented in the government land office. The documents show A. B. Hammond, the lumber king, receiving much of the Cedar Creek ranch in an exchange of Washington forest land in 1904. Cato's wife, Julia, is shown as the grantee of the Hatchet Creek location in 1909. Much of the Big Open was not fully "officially" surveyed before 1900. On Hammond, for whom an endowed chair in the History Department of the University of Montana is named, see Miller, *Illustrated History*, 556–57; Vertical Files, "A. B. Hammond," MHS; Gordon, *When Money Grew on Trees.*

10. Haley, *XIT Ranch*, 143.

11. Ab Owings, XIT Trail Boss, to Findlay, May 24, 1891; Accounts, Ranch, Journal #1, 1889–1892, 159, 169 [June, July], XIT Papers, PPHM.

12. Haley, *XIT Ranch*, 239–40; J. E. Moore, "Diary of a Trail Trip to Montana, 1892" (Typescript, n.d. [1922]), XIT Papers, PPHM (copies also at DBCAH and NSHL): J. Ealy

Moore Diary, 1892, DBCAH; J. E. Moore to J. Evetts Haley, February 26, 1927, J. Evetts Haley Collection V, NSHL.

13. Haley, *XIT Ranch*, 143; Nordyke, *Cattle Empire*, 241; Duke and Frantz, *6,000 Miles*, 20; "Mon Tana Lou Grill," *Montana News Association*, September 26, 1938, Vertical Files: XIT Papers, MHS; XIT Association, "'Scandlous John': Familiar Western Character," and "No Such Thing as XIT Brand Recorded in Dallam County," in *XIT Brand*, 12, 50; "Brand Listings," *Stock Growers Journal*, May 4, 1905; *Dawson County Review*, June 25, 1903, in Scherger, *Synopsis*, 231.

14. F. W. Farwell to Boyce, August 9, 1890, XIT Papers, PPHM. Farwell signs correspondence "F.W." and is also referred to as Frank. Attempts to discover F.W.'s specific relationship to either Farwell brother are inconclusive. He is not either man's son.

15. F. W. Farwell to Findlay, July 28, 1893, XIT Papers, PPHM; "Hicks Stock Car Company," *Mid-Continent Railway Museum*, April 9, 2006, www.midcontinent.org/rollingstock /builders/hicks_stockcar.htm; Conard et al., *Official Railway Equipment Registry*, lxxxi.

16. W. M. Sage, Traffic Manager, Chicago, Rock Island & Pacific Railway Co., Chicago, to F. W. Farwell, July 10, 1893; Y. A. Whitmore, Assistant to the President, Hick's Stock Car Co., Chicago, to Findlay, July 28, 1893; Findlay to Boyce, Liberal, KS [telegram], July 29, 1893; F. W. Farwell to Findlay, July 31, 1893; F. W. Farwell to Findlay, August 3, 1893, XIT Papers, PPHM.

17. Martin A. Knapp, "Car Shortage, Etc: Letter from the Chairman of the Interstate Commerce Commission Transmitting a Transcript of the Testimony Taken by the Commission at St. Louis, Etc., in the Matter of Car Shortage and Other Insufficient Transportation Facilities, December 18–19, 1906," in U.S. Senate. Select Committee on Transportation and Sale of Meat Products, *Investigation*, 149–53.

18. F. W. Farwell to W. D. Jordan, National Stock Yards, St. Claire Co., IL, July 23, 1890; F. W. Farwell to Fred W. De Boice, July 24, 1890; William G. (Green) Preuitt, State of Montana, Board of Stock Commissioners, to Findlay, August 29, 1893, XIT Papers, PPHM; O. C. Cato, Miles City, to John T. Murphy, Helena, MT, July 28, November 15, 1909, John T. Murphy Papers, Incoming Correspondence, 1908–1914, MHS; Clay, *My Life on the Range*, 345; J'Nell L. Pate, "Stockyards Cowboys," in Carlson, *Cowboy Way*, 119–29. Pate's essay is not really about stockyard brand inspectors, but it gives a sense of the conditions in which the inspectors operated.

19. Schofield, *Indians, Cattle, Ships, and Oil*, 89–90; Haley, *Charles Goodnight*, 383; Sullivan, *LS Brand*, 127; Haley, *XIT Ranch*, 204–10. For a further reference to Cheyenne Pens, see chapter 6.

20. *CFLIC Proceedings (Fourth)*, 1889, 12–13; "Report of the Hon. John V. Farwell," in *CFLIC Proceedings (Sixth)*, 1891, 25, XIT Papers, PPHM.

21. *Fort Worth Daily Gazette*, January 30, 1890; September 6, September 22, 1890; December 17, 1890.

22. Henry M. Robert, Stehman Forney, and Robert Moore, Board of Engineers, U.S. Army, in U.S. Senate, Committee on Commerce, *Improvements at the Mouth*, 1–63; John M. Wilson, Chief of Engineers, U.S. Army, in U.S. House, Committee on Rvers and Harbors, *Examination and Survey*, 6, 1–36.

23. Robert et al. in U.S. House, *Examination and Survey*, 9–11, 14–19, 40–48.

24. *Chicago Tribune*, February 26, 1899. After serving several years in the House of Representatives, Farwell took a break from officeholding. He returned to Congress as a senator in 1887 to complete the term of the deceased Gen. John A. Logan. Farwell did not seek reelection in 1891, instead becoming the president of the John V. Farwell & Co. See Arthur H. Miller, "Charles B. Farwell," 2010, Lake Forest College Library Archives and Special Collections, Lake Forest, IL; Lusk, *History of the Contest for United States Senator*. Taylor served in the 51st and 52nd Congresses from 1889 to 1893.

25. *New York Times*, October 23, 1889; Farwell, *Some Recollections*, 41.

26. Farwell, *Some Recollections*, 202–6; *New York Daily Tribune*, March 15, 1886; *National Republican* (Washington, DC), March 16, 1886. "Sturgis" is sometimes written "Sturges"; see *New York Times*, June 22, 1894; *Decatur* (TX) *Daily Republican*, June 22, 1894. See also *Farwell v. Sturges*, 58 Ill. App. 462, 1895 Ill. App. Lexis 74.

27. Texas Constitution, Article XIV, "Public Lands and Land Office," Section 3, Part 2, Section 5; James S. Hogg, "State of the State Message, 1893," *Legislative Reference Library of Texas*, www.lrl.state.tx.us/scanned/govdocs/James%20Stephen%20Hogg/1893/SOS_Hogg_1893.pdf; Atherton, *Cattle Kings*, 198; Cotner, *James Stephen Hogg*, 105–17, 133–38; Robert C. Cotner, "Hogg, James Stephen," *Handbook of Texas Online*, mod. November 6, 2019, www.tshaonline.org/handbook/online/articles/fho17; *Texas Senate Journal, Twenty-third Legislature, January 10, 1893–May 9, 1893* (Austin: State Printer, 1893), 14–16.

28. Dr. William Green, conversation with author, March 12, 2014; *Austin Weekly Statesman*, April 6, 1893.

29. Cotner, *James Stephen Hogg*, 341–42; *Fort Worth Daily Gazette*, April 16, 1893; *Waco* (TX) *Evening News*, April 7, 1893; Nordyke, *Cattle Empire*, 218–21.

30. *Fort Worth Daily Gazette*, June 16, 1890; *Weekly Statesman*, July 3, 1890; Cotner, *James Stephen Hogg*, 209–19; Findlay to Matlock, Texline, TX, August 13, 1890, XIT Papers, PPHM.

31. Cotner, *James Stephen Hogg*, 137–38, 169–71; "The Fight for the Commission," [*Hazardous Business: Industry, Regulation, and the Texas Railroad Commission*, online exhibit] Texas State Library and Archives Commission, 5–6, www.tsl.texas.gov/exhibits/railroad/fight/page5.html.

32. Taylor to James S. Hogg, Attorney General, Austin, TX, August 3, 1889, XIT Papers, PPHM; State of Texas, *Biennial Report* (1886), 195–205; Cotner, *James Stephen Hogg*, 210–11.

33. Taylor to Matlock, June 21, 1890, XIT Papers, PPHM; Cotner, *James Stephen Hogg*, 209–11, 219; Cunningham, *Cowboy Conservatism*, 15–16.

34. *Weekly Statesman*, August 18, November 10, 1892; Cotner, *James Stephen Hogg*, 295–303, 402, 439–442.

35. Cotner, *James Stephen Hogg*, 312–19; *Weekly Statesman*, November 17, 1892; *Greer County v. Texas*, 31 Tex. Civ. App. 223; 72 S.W. 104; 1903 Tex. App. LEXIS 27. For a good summary of the Greer County story, see Webb L. Moore, "Greer County," *Handbook of Texas Online*, June 15, 2010, https://tshaonline.org/handbook/online/articles/hcg81.

36. Findlay to Matlock, January 13, 1890; Findlay to H. H. Wallace, President, Oldham County Commissioners, Tascosa, TX, January 13, 1890, XIT Papers, PPHM; Nordyke, *Cattle Empire*, 214–22.

37. Haley, *XIT Ranch*, 111–12; Nordyke, *Cattle Empire*, 233–35; Findlay to James M. Cook, Foreman, Escarbada Division, January 4, 1890, XIT Papers, PPHM; Alexander, *Rawhide Ranger*, 264, 280–83; Aten, "Six and One-Half Years."

38. *Wallace's Farmer and Dairyman* (Des Moines, IA), January 18, 1901. Cattle rustling remains a problem for modern ranchers, albeit not on the scale that plagued the owners and managers of the XIT; see Herskovitz and Brandes, "Cattle Rustling U.S.A."

39. *Weekly Statesman*, November 16, 1893; Nordyke, *Cattle Empire*, 222–23.

40. Nordyke, *Cattle Empire*, 251; *Amarillo News-Globe*, August 14, 1938, sec. D, 22; *An Act Making Appropriations For Sundry Civil Expenses of the Government For the Fiscal Year Ending June Thirtieth, Eighteen Hundred and Ninety-two, and For Other Purposes*, Public Law 51–542, 26 Stat. 948 (1891): 971.

41. W. S. Mabry to Findlay, September 9, 1893, XIT Papers, PPHM.

42. W. S. Mabry, Sales Agent, Vernon, Texas to Findlay, June 5, 1893; Charles Hamilton, General Manager, Texas Central Railway, Waco, to Findlay, March 31, 1893, XIT Papers, PPHM; Nancy Beck Young, "Texas Central Railroad," *Handbook of Texas Online*, mod. May 20, 2019, www.tshaonline.org/handbook/online/articles/eqt11.

43. Matlock to Findlay, February 27, 1893, XIT Papers, PPHM; "Sue Greenleaf" and "Mary [Sweet] Greenleaf," *1900, 1910, 1920, 1930 United States Federal Census* [database on-line], *California, Death Index, 1905–1939* [database on-line] (Provo, UT: Ancestry.com Operations Inc, 2004, 2013); *Weekly Statesman*, July 27, 1893; *Fort Worth Daily Gazette*, December 10, 1893; *San Francisco Call*, October 14, 18, 1911; Di Cola and Stone, *Chicago's 1893 World's Fair*, 79. A collection of articles regarding suffrage and the women's movement—Ruthe Winegarten et al., eds., *Citizens at Last*, 107–12—includes an article by Greenleaf, "Equal Suffrage Means Purer Laws: Women Should Vote," from *Dallas Morning News*, June 8, 1894. See also Greenleaf, *Future Metropolis*. Greenleaf supported herself and her mother as a writer throughout her life. Her mother died in 1918, and Sue later moved to Los Angeles, where she died at the age of seventy-two on March 2, 1935.

44. Sue Greenleaf to Findlay, October 13, 1893; Greenleaf to Findlay, November 3, 1893, XIT Papers, PPHM.

45. Hugo Dunfalvy, Chicago to Findlay, December 6, 1893, XIT Papers, PPHM; Haley and Holden, *Flamboyant Judge*, 173. Hamlin was a huge figure in Panhandle business and politics. He acted as a lawyer and land agent for Capitol Freehold, later Capitol Reservation Lands. The *Flamboyant Judge* documents Hamlin's extensive association with the Farwell brothers, their heirs, and the Capitol Freehold land.

46. F. W. Farwell to Findlay, August 5, 1893, XIT Papers, PPHM.

47. *CFLIC Proceedings (Eighth)*, 1894, 2–4, XIT Papers, PPHM.

48. John V. Farwell, "Report to the Board of Directors of the Capitol Freehold Land and Investment Company, Limited" (typed draft), December 31, 1892, XIT Papers, PPHM; "About Texas Wine Grapes," *Texas Wine and Grape Growers Association*, www.txwines.org /about-texas-wine (accessed May 27, 2017).

49. Findlay to Postmaster, Anthony, NM [Charles E. Miller], February 24, 1893; [Miller to Findlay, undated], XIT Papers, PPHM.

50. Hiram Hadley, President, New Mexico A&M College, Las Cruces, NMT, to Findlay, March 9, 1893, XIT Papers, PPHM.

51. J. P. Onstott, Yuba City, CA, to Findlay, April 3, 5, 1893; F. W. Farwell to Findlay, July 28, 1893, XIT Papers, PPHM.

52. John V. Farwell, "Report to the Board of Directors of the Capitol Freehold Land and Investment Company, Limited," December 31, 1892; *CFLIC Proceedings (Sixth)*, 1891, 18–25; *CFLIC Proceedings (Eighth)*, 1894, 5–7; *CFLIC Proceedings (Seventh)*, 1892, 2, 18–19, XIT Papers, PPHM.

53. Taylor to Findlay, March 26, 1889; Boyce to John V. Farwell, January 13, 1891; F. W. Farwell to Findlay, August 1, 1893; *CFLIC Proceedings (Fourth)*, 1889, 32–33; *CFLIC Proceedings (Sixth)*, 1891, 25–32, XIT Papers, PPHM; Findlay, "Famous XIT Range Classic"; T. F. B. Sotham, "The Grade Bull," *De Moines Homestead*, July 27, 1899; *Dawson County Review*, November 20, 1902, in Scherger, *Synopsis*, 223; Haley, *XIT Ranch*, 218–21.

54. Haley, *XIT Ranch*, 131, 146–48; Milner and O'Connor, *As Big as the West*, 259; *Helena Independent*, June 4, 1891.

55. Paul H. Carlson, "Myth and the Modern Cowboy" and "Cowboys and Sheepherders," in Carlson, *Cowboy Way*, 4, 115–16. A detailed study of the Matador finances from the Scottish company's perspective is Swan, *Scottish Cowboys*.

56. Carlson, "Myth and the Modern Cowboy," in Carlson, *Cowboy Way*, 5; Ward, *Cowboy at Work*, 4.

57. Carlson, "Myth and the Modern Cowboy," in Carlson, *Cowboy Way*, 5–6. See also Slatta, *Cowboys*, 4, 30, 47.

58. Forbis, *Cowboys*, 20; Starrs, *Let the Cowboy Ride*, 2; James R. Wagner, "Cowboy: Origin and Early Use of the Term," in Carlson, *Cowboy Way*, 11–20.

59. Forbis, *Cowboys*, 17–18; Starrs, *Let the Cowboy Ride*, 5.

60. Atherton, *Cattle Kings*, 227–35; Robert E. Zeigler, "The Cowboy Strike of 1883," in Carlson, *Cowboy Way*, 80–81; *News-Globe*, August 14, 1938, sec. E, 14; "Prices Paid per Month for the Following Classes of Employees" [handwritten notation of "Pay Roll Average 1888"], XIT Papers, PPHM.

61. Duke and Frantz, *6,000 Miles*, 142–45, 149; Kennedy, *Cowboys and Cattlemen*, 136. Mrs. Duke's segment on Montana, primarily the recollections of cowboy Al Denby, is one of the best descriptions of the Montana operation and its men; see Duke and Frantz, *6,000 Miles*, 139–53. See also Russell, *Bob Fudge;* Wollaston, *Homesteading*, 65.

CHAPTER 8. CLOSEOUT

1. Dr. William Green, conversation with author, March 12, 2014; *Austin Weekly Statesman*, April 6, 1893; Nordyke, *Cattle Empire*, 220; Haley and Holden, *Flamboyant Judge*, 169; Kent Biffle, "Capitol Trade a Twisted Tale," *Dallas Morning News*, May 12, 1996; *Stock Growers Journal*, September 3, 1892; *Daily Yellowstone Journal*, August 14, 1895.

2. Taylor to Findlay, March 26, 1889; Boyce to J. V. Farwell, January 13, 1891 ("The more I see of the black cattle the more I like them."); H. Milner Willis, Secretary, Capitol Freehold, London, to Findlay June 7, 1900; Cash, Stone, & Co., Auditors to Willis, May 18, 1900;

Findlay to Willis, June 25, 1900; *CFLIC Proceedings (Twentieth)*, 1907, 3, XIT Papers, PPHM; T. F. B. Sotham, "The Grade Bull," *Des Moines Homestead*, July 27, 1899; *Dawson County Review* (Glendive, MT), November 20, 1902, quoted in Scherger, 223; Haley, *XIT Ranch*, 187–93, 218–21.

3. H. Milner Willis, Secretary, Capitol Freehold, London, to Findlay June 7, 1900; Cash, Stone, & Co., Auditors to Willis, May 18, 1900; Findlay to Willis, June 25, 1900, XIT Papers, PPHM.

4. Findlay, "Famous XIT Range Classic"; R. L. Duke to Capitol Freehold, Chicago, June 24, August 16, 1912 ["Spring Tallies" and "Montana Sales"], XIT Papers, PPHM.

5. Tower & Collins, Livestock and Real Estate Brokers, Miles City, MT, to George Findlay, January 21, 1898, XIT Papers, PPHM.

6. Haley, *XIT Ranch*, 206–11; A. G. Boyce, Wm. Boyce, Geo. Findlay, "3,000,000 Acres Fine Agricultural and Grazing Land," Promotional booklet w/photographs, J. Evetts Haley Collection IV-A-1, W.6, F.6, XIT Ranch, NSHL.

7. Skaggs, *Cattle-Trailing Industry*, 4, 11, 71; Brayer, "Influence of British Capitol," 91–93; "Owns 1,250,000 Acres," *Pittsburg* (PA) *Press*, June 21, 1901; J. Marvin Hunter, "Major George Washington Littlefield," in *Trail Drivers*, 700–702; Blodgett, *Land of Bright Promise*, 43; David B. Gracy II, "Littlefield, George Washington," *Handbook of Texas Online*, June 15, 2020, www.tshaonline.org/handbook/online/articles/fli18; *Amarillo News-Globe*, August 14, 1938, sec. E, 10, 14; Haley, *XIT Ranch*, 218; Nordyke, *Cattle Empire*, 246–47.

8. Chicago [Findlay?] to John V. Farwell Jr., London, August 30, 1905, XIT Papers, PPHM; Blodgett, *Bright Promise*, 41–42; Haley, *XIT Ranch*, 218–20; *News-Globe*, August 14, 1938. Fred W. Browne, J. M. Lyon, and Bert E. Nash led the South and West Land Company.

9. Haley and Holden, *Flamboyant Judge*, 169–73; Haley, *XIT Ranch*, 221–25; *News-Globe*, August 14, 1938; H. Allen Anderson, "XIT Ranch," *Handbook of Texas Online*, mod. December 9, 2015, www.tshaonline.org/handbook/online/articles/apx01.

10. Cato to Findlay, March 16, 1891, XIT Papers, PPHM; "Local Items," *Daily Yellowstone Journal*, August 29, 1896; *Billings Gazette*, February 5, 1901; "It's Twenty-Two Times," *Stock Growers Journal*, April 17, 1907; Advertisement, "The O. C. Cato Ice Company," *Stock Growers Journal*, September 18, 1907.

11. "Legislative Biographies," vol. 1 (1897–1915), s.v. "Cato," Montana Historical Society Library, MHS; *Terry* (MT) *Tribune*, May 7, 1915; A. W. Bowen & Co., *Progressive Men*, 242–43; *Daily Yellowstone Journal*, April 19, 1892, August 29, 1896; "It's Twenty-Two Times," *Stock Growers Journal*, April 17, 1907.

12. *Weekly Yellowstone Journal* (Miles City, MT), November 10, 1898.

13. *Glendive Independent*, December 24, 31, 1898.

14. *Glendive Independent*, December 31, 1898, January 14, 21, 28, February 18, March 25, 1899.

15. *Anaconda* (MT) *Standard*, May 17, June 13, 1899; *Butte* (MT) *Daily Inter Mountain*, January 29, March 30, 31, 1900.

16. *Weekly Yellowstone Journal*, April 6, 1899; *Billings Gazette*, January 9, 1900; Cato to Findlay, August 25, 1899, XIT Papers, PPHM; *Billings Gazette*, August 29, 1899; *Anaconda Standard*, August 23, December 31, 1899.

17. Howard, *Montana*, 112–13, 320; Brown, *Plainsmen of the Yellowstone*, 422–23; Freese et al., *Centennial Roundup*, 67; Brown and Felton, *Before Barbed Wire*, 93, 221.

18. Findlay to Boyce, April 1, May 6, 9, 17, 1901, XIT Papers, PPHM; Marsh, *Loco Weed Disease*; Agricultural Research Service, "Locoweed," Department of Agriculture, USDA.gov, 2014, http://ars.usda.gov/services/docs.htm?docid=9948.

19. Findlay to Boyce, April 1, May 6, 9, 17, 1901, XIT Papers, PPHM; Dr. William Green, conversation with Author, March 12, 2014; Haley and Holden, *Flamboyant Judge*, 169; Nordyke, *Cattle Empire*, 244–50.

20. C. B. Farwell to Boyce, April 10, 1902, Boyce, A. G., J. Evetts Haley Collection II-B, NSHL.

21. *Billings Gazette*, April 12, 1901.

22. Findlay to H. R. McCullough, Chicago & North Western RR, Chicago, April 21, 1902, XIT Papers, PPHM. It sometimes becomes difficult to distinguish the Syndicate lessees of the ranch from Capitol Freehold and the local lessees the ranch offered land for pasturage.

23. Findlay to Boyce, April 3, 29, May 7, 15, 29, 1902, XIT Papers, PPHM. Findlay hoped the shipments would take about five days. The cattle would be fed at Herington, Sioux City, and Jamestown. Findlay expressed concern not to draw the attention of the Humane Society. Cattle were unloaded and rested for twelve hours at least once on the way.

24. Findlay to Boyce, May 31, June 12, 25, 1902, July 9, 1902, XIT Papers, PPHM; Findlay to Boyce (telegrams), June 24, 25, 1902, J. Evetts Haley Collection IV-A, NSHL. Some explanation of the route for the XIT's return to Montana may come in Capitol Freehold's long-running dispute with C. F. Meek, the one-time president of the FW&DC. The company ultimately wrote of charges for some 6,400 acres Meek agreed to purchase in 1889. The Syndicate continually sparred with the railroads about rates anyway, and this was probably just that simple. John V. Farwell Jr. was later on the board of the Chicago & North Western. See Chicago and North Western Railway, *Yesterday and Today*, 5, 173.

25. Findlay to Cato, April 1, 1895, XIT Papers, PPHM; Evelyn Jephson Cameron Collection, Photographs Collection, and Evelyn Cameron, 1868–1928, Diaries (1893–1928), [September 22, 1903], MHS; Chicago Report prepared for Twenty-First Annual Meeting, dated October 14, 1908, XIT Papers, PPHM.

26. Willis to Findlay, August 23, December 1, 1904; Willis to Findlay, December 20, 1905; Jonathon W. Donnelly, John V. Farwell Co., Liverpool, to Findlay, May 18, June 13, 1906; [Treasurer, Chicago] to Donnelly, March 16, May 7, 1906; Donnelly to John V. Farwell Jr., April 25, 1906, XIT Papers, PPHM; Blodgett, *Bright Promise*, 58–59.

27. Haley, *XIT Ranch*, 217; Nordyke, *Cattle Empire*, 247; Duke and Frantz, *6,000 Miles*, 180–83; *Daily Yellowstone Journal*, July 26, 1901. Boyce was never happy with the land sales aspect of his duties in Texas. W. S. Mabry, a surveyor and sometimes Syndicate employee, reported on Boyce's curmudgeonly attitude on the role yet wrote that Boyce would "make as good a land man as a cattle man." W. S. Mabry to Findlay, September 9, 1893, XIT Papers, PPHM; H. Allen Anderson, "Boice, Henry S.," *Handbook of Texas Online*, June 12, 2010, www.tshaonline.org/handbook/online/articles/fbo89. On the murder of the Boyces, see Neal, *Vengeance Is Mine*. Growing up a cowboy, Al Boyce visited Montana often and may have been employed for a time by Cato.

28. *Dallas Morning News*, November 19, 1892, July 31, 1901, February 2, 1916; Haley, *XIT Ranch*, 215; *Babcock v. Farwell*, 146 Ill. App. 307, LEXIS 359 [Ill. App. Ct. 1909]; *Babcock v. Farwell* [1913], 1, 1170, 1183; *Babcock v. Farwell*, 189 Ill. App. 279, 1914 LEXIS 316 [Ill. App. Ct. 1914].

29. Howard, *Montana*, 164–66; Wollaston, *Homesteading*, 63; "History of Custer County [Winter of 1906–1907]," U.S. Work Projects Administration, Montana Writers Program Records, 1939–1941, Microfilm 250, Reel 18, MHS; William Floyd Hardin (1890–1974), "Reminiscence, 1951," 98, MHS; Hartmann, "'Our Snow Covered Trail'; *Babcock v. Farwell*, 190 1d 19580 [Ill. App. Ct. 1913]; Nordyke, *Cattle Empire*, 247; *Chicago Tribune*, February 26, 1899; "Obituary [C. B. Farwell], *New York Daily Tribune* and *New York Sun*, September 24, 1903; "Ex-Congressman Abner Taylor [obituary]," *New York Times*, April 14, 1903; Bill McKern, "Abner Taylor," *Find A Grave* [online], Mar 15, 2008, www.findagrave.com/cgi-bin /fg.cgi?page=gr&GRid=25294639.

30. Agreement for Ferry and Corral Service, Seth Mabry, H. R. Phillips, O. C. Cato, and George Lennare [Larrabee?], May 2, 1892, "Mont Sales 1909 [Cattle Sales]," XIT Papers, PPHM; *Babcock v. Farwell*, 1913, 588; *Dawson County Review*, February 25, 1910, in Scherger, *Synopsis*, 324; Matt J. Roke, Foreman, Montana Cattle Co. to John T. Murphy, Helena, May 14, 1909, John T. Murphy Papers, MC 84 Box 5 Folder 22, MHS; *Stock Growers Journal*, April 17, 1907, October 17, 1908.

31. Notice, *London Standard*, April 6, 1907; *CFLIC Proceedings (Twenty-Second)*, 1909, 5, XIT Papers, PPHM; Haley, *XIT Ranch*, 73, 223; Dan Packard, "XIT's Home on the Range Moving," *Amarillo Globe-News*, April 13, 2008. For more on the land operation, see James D. Hamlin Papers, Southwest Collection, Texas Tech University.

32. Osgood, *Day of the Cattleman*, 177–215.

33. *CFLIC Proceedings (Twenty-Sixth)*, 1913, 5; R. L. Duke to Capitol Freehold, Chicago, June 24, August 16, 1912, XIT Papers, PPHM; Nordyke, *Cattle Empire*, 241. The actual Montana count is 460 steers, spayed heifers, and cows. An additional fifty-seven calves were not figured in the sales count, as was customary. For spaying information, see Ben Woodcock, "Cattle Spaying," Montana Writers Project, Reel 18, MHS; C. O. Netherton, *Cattle Spaying* (Gallatin, MO: Democrat Print, 1906), XIT Museum, Dalhart, TX.

34. Robbins, *Colony and Empire*, 88–89.

35. Kramer, "Power and Connection," 1354–65, 1376–78, 1383; Robbins, *Colony and Empire*, 169–73. For another succinct summation of the end of the imperial ranch, see Jordan, *North American Cattle-Ranching*, 236–40.

36. Worster, *Dust Bowl*; Egan, *Worst Hard Time*.

37. Malin, *Grassland*, 62–81; Webb, *Great Plains*, 29–33; Osgood, *Day of the Cattleman*, 217; Lewis, "Cattle Trail," 212; Richardson, *Compilation*, 9:97–98.

Bibliography

ARCHIVES AND MANUSCRIPTS

Austin History Center, Austin Public Library, Austin, Texas

Dolph Briscoe Center for American History, The University of Texas at Austin, Austin, Texas

    Moore, J. E. "Ealy." Diary, 1892

    XIT Ranch. Records, 1885–1889

Nita Stewart Haley Memorial Library & J. Evetts Haley Research Center, Midland, Texas

    J. Evetts Haley Collection

        Series I, Photographs

        Series II, Research Files

        Series IV, Literary Productions of J. Evetts Haley

        Series V, Correspondence Files

    Alexander and Lucy Hatch Collection

        Series I, Hatch, McCormick, Streeter, Boice

        Series IV, Materials from Relevant Collections

        Series V, Boice Family Tree

        Series VI, Boice Materials from Miriam Boice

        Series VIII, Boice Ranching Material (Montana and Wyoming)

        Series X, Artifacts

Montana Historical Society, Research Center, Helena, Montana

    Abbott, Edward Charles "Teddy Blue" Papers

    Cameron, Evelyn Jephson. Photographs and Diaries

    Hardin, William Floyd. "Reminiscence, 1951"

    Huffman, L. A. (Laton Alton). Photographs

    Murphy, John T. Papers

    Power, Thomas Charles Papers

    Rutter, Harry J. "Reminiscence, 1931"

    United States. Work Projects Administration. Montana Writers Program Records, 1939–1941

National Portrait Gallery, London, England
Panhandle-Plains Historical Museum, Canyon, Texas
    XIT Ranch. Papers, 1882–1917
    William Benjamin Munson Sr. Papers
Prairie County Museum, Terry, Montana
    Evelyn Cameron Gallery
Range Riders Museum, Miles City, Montana
Ryerson and Burnham Libraries, The Art Institute of Chicago, Chicago, Illinois
Southwest Collection, Texas Tech University, Lubbock, Texas
    Hamlin, James D. Papers
Texas General Land Office, Archives and Records Program, Austin, Texas
    Twichell Survey Records (AR.16.TSR)
Texas State Library and Archives, Austin, Texas
    Texas. Capitol Building Commission. Competition Drawings, Blueprints, and Records,
        1879–1889
    Texas. Governor. Records and Papers [Richard Coke, John Ireland, and Oran M. Roberts]
XIT Museum, Dalhart, Texas

NEWSPAPERS
Chicago Tribune
Daily Gazette, Fort Worth, Texas
Daily Inter Mountain, Butte, Montana
Daily News, Dennison, Texas
Daily News, Galveston, Texas
Daily News, London
Daily Republican, Decatur, Texas
Daily Tribune, New York
Daily Yellowstone Journal, Miles City, Montana
Dawson County Review, Glendive, Montana
Enterprise, Malta, Montana
Evening News, Waco, Texas
Examiner, Waco, Texas
Financial News, London
Gazette, Billings, Montana
Gazette, Las Vegas, New Mexico
Globe-New, Amarillo, Texas
Herald, Glasgow, Scotland
Herald Democrat, Sherman, Texas
Homestead, Des Moines, Iowa
Independent, Glendive, Montana
Independent, Helena, Montana
Morning News, Dallas, Texas
New York Times

News-Argus, Lewistown, Montana

News-Globe, Amarillo, Texas

Pittsburg Press, Pittsburgh, Pennsylvania

River Press, Fort Benton, Montana

Standard, Anaconda, Montana

Standard, London

Stock Growers Journal, Miles City, Montana

Sun, New York

Texan, Shamrock, Texas

Union, Princeton, Minnesota

Wallace's Farmer and Dairy Man, Des Moines, Iowa

Weekly Banner, Brenham, Texas

Weekly Chronicle, Bozeman, Montana

Weekly Crisis, Chillicothe, Missouri

Weekly Herald, Helena, Montana

Weekly Statesman, Austin, Texas

Weekly Yellowstone Journal, Miles City, Montana

PUBLICATIONS AND DISSERTATIONS

A. W. Bowen & Co. *Progressive Men of the State of Montana.* Chicago: A. W. Bowen, 1902.

Abbott, E. C., and Helena Huntington Smith. *We Pointed Them North: Recollections of a Cowpuncher.* Norman: University of Oklahoma Press, 1955.

Adams, James Truslow. *The Epic of America.* Boston: Little Brown, 1931.

Adams, James Truslow, and Howard Schneiderman. *The Epic of America.* New Brunswick, N.J.: Transaction, 2012.

Alexander, Bob. *Rawhide Ranger, Ira Aten: Enforcing Law on the Texas Frontier.* Denton: University of North Texas Press, 2011.

Anderson, Terry L., and Peter J. Hill. "Cowboys and Contracts." *Journal of Legal Studies* 31 (June 2002): S489–514.

Andreas, Alfred Theodore. *History of Chicago.* 3 vols. 1884. Reprint, New York: Arno Press, 1975.

Archive and History Department of the Texas State Library. *Governors' Messages: Coke to Ross, 1874–1891.* Austin, Tex.: Baldwin and Sons, 1916.

Armitage, George T. "Prelude to the Last Roundup. The Dying Days of the Great 79." *Montana: The Magazine of Western History* 11 (Autumn 1961): 66–75.

Aten, Ira. "Six and One-Half Years in the Ranger Service: Memoirs of Sergeant Ira Aten." *Frontier Times* 22 (March 1945): 157–165.

Athearn, Robert G. *Union Pacific Country.* New York: Rand McNally, 1971.

Atherton, Lewis. "Cattleman and Cowboy: Fact and Fancy." *Montana: The Magazine of Western History* 11 (Autumn 1961): 2–17.

———. *The Cattle Kings.* Bloomington: Indiana University Press, 1961.

Baker, E. T. *Adventures on the King Ranch and Armstrong Ranch.* Austin: E. T. Baker, 2009.

Baker, T. Lindsay. *Building the Lone Star: An Illustrated Guide to Historic Sites.* College Station: Texas A&M University Press, 1986.

———. "An Inventory of Windmills on Part of the XIT Ranch of Texas in 1912." *Windmillers' Gazette* 23 (Summer 2004): 8–14.

Ball, C. E. "Historical Overview of Beef Production and Beef Organization in the United States." *Proceedings of the Western Section, American Society of Animal Science, 2000* (2001).

Barnes, Ian. *The Historical Atlas of Native Americans*. New York: Hartwell Books, 2009.

Belgrad, Daniel. "'Power's Larger Meaning': The Johnson County War as Political Violence in an Environmental Context," *Western Historical Quarterly* 33 (Summer 2002): 159–77.

Belich, James. *Replenishing the Earth: The Settler Revolution and the Rise of the Anglo-World, 1783–1939*. Oxford: Oxford University Press, 2009.

Bjerga, Alan. "The Great Plains' Looming Water Crisis." *Bloomberg Businessweek*, July 2, 2015.

Blodgett, Jan. *Land of Bright Promise: Advertising the Texas Panhandle and South Plains, 1870–1917*. Austin: University of Texas Press, 1988.

Bobrow-Strain, Aaron. "Logics of Cattle–Capital." *Geoforum* 40 (2009): 778–80.

Brands, H. W. *American Colossus: The Triumph of Capitalism, 1865–1890*. New York: Anchor Books, 2010.

Brayer, Herbert O. "The Influence of British Capitol on the Western Range Cattle Business." *Journal of Economic History* 9 (1949): 85–98.

———. "Review of *Cattle Empire: The Fabulous Story of the 3,000,000 Acre XIT* by Lewis Nordyke." *Pacific Historical Review* 19 (August 1950): 299–300.

Brinkman, Bob, and Dan K. Utley. "A Name on the Cornerstone: The Landmark Texas Architecture of Jasper Newton Preston." *Southwestern Historical Quarterly* 110 (July 2006): 1–37.

Brisbin, James S. *The Beef Bonanza; Or, How to Get Rich on the Plains, Being a Description of Cattle Growing, Sheep-Farming, Horse-Raising, and Dairying in the West*. 1881. Reprint, Norman: University of Oklahoma Press, 1959.

Brown, Dee, and Martin F. Schmitt. *Trail Driving Days*. New York: Charles Scribner, 1952.

Brown, Mark H. *The Plainsmen of the Yellowstone: A History of the Yellowstone Basin*. New York: G. P. Putnam's Sons, 1961.

Brown, Mark H., and W. R. Felton. *Before Barbed Wire: L. A. Huffman, Photographer on Horseback*. New York: Bramhall House, 1956.

Burns, Robert H. "The Newman Brothers: Forgotten Cattle Kings of the Northern Plains." *Montana: The Magazine of Western History* 11 (Autumn 1961): 28–36.

Campbell, Randolph B. *Gone to Texas: A History of the Lone Star State*. New York: Oxford University Press, 2003.

———. *Grass-Roots Reconstruction in Texas*. Baton Rouge: Louisiana State University Press, 1997.

Carlson, Paul Howard, ed. *The Cowboy Way: An Exploration of History and Culture*. Lubbock: Texas Tech University Press, 2000.

———. *The Plains Indians*. College Station: Texas A&M University Press, 1998.

Carter, Sarah, S. M. Evans, and Bill Yeo. *Cowboys, Ranchers and the Cattle Business: Cross-Border Perspectives on Ranching History*. Calgary: University of Calgary Press, 1999.

Carter, Susan B., et al. "Table Da968–982: Cattle, Hogs, Sheep, Horses, and Mules—Number on Farms: 1868–2000 [Annual]." In *Historical Statistics of the United States Millennial Edition.* New York: Cambridge University Press, 2006.

Cashion, Ty. "What's the Matter with Texas?" *Montana: The Magazine of Western History* 55 (Winter 2005): 2–15.

Cates, Ivan. *The XIT Ranch: A Texas Legacy.* Channing: Hafabanana Press, 2008.

Chicago and North Western Railway and the Compiler. *Yesterday and Today: A History of the Chicago and North Western Railway System,* 3rd ed. Chicago: Chicago and North Western Railway, 1910.

Chicago Railways Company. *Chicago Railways Company Report of Henry A. Blair, Chairman to the Board of Directors, Dated April 23, 1913.* Chicago: Chicago Railways, 1913.

Clark, Jonas. "In Search of the American Dream." *Atlantic,* June 2007. www.theatlantic.com /magazine/archive/2007/06/in-search-of-the-american-dream/305921.

Clay, John. *My Life on the Range.* 1924. Reprint, New York: Antiquarian Press, 1961.

Clay, T. A. "A Call to Order: Law, Violence, and the Development of Montana's Early Stockmen's Organizations." *Montana: The Magazine of Western History* 58 (Autumn 2008): 40–63, 95–96.

Clayton, Lawrence, and J. U. Salvant. *Historic Ranches of Texas.* Austin: University of Texas Press, 1993.

Clements, Roger V. "British-Controlled Enterprise in the West between 1870 and 1900, and Some Agrarian Reactions." *Agricultural History* 27 (October 1953): 132–41.

———. "British Investment and American Legislative Restrictions in the Trans-Mississippi West, 1880–1900." *Mississippi Valley Historical Review* 42 (September 1955): 207–28.

Collins, Michael L. *That Damned Cowboy: Theodore Roosevelt and the American West, 1883–1898.* New York: Peter Lang, 1991.

Conard, G. P., et al. *The Official Railway Equipment Registry.* New York: Railway and Equipment Publications, 1903.

Connor, Seymour Vaughan. *A Guide to the XIT Papers in the Panhandle-Plains Historical Museum.* Canyon, Tex.: Panhandle-Plains Historical Museum, 1953.

Cotner, Robert Crawford. *James Stephen Hogg: A Biography.* Austin: University of Texas Press, 1959.

Cram, George Franklin, and Oscar Hinrichs. *Cram's Standard American Atlas of the World. Accompanied by a Complete and Simple Index.* New York: George F. Cram, 1889.

Cronon, William. *Nature's Metropolis: Chicago and the Great West.* New York: W. W. Norton, 1992.

Crosby, Alfred W. *The Columbian Exchange: Biological and Culture Consequence of 1492.* Westport, Conn: Greenwood Press, 1973.

Cullen, Jim. *The American Dream.* New York: Oxford University Press, 2003.

Cunningham, Sean P. *Cowboy Conservatism: Texas and the Rise of the Modern Right.* Lexington: University Press of Kentucky, 2010.

Dale, Edward E. *Cattle-Raising on the Plains of North America.* Norman: University of Oklahoma Press, 1964.

———. *The Range Cattle Industry: Ranching on the Great Plains from 1865 to 1965.* Norman: University of Oklahoma, 1960.

Dalrymple, William Haddock, Harcourt A. Morgan, and W. R. Dodson. *Cattle Tick and Texas Fever: Results of Experiments at State Experiment Station, Baton Rouge, LA.* Baton Rouge: Louisiana Bureau of Agriculture and Immigration, 1898.

Daniell, L. E. *Personnel of the Texas State Government, with Sketches of Distinguished Texans, Embracing the Executive and Staff, Heads of Departments, United States Senators and Representatives, Members of the XXth Legislature.* Austin: Press of the City, 1887.

Davis, John W. *Wyoming Range War: The Infamous Invasion of Johnson County.* Norman: University of Oklahoma Press, 2010.

Denoon, Donald. *Settler Capitalism: The Dynamics of Dependent Development in the Southern Hemisphere.* New York: Oxford University Press, 1983.

Di Cola, Joseph M., and David Stone. *Chicago's 1893 World's Fair.* Charleston, S.C.: Arcadia, 2012.

Dobie, Frank J. *Cow People.* Boston: Little Brown, 1964.

Dobie, Frank J., and Tom Lea. *The Longhorns.* Austin: University of Texas Press, 1990.

Duke, Cordia Sloan, and Joe B. Frantz. *6,000 Miles of Fence: Life on the XIT Ranch of Texas.* Austin: University of Texas Press, 1961.

Dumbauld, Edward. *The Political Writings of Thomas Jefferson: Representative Selections.* Indianapolis: Bobbs-Merrill, 1976.

Egan, Timothy. *The Worst Hard Time: The Untold Story of Those Who Survived the Great American Dust Bowl.* New York: Mariner Books, 2006.

Elofson, W. M. *Cowboys, Gentlemen and Cattle Thieves: Ranching on the Western Frontier.* Montréal: McGill-Queen's University Press, 2000.

———. *Frontier Cattle Ranching in the Land and Times of Charlie Russell.* Seattle: University of Washington Press, 2004.

Ely, Glen Sample. *Where the West Begins: Debating Texas Identity.* Lubbock: Texas Tech University Press, 2011.

Evans, Keith. "Angus Origins." *Angus Journal,* February 2005: 215–18.

Farwell, John Villiers, Jr. *Some Recollections of John V. Farwell: A Brief Description of His Early Life and Business Reminiscences.* Chicago: R. R. Donnelley and Sons, 1911.

Ferry, Abby Farwell. *Reminiscences of John V. Farwell.* Chicago: Ralph Fletcher Seymour, 1928.

Findlay, George. "The Aberdeen-Angus on the Range." In *Thirteenth Biennial Report of the Kansas State Board of Agriculture to the Legislature of the State.* Topeka: Kansas Department of Agriculture, 1902.

———. "Famous XIT Range Classic of Angus Cattle." *Aberdeen-Angus Journal* 2, no. 10 (December 13, 1920): 7, 48, 50; no. 11 (December 27, 1920): 3, 21–23; no. 12 (January 10, 1921): 3, 25–27 (there is also editorial on Findlay on 8–9).

Fink, Tiffany Marie Haggard. "The Fort Worth and Denver City Railway: Settlement, Development, and Decline on the Texas High Plains." Ph.D. Diss., Texas Tech University, 2004.

Fleischner, Thomas L. "Ecological Costs of Livestock Raising in Western North America." *Conservation Biology* 8 (September 1994): 629–44.

Fletcher, Robert H. "The Day of the Cattlemen Dawned Early: In Montana." *Montana: The Magazine of Western History* 11 (Autumn 1961): 22–28.

Fletcher, Robert H., and Charles M. Russell. *Free Grass to Fences: The Montana Cattle Range Story.* New York: Published for the Historical Society of Montana, University Publishers, 1960.

Fletcher, Robert S. "The End of the Open Range in Eastern Montana." *Mississippi Valley Historical Review* 16 (September 1929): 188–211.

————. "That Hard Winter in Montana, 1886–1887." *Agricultural History* 4 (October 1930): 123–30.

Foran, Maxwell. *Trails and Trials: Market Land Use in Alberta Beef Cattle Industry.* Calgary: University of Calgary Press, 2003.

Forbis, William H. *The Cowboys.* 1973. Reprint, London: Time-Life Books, 2004.

Frantz, Joe B. "Texas's Largest Ranch: In Montana." *Montana: The Magazine of Western History* 11 (Autumn 1961): 46–56.

Freese, Jean, John Halbert, et al. *Centennial Roundup: A Collection of Stories Celebrating the 100th Anniversary of the Incorporation of Miles City, Montana.* Miles City: Miles City Star, 1987.

Gammel, Hans Peter Marcus Neilsen, and Cadwell Walton Raines. *The Laws of Texas, 1822–1897.* 10 vols. Austin: Gammel Book, 1898.

Garland, Hamlin. *Jason Edwards: An Average Man.* Boston: Arena, 1892.

Gavett, Joseph L. *North Dakota: Counties, Towns and People,* pt. 3. Tacoma, Wash.: Judd's Workshop, 2010.

Gilbert, Fabiola Cabeza de Baca. *We Fed Them Cactus.* Albuquerque: University of New Mexico Press, 1994.

Gordon, David. "Swift & Co. v. United States: The Beef Trust and the Stream of Commerce Doctrine." *American Journal of Legal History* 28 (July 1984): 244–79.

Gordon, Greg. *When Money Grew on Trees: A. B. Hammond and the Age of the Timber Baron.* Norman: University of Oklahoma Press, 2014.

Graham, Richard. "The Investment Boom in British-Texan Cattle Companies, 1880–1885." *Business History Review* 34 (Winter 1960): 421–45.

Grant, Richard. "Recollections of a Cowpuncher." *Cowboys & Indians: The Premier Magazine of the West,* November/December 2013. www.cowboysindians.com/2016/03/recollections -of-a-cowpuncher.

Graybill, Andrew R. *Policing the Great Plains: Rangers, Mounties, and the North American Frontier, 1875–1910.* Lincoln: University of Nebraska Press, 2007.

Grayson County Frontier Village. *The History of Grayson County, Texas.* Dallas, Tex.: Curtis Media, 1981.

Greenleaf, Sue. *The Future Metropolis of Texas.* Fort Worth: H. B. Chamberlain, 1893.

Greer, Joubert Lee. "The Building of the Texas State Capitol, 1882–1888." M.A. Thesis, University of Texas, 1932.

Gunter, Pete A. Y. "Jot Gunter: Sherman Rancher and Land Speculator." In *History of Grayson County Texas,* vol. 2. Sherman, Tex.: Grayson County Frontier Village, 1981.

Gunter, P. A. Y., and Max Oelschlaeger. *Texas Land Ethics.* Austin: University of Texas Press, 1997.

Gwynne, S. C. "Rain of Error: Dry Enough for You?" *Texas Monthly* 31 (August 2003): 38–44.

Hagan, William T. *Charles Goodnight: Father of the Texas Panhandle.* Norman: University of Oklahoma Press, 2007.

Haley, J. Evetts. *Charles Goodnight: Cowman and Plainsman.* Boston: Houghton Mifflin, 1936.

———. *The XIT Ranch of Texas and the Early Days of the Llano Estacado.* Norman: University of Oklahoma Press, 1953.

Haley, J. Evetts, and William Curry Holden. *The Flamboyant Judge: James D. Hamlin, A Biography.* Canyon, Tex.: Palo Duro Press, 1972.

Hämäläinen, Pekka. *The Comanche Empire.* New Haven, Conn.: Yale University Press, 2008.

———. "The Rise and Fall of Plains Indian Horse Cultures." *Journal of American History* 90 (December 2003): 833–62.

Hartmann, Joseph M. "'Our Snow Covered Trail': A Montana Freighter Recalls the Hard Winter of 1906–1907." *Montana: The Magazine of Western History* 61 (Winter 2011): 34–54, 94.

Harvey, T. Fred. "George Findlay, General Manager of the XIT Ranch, 1888–1889." M.A. Thesis, West Texas State College, 1950.

Hazel, G. H. *Public Land Laws of Texas; An Examination of the History of the Public Domain of This State, with the Constitutional and Statutory Provisions, and Leading Cases, Governing Its Use and Disposition.* Austin, Tex,: Gammel's, 1938.

Herskovitz, Jon, and Heidi Brandes. "Cattle Rustling U.S.A.: Where 'Rawhide' Meets 'Breaking Bad.'" *Reuters,* October 20, 2015, http://reut.rs/1MB4xhm.

Hoopes, Lorman L. *This Last West: Miles City, Montana Territory, and Environs, 1876–1886: The People, the Geography, the Incredible History.* Miles City, Mont: L. L. Hoopes, 1990.

Hopkins, James D. "Veterinarian's Report." In *List of Members, By-Laws, and Reports of the Wyoming Stock Growers Association.* Cheyenne, Wyo.: Bristol and Kanabe, 1887.

Howard, Joseph Kinsey. *Montana High, Wide, and Handsome.* New Haven, Conn.: Yale University Press, 1943.

Hughey, Sue C. "Texas: The Lonestar State" [map]. In *Sesquicentennial Projects.* Lakewood, Colo.: Associated Arts, 1985.

Hunter, J. Marvin. "Captain Arrington's Expedition." *Frontier Times* 6 (December 1928): 97–101.

———. *The Trail Drivers of Texas: Interesting Sketches of Early Cowboys and Their Experiences on the Range and on the Trail during the Days That Tried Men's Souls: True Narratives Related by Real Cow-Punchers and the Men Who Fathered the Cattle Industry in Texas.* 1924. Reprint, Austin: University of Texas Press, 1985.

Hutson, Cecil Kirk. "Texas Fever in Kansas, 1866–1930." *Agricultural History* 68 (Winter 1994): 74–104.

Igler, David. *Industrial Cowboys: Miller and Lux and the Transformation of the Far West, 1850–1920.* Berkeley: University of California Press, 2001.

Interstate Convention of Cattlemen. *Proceedings of an Interstate Convention of Cattlemen, Held at Fort Worth, Texas, March 11, 12, 13, 1890.* Washington: Government Printing Office, 1890.

Isenberg, Andrew C. *The Destruction of the Bison: An Environmental History, 1750–1920.* Cambridge: Cambridge University Press, 2010.

Jackson, Jack. *Los Mesteños: Spanish Ranching in Texas, 1721–1821.* College Station: Texas A&M University Press, 1986.

Jordan, Terry G. *North American Cattle-Ranching Frontiers: Origins, Diffusion, and Differentiation.* Albuquerque: University of New Mexico Press, 1993.

———. "Windmills in Texas." *Agricultural History* 37 (April 1963): 80–85.

Joseph, Donald, and Mary Tonkin Smith. *Ten Million Acres: The Life of William Benjamin Munson.* [Privately published, New York: William E. Rudge's Sons], 1946.

Judd, Cornelius D., and Claude V. Hall. *The Texas Constitution Explained and Analyzed.* Dallas: Bank Upshaw, 1932.

Kennedy, Michael S. *Cowboys and Cattlemen: A Roundup from* Montana: The Magazine of Western History. New York: Hastings House, 1964.

Kens, Paul. "Wide Open Spaces? The Texas Supreme Court and the Scramble for the State's Public Domain, 1876–1898." *Western Legal History: The Journal of the Ninth Judicial Circuit Historical Society* 16 (June 2003): 159–87.

Kingston, C. S. "Introduction of Cattle into the Pacific Northwest." *Washington Historical Quarterly* 14 (July 1923): 164–85.

Klein, Kerwin Lee. *Frontiers of Historical Imagination: Narrating the European Conquest of Native America, 1890–1990.* Berkley: University of California Press, 1999.

Kramer, Paul A. "Power and Connection: Imperial Histories of the United States and the World." *American Historical Review* 116 (December 2011): 1348–91.

Lea, Tom. "Prodigious Growth of Cattle Domain." *Life* 43 (July 15, 1957): 70–88.

Lewis, Theodore B. "The National Cattle Trail, 1883–1886." *Nebraska History* 52 (Summer 1971): 205–20.

Libecap, Gary D. "The Rise of the Chicago Packers and the Origins of Meat Inspection and Antitrust." *Economic Inquiry* 30 (April 1992): 242–62.

Limerick, Patricia Nelson. *The Legacy of Conquest: The Unbroken Past of the American West.* New York: W. W. Norton, 1987.

Liu, Joanne S. *Barbed Wire: The Fence That Changed the West.* Missoula, Mont.: Mountain Press, 2009.

Lohse, Joyce B. *First Governor, First Lady: John and Eliza Routt of Colorado.* Palmer Lake, Colo.: Filter Press, 2002.

Lucey, Donna M. *Photographing Montana, 1894–1928: The Life and Work of Evelyn Cameron.* Missoula, Mont.: Mountain Press, 2001.

Lusk, D. W. *History of the Contest for United States Senator, before the Thirty-Fourth General Assembly of Illinois, 1885.* Springfield, Ill.: H. W. Rokker, 1885.

Mabry, Robert Smith. "Capitol Context: A History of the Texas Capitol Complex." M.Arch. Thesis, University of Texas at Austin, 1990.

Mabry, W. S. "Early Surveying in the Texas Panhandle." *Frontier Times* 15 (March 1938): 245–55.

MacMillan, D. "The Gilded Age and Montana's DHS Ranch." *Montana: The Magazine of Western History* (Spring 1970): 52.

Malin, James Claude. *The Grassland of North America; Prolegomena to Its History, with Addenda and Postscript.* Lawrence, Kans.: James C. Malin, 1947, 1956.

Malone, Michael P., and Richard B. Roeder. *Montana: A History of Two Centuries.* Seattle: University of Washington Press, 1976.

Marsh, Charles Dwight. *The Loco Weed Disease of the Plains.* U.S. Department of Agriculture, Bureau of Animal Industry, Bulletin 112. Washington, D.C.: Government Printing Office, June 1909.

Marx, Karl, and E. J. Hobsbawm. *Pre-capitalist Economic Formations.* New York: International, 1965.

McCoy, Joseph G. *Historic Sketches of the Cattle Trade of the West and Southwest.* 1874. Reprint, Columbus, Ohio: Long's College Book, 1951.

McCumsey, John S., Robert H. Burns, et al. "Cowboy and Cattleman's Edition Strikes a Responsive Chord." *Montana: The Magazine of Western History* 12 (Winter 1962): 60–64.

McKay, Seth Shepard. *Debates in the Texas Constitutional Convention of 1875.* Austin: University of Texas Press, 1930.

———. "Making the Texas Constitution of 1876." Ph.D Diss., University of Texas/Ohio State University, 1924.

Miller, David, Dennis Smith, et al. *The History of the Assiniboine and Sioux Tribes of the Fort Peck Indian Reservation, Montana, 1800–2000.* Poplar, Mont.: Fort Peck Community College, 2007.

Miller, Joaquin. *An Illustrated History of the State of Montana.* Chicago: Lewis, 1904.

Miller, Michael M. "Cattle Capitol: Misrepresented Environments, Nineteenth Century Symbols of Power, and the Construction of the Texas State House, 1879–1888." M.A.Thesis, University of North Texas, 2011.

———. "Cowboys and Capitalists: The XIT Ranch in Texas and Montana, 1885–1912." *Montana: The Magazine of Western History* 65 (Winter 2015): 3–28.

Miller, Thomas Lloyd. *Bounty and Donation Land Grants of Texas, 1835–1888.* Austin: University of Texas Press, 1967.

———. *The Public Lands of Texas, 1519–1970.* Norman: University of Oklahoma Press, 1972.

Milner, Clyde A., and Carol A. O'Connor. *As Big as the West: The Pioneer Life of Granville Stuart.* Oxford: Oxford University Press, 2009.

Monday, Jane Clements, and Frances Brannen Vick. *Petra's Legacy: The South Texas Ranching Empire of Petra Vela and Mifflin Kenedy.* College Station: Texas A&M University Press, 2007.

Moneyhon, Carl H. *Texas after the Civil War: the Struggle of Reconstruction.* College Station: Texas A&M University Press, 2004.

Montana Stock Growers Association. *Brand Book of the Montana Stock Growers Association for 1899.* Helena, Mont.: Independent, 1899.

Moore, Gary, Frank A. Weir, et al. *Temporary Capitol of Texas, 1883–88: History and Archaeology.* Austin: Texas Highway Department, 1972.

National Convention of Cattlemen (Cattlemen). *Proceedings of the First National Convention of Cattlemen and of the First Annual Meeting of the National Cattle and Horse Growers Association of the United States, Held in St. Louis, Mo., November 17th to 22d, 1884.* St. Louis: R. P. Studley, 1884.

Neal, Bill. *Vengeance Is Mine: The Scandalous Love Triangle That Triggered the Boyce-Sneed Feud.* Denton: University of North Texas Press, 2011.

Netherton, C. O. *Cattle Spaying.* Gallatin, Mo.: Democrat Print, 1906.

Nevins, Allan. *James Truslow Adams: Historian of the American Dream.* Urbana: University of Illinois Press, 1968.

Niedringhaus, Lee I. "N Bar N Ranch: A Legend of the Open-Range Cattle Industry, 1885–1899." *Montana: The Magazine of Western History* 60 (Spring 2010): 3–23.

Nolan, Frederick W. *Tascosa: Its Life and Gaudy Times.* Lubbock: Texas Tech University Press, 2007.

Nordyke, Lewis. *Cattle Empire: The Fabulous Story of the 3,000,000 Acre XIT.* New York: William Morrow, 1949.

———. *Great Roundup: The Story of Texas and Southwestern Cowmen.* New York: William Morrow, 1955.

Olmstead, Alan L. "The First Line of Defense: Inventing the Infrastructure to Combat Animal Disease." *Journal of Economic History* 69 (June 2009): 327–57.

Olmstead, Alan L., and Paul W. Rhode. *Arresting Contagion: Science, Policy, and Conflicts over Animal Disease Control.* Cambridge: Harvard University Press, 2015.

Osgood, Ernest Staples. *The Day of the Cattleman.* 1929. Reprint, Chicago: University of Chicago Press, 1957.

Ostler, Jeffrey. *The Plains Sioux and U.S. Colonialism from Lewis and Clark to Wounded Knee.* Cambridge: Cambridge University Press, 2004.

Paladin, Vivian A. *From Buffalo Bones to Sonic Boom. Glasgow Diamond Jubilee. 75th Anniversary Souvenir.* Glasgow, Mont.: Glasgow Jubilee Committee, 1962.

———. *Montana Stockgrowers Association, 1884–1984: A Century of Service to Montana's Cattle Industry.* Helena, Mont.: Montana Stockgrowers Association, 1984.

Parker, E. S. *Report of the Commissioner of Indian Affairs for the Year 1869.* Washington: Government Printing Office, 1870.

Paul, Rodman W. *The Far West and the Great Plains in Transition, 1859–1900.* Norman: University of Oklahoma Press, 1998.

Pearce, William Martin. *The Matador Land and Cattle Company.* Norman: University of Oklahoma Press, 1964.

Pringle, Henry F. *Theodore Roosevelt.* New York: Harvest Books, 1956.

Rackley, Barbara Fifer. "The Hard Winter: 1886–1887." *Montana: The Magazine of Western History* 21 (Winter 1971): 50–59.

Rarick, Ronald D. "A Michigan Architect in Indiana: Elijah E. Myers and the Business of Public Architecture in the Gilded Age." *Michigan Historical Review* 26 (Fall 2000): 148–59.

Rathjen, Frederick W. *The Texas Panhandle Frontier.* Austin: University of Texas Press, 1973.

————. "The Texas State House: A Study of the Texas Capitol Based on the Reports of the Capitol Building Commissioners." *Southwestern Historical Quarterly* 60 (April 1957): 434–62.

Reeves, T. V. "The Transformation of the XIT Ranch." *Frontier Times* 4 (June 1927): 4–7.

Rhodes, Andy. "Alive and Well in Austin." *American Cowboy,* Texas Rangers Special Issue (2014): 21–22.

Richardson, James Daniel. *A Compilation of the Messages and Papers of the Presidents.* 10 vols. New York: Bureau of National Literature, 1897.

Richardson, John G. *Handbook of Theory and Research for the Sociology of Education.* Westport Conn.: Greenwood Press, 1986.

Robbins, Paul. *Encyclopedia of Environment and Society.* 5 vols. Thousand Oaks, CA: Sage, 2007.

Robbins, Roy M. "The Public Domain in the Era of Exploitation, 1862–1901." *Agricultural History* 13 (April 1939): 100–101.

Robbins, William G. *Colony and Empire: The Capitalist Transformation of the American West.* Lawrence: University Press of Kansas, 1994.

Robertson, Pauline Durrett, and R. L. Robertson. *Panhandle Pilgrimage: Illustrated Tales Tracing History in the Texas Panhandle.* Amarillo, Tex.: Paramount, 1978.

Rockwell, Ronald V. *The U.S. Army in Frontier Montana.* Helena, Mont.: Sweetgrass Books, 2009.

Russell, Jim. *Bob Fudge, Texas Trail Driver, Montana-Wyoming Cowboy, 1862–1933.* Denver: Big Mountain Press, 1962.

Sabin, Paul. "Home and Abroad: The Two 'Wests' of Twentieth-Century United States History." *Pacific Historical Review* 66 (August 1997): 305–35.

Sanders, Alvin Howard. *A History of Aberdeen-Angus Cattle With Particular Reference to Their Introduction, Distribution and Rise to Popularity in the Field of Fine Beef Production in North America.* Chicago, Ill.: New Breeder's Gazette, 1928.

Sandoz, Mari. *The Cattlemen: From the Rio Grande across the Far Marias.* Lincoln: University of Nebraska Press, 1958.

Scherger, R. H. *Synopsis of Old Glendive (Old Dawson County) Newspapers, 1882–1910: About Indians, Railroaders, Soldiers, Cowboys, Businessmen and Ranchers: Eastern Montana History.* [Glendive, Mont.:] R[obert] H. Scherger, 1996.

Schneiders, Robert Kelley. *Big Sky Rivers: The Yellowstone and Upper Missouri.* Lawrence: University Press of Kansas, 2003.

Schofield, Donald F. *Indians, Cattle, Ships, and Oil: The Story of W. M. D. Lee.* Austin: University of Texas Press, 1985.

Seale, William. "Symbol as Architecture." *Design Quarterly* 94/95 (1975): 14–15.

Sherow, James E. *The Chisholm Trail: Joseph McCoy's Great Gamble.* Norman: University of Oklahoma Press, 2018.

Skaggs, Jimmy M. *The Cattle-Trailing Industry: Between Supply and Demand, 1866–1890.* Lawrence: University Press of Kansas, 1973.

————. *Prime Cut: Livestock Raising and Meatpacking in the United States, 1607–1983.* College Station: Texas A&M University Press, 1986.

Slatta, Richard W. *Cowboys of the Americas*. New Haven, Conn.: Yale University Press, 1990.

Smith, Duane A. *Rocky Mountain West: Colorado, Wyoming, and Montana, 1859–1915*. Albuquerque: University of New Mexico Press, 1992.

Smith, Thomas T. *The U.S. Army and the Texas Frontier Economy, 1845–1900*. College Station: Texas A&M University Press, 1999.

Specht, Joshua. *Red Meat Republic: A Hoof-to-Table History of How Beef Changed America*. Princeton, N.J.: Princeton University Press, 2019.

Stanley, F. *Story of the Texas Panhandle Railroads*. Borger, Tex.: Hess, 1976.

Starrs, Paul F. *Let the Cowboy Ride: Cattle Ranching in the American West*. Baltimore: Johns Hopkins University Press, 1998.

State of Texas. Capitol Building Commission. *Biennial Report of the Capitol Building Commission Comprising the Reports of the Commissioners, Superintendent, and the Secretary, to the Governor of Texas*. Austin: Triplett and Hutchings, State Printers, 1883–88.

———. Senate. *Journal of the Senate of Texas, Regular Session of the Eighteenth Legislature*. Austin: E. W. Swindells, 1883.

———. State Library and Archives. *Governor's Messages: Coke to Ross, 1874–1891*. Austin: Baldwin and Sons, 1916.

Streeter, Floyd Benjamin. "The National Cattle Trail." *Cattleman*, June 1951: 26–27, 59–74.

Stuart, Granville, and Paul C. Phillips. *Forty Years on the Frontier: As Seen in the Journals and Reminiscences of Granville Stuart, Gold-Miner, Trader, Merchant, Rancher and Politician*. Lincoln: University of Nebraska Press, 2004.

Stuart, Leland E. "The Winter of 1886–1887: The Last of Whose 5,000?" *Montana: The Magazine of Western History* 38 (Winter 1988): 32–41.

Sullivan, Dulcie. *The LS Brand*. Austin: University of Texas Press, 1968.

Swan, Claire E. *Scottish Cowboys and the Dundee Investors: [Dundee Investment in the Texas Panhandle, a Case Study: The Matador Land and Cattle Company]*. Dundee, U.K.: Abertay Historical Society, 2004.

Teigen, Mons L. "A Century of Striving to Organized Strength." *Montana Stockgrower*, Special Centennial Edition 55 (June 1984): 11–13.

Texas Legislative Council and Texas Highway Department. *The Texas Capitol: Symbol of Accomplishment or Building a Capitol and a Great State*. [Austin]: Texas Legislative Council, 1975.

Texas State Historical Association (TSHA). *The Texas State Capitol: Selected Essays from the Southwestern Historical Quarterly*. Austin: Texas State Historical Association, 1995.

Toole, K. Ross. *Montana: An Uncommon Land*. Norman: University of Oklahoma Press, 1959.

Turner, Frederick Jackson. *The Frontier in American History*. 1920. Reprint, New York: Barnes and Noble, 2009.

U.S. Congress. House. Committee on Agriculture. *Memorial in Regard to the Texas Fever or Cattle Plague by O. M. Wozencraft, M.D.* 49th Cong., 1st sess., 1886. H. Misc. Doc.127.

———. House. Committee on Agriculture. *Report on Texas Fever or Cattle Plague*. 49th Cong., 1st sess., 1886. H. Rpt. 718.

———. House. Committee on Commerce. *National Live-stock Highway in Colorado for Cheap Transportation of Cattle*. 49th Cong., 1st sess., 1886. H. Rpt. 1228.

————. House. Committee on Rivers and Harbors. *Examination and Survey of Brazos River, Texas.* 56th Cong., 2nd Sess., 1901, H. Doc. 283.

————. House. Select Committee on the Texas Frontier Troubles. *Depredations on the Texas Frontier,* 44th Cong., 1st Sess., 1875, H. Misc. Doc. 37.

————. Senate. Committee on Commerce. *Improvements at the Mouth of the Brazos River, Texas.* 54th Cong. 2nd Sess., 1897, S. Doc. 138.

————. Senate. Committee on Interstate Commerce. *Testimony Before the Interstate Commerce Commission at St. Louis and Kansas City on [Rail] Car Shortages, Etc.* 59th Cong., 2d Sess., 1907, S. Doc. 233.

————. Senate. Select Committee on Transportation and Sale of Meat Products. *Investigation of Transportation and Sale of Meat Products, with Testimony* [Vest Committee]. 51st Cong., 1st sess., 1890. S. Rpt. 829.

U.S. Department of Agriculture. *Annual Report of the Commissioner of Agriculture, 1885.* 48th Cong., 2nd sess., 1885. H. Exec. Doc. 269.

————. Bureau of Animal Industry. *Annual Report of Bureau of Animal Industry, 1884.* 48th Cong., 2nd sess., 1890. H. Misc. Doc. 25.

U.S. Department of the Interior. *Annual Report of Director of Geological Survey, 1900, pt. 4; Hydrography.* 56th Cong., 2nd sess., 1900. H. Doc. 5/32.

————. *Report from the Acting Commissioner of the General Land Office, in Response to a Resolution of the House Calling for Information Relative to the Use of Public Lands by Cattle Graziers.* 50th Cong., 1st sess., 1888. H. Exec. Doc. 232.

U.S. Department of the Treasury. *A Report from the Chief of the Bureau of Statistics, in Response to a Resolution of the House Calling for Information in Regard to the Range and Ranch Cattle Traffic in the Western States and Territories* [Nimmo Report]. 48th Cong., 2nd sess., 1885. H. Exec. Doc. 267.

Wallis, George A. *Cattle Kings of the Staked Plains.* Denver: Sage Books, 1964.

Walsh, John, and Jane Braxton Little. "The Ogallala Aquifer: Saving a Vital U.S. Water Source." *Scientific American* 300 (Special Editions, March 1, 2009). www.scientificamerican.com /article/the-ogallala-aquifer.

Ward, Fay E. *The Cowboy at Work: All about His Job and How He Does It, with 600 Drawings by the Author.* 1958. Reprint, Mineola, N.Y.: Dover, 2003.

Waterhouse, S. *Address of S. Waterhouse before the First National Convention of American Cattlemen: St. Louis, November 18th, 1884.* St. Louis, Mo.: R. P. Studley, 1885.

Webb, Walter Prescott. *The Great Plains.* 1931. Reprint, Lincoln: University of Nebraska Press, 1981.

Welsh, Donald H. "Cosmopolitan Cattle King: Pierre Wibaux and the W Bar Ranch." *Montana: The Magazine of Western History* 5 (Spring 1955): 1–15.

West, Elliott. *The Contested Plains: Indians, Goldseekers, and the Rush to Colorado.* Lawrence: University Press of Kansas, 1998.

Western Historical Publishing Company. *An Illustrated History of the Yellowstone Valley: Embracing the Counties of Park, Sweet Grass, Carbon, Yellowstone, Rosebud, Custer and Dawson, State of Montana.* Spokane, Wash.: Western Historical, 1907.

Weston, Jack. "The Cowboy Western and the Utopian Impulse." *Monthly Review* 53 (March 202): 51–55.

Wheeler, David L. "The Blizzard of 1886 and Its Effect on the Range Cattle Industry in the Southern Plains," *Southwestern Historical Quarterly* 94 (Winter 1991): 415–34.

White, Richard. *"It's Your Misfortune and None of My Own": A History of the American West.* Norman: University of Oklahoma Press, 1991.

Winegarten, Ruthe, and Judith N. McArthur, eds. *Citizens at Last: The Woman Suffrage Movement in Texas.* College Station: Texas A&M University Press, 2015.

Wollaston, Percy. *Homesteading: A Montana Family Album.* New York: Penguin Books, 1997.

Woods, Lawrence M. *British Gentlemen in the Wild West: The Era of the Intensely English Cowboy.* London: Robson, 2003.

Worster, Donald. *Dust Bowl: The Southern Plains in the 1930s.* New York: Oxford University Press, 1979.

XIT Association, Capitol Freehold Land Trust, Harold Bugbee, H. H. Hutson, et al. *The XIT Brand: Annual XIT Cowboy Reunion and Rodeo.* Dalhart, Tex.: Dalhart, 1939.

Yellowstone Corral Posse. "XIT." *Hoofprints from the Yellowstone Corral of the Westerners* 18 (Spring/Summer 1988): 1–19.

Index

References to illustrations appear in *italics*; references to tables are followed by a *t*.